Murder in a Small Town

The Kyson Rice Case

Larry Scheckel

Oak Grove Press

Copyright © 2025 Larry Scheckel

All rights reserved.

No portion of this book may be reproduced in any form without written permission from the publisher or author, except as permitted by U.S. copyright law.

Liability Statement: The author has made every effort to ensure that the information within this book is accurate at the time of publication. The author does not assume and hereby disclaims any liability to any party for any loss, damage, or disruption caused by errors or omissions, whether such errors or omissions result from accident, negligence, or any other cause.

ISBN Paperback: 979-8-9922383-0-3

ISBN eBook: 979-8-9922383-1-0

Contents

Foreword	1
Introduction	4
1. Jessica Rice	9
2. Marcus Anderson	14
3. Marcus Comes to Wisconsin	19
4. Prelude to Murder	25
5. Murder on Jodi Circle	30
6. Ambulance to Tomah Hospital	38
7. Search for a Killer	42
8. Jessica Talks	54
9. Tomah PD, Ambulance, Sparta Mayo Hospital	62
10. Crime Scene Search	71
11. Marcus Anderson is Booked Into Prison	76
12. The Investigation Switches into High Gear	79
13. Tomah Detectives Seek Answers	87
14. Evidence Seized	94
15. The Final Farewell	98

16.	Surveillance Cameras Produce Evidence	103
17.	Anderson Works the Phones from Prison	107
18.	Shelby Anderson Reveals a Monster	116
19.	Anderson Continues Calling	120
20.	Interviews in Arizona	122
21.	Interviews Reveal Anderson's Character	126
22.	The Investigation Deepens	129
23.	The Investigation Continues	133
24.	A Jury Is Selected	137
25.	The Trial Begins - Day 2: Morning Session	144
26.	Day 2: Afternoon Session	155
27.	Day 3: Five Witnesses in the Morning	166
28.	Jessica Takes the Stand	174
29.	Five Witnesses Testify	185
30.	The State Pushes Its Case	191
31.	Day 5: Eight Witnesses Called by the State	200
32.	A Reluctant Stellar Witness	215
33.	Investigator Walensky Takes the Stand	229
34.	The Trial Resumes	235
35.	The Defendant's Day in Court	251
36.	Jury Instructions	261
37.	Day 8: Croninger's Closing Arguments	267
38.	The Verdict	277

39. Victim Impact Statements	281
40. The Guilty One Speaks	292
41. The June 29th Sentencing	295
Epilogue	308
Press Release Upon Conviction	312
Acknowledgments	314
Biographies	315
Why Do People Commit Murder?	322
Wisconsin Prison System	326
Death Penalty in Wisconsin	329
Books by Larry and Ann Scheckel	331

Foreword

Dear Reader,

I am grateful that Larry Scheckel wrote this book so that people can learn from this horrific tragedy. So many lessons to be learned. An unthinkable thing happened in our community, and true heroes answered the call to action. Our Police and EMS quickly responded and tried valiantly to save our beloved, vulnerable, Kyson. The hospital staff worked very hard providing Kyson with fantastic medical care but sometimes evil in this world wins a battle. Our city of Tomah and Monroe County Police Officers and Detectives demonstrated strength and restraint beyond belief for hours as I observed, later during the trial through videos submitted as evidence, by treating the prime suspect with the highest level of respect and patience. Only a police department run with the highest level of leadership that instilled professionalism could possibly train and demand to suppress normal human reactions after viewing such injuries. I saw Kyson that day at the hospital, after losing his battle with evil, and trust me the normal gut human reaction was to respond immediately with swift permanent revenge. We all unfortunately had to learn that justice can be very slow moving. Answers to questions take a long time and some questions will never be answered. We are forever grateful that justice patiently moved doggedly forward for three years, determined to carefully expose the truth about the monster and his crimes against our most innocent three-year-old boy. Kyson's murder happened before many other high-profile murders in many cities around the country at the same time. Many of these murders were picked up by the national news media and given society's focus they were all tried, prosecuted, and sentenced, prior to Kyson's case. I personally found that hard to deal with and justify. I suppose I value young innocent life more than some mainstream media outlets. Sad that society does not value innocent three-year-old lives as much as some criminals. We are blessed to have a prosecution team that diligently sought out justice for Kyson. Judge Goodman created an environment in the courtroom that enabled the truth to be told. Not every decision during the trial went in Kyson's favor but Judge Goodman carefully explained what was fair and why he ruled as he did with his decisions. I felt the truth would come out and every attempt was made to ensure the trial followed the rules that everyone is innocent until proven guilty. The verdict would be just. The Juror's called to duty, rose to an occasion that I wouldn't have wished on anyone. No human that reviewed the evidence, and listened to the testimony in this case can leave without forever being changed by the photos and video results of witnessing what atrocities true evil is capable of. Everything learned about Kyson's murder is stained by his blood. I want to share with you the Kyson that we, his family were privileged to know about the amazing little man Kyson. Please do not remember Kyson after facing a one-sided battle with an evil monster but remember him as who we were blessed to know and love.

Kyson was an unusually thoughtful caring little boy who found true joy in others. First of all, Kyson loved his mother Jessica with all his heart. Kyson also loved his Great Grandma and Grandpa and was often found happy on their laps. Kyson loved his Nana, my wife Jolene, in a very special way and many times I was fortunate enough to witness their special bond. Kyson loved his cousins and family all so much and we all very easily loved him back. Words cannot describe our feelings for Kyson, just as many of you readers know how blessed you are to have children in your lives. Kyson had a most unusual low voice and deep heartfelt laugh. You could not listen to his infectious, deep, low toned laugh and not smile. Kyson loved playing with all his cousins. Kyson shared, Kyson tried to help other kids, Kyson found true joy in his cousin's achievements no matter how small, even one cousin who just learned to only say the word "Hi." Kyson had dreams that were fun to listen to (helicopters and Spiderman). Please remember Kyson for the wonderful little boy he was and not for the things you will learn about that are indelibly etched into your brain, when exposed to in this book.

Use what you learn in this book to make yourself spend more time with kids, be grateful for the children you have in your life. Stand up for children. Value their lives. Hug them, protect them, and love them. Make a difference in your community and make your community a safe place for children. Support your Law enforcement, EMS, and Justice system. Answer the call to jury duty and get involved. I pray for all touched by this tragedy, I pray for you the reader that you can learn from Kyson's tragedy and make things safer for all children who are still with us today. Remember that praying is the most powerful tool a person has to deal with situations like this. Sometimes evil wins battles but love wins wars. Remember Kyson for his love, laughter, and for finding joy in others. Trust me, Kyson would like that.

Sincerely,

John Glynn

Introduction

Cain and Abel

Murder, the taking of human life, is the ultimate evil act. Murder is not new, not something invented in modern times. It goes back to the time of Cain and Abel in Genesis. Why did Cain kill Abel? Cain and Abel are the first two sons of Adam and Eve. Cain, the firstborn, was a farmer, and his brother Abel was a shepherd. The brothers made sacrifices to God, but God favored Abel's sacrifice instead of Cain's. Cain then murdered Abel out of jealousy, whereupon God punished Cain by condemning him to a life of wandering. Cain then dwelt in the land of Nod, where he built a city and fathered the line of descendants beginning with Enoch.

Precautions

I strived for accuracy in this narrative. I obtained the entire transcript of the trial, some 2,000 pages and 400,000 words. I attended two days of the trial. Most of the people I interviewed were open and friendly. I told every individual that I interviewed, "I will allow you to read the manuscript before publishing. If there was anything that you object to, I will take it out." I did this to check factual accuracy and remain sensitive to people's feelings.

People have long memories. Many of these cases cut deep into the psyche and leave lasting scars. Telling those I talked to about the case ahead of time that they have a veto option may have made them more open and comfortable. I believe that strategy was successful and the right way to go. When the information passed on to me was more along the lines of gossip, I left that stuff out.

The manuscript has been proofread several times by those in different professions. I used as many good quality photographs as I could, which is not as easy to do as you might think with newspaper photos sometimes being produced at lower resolutions than necessary for book publishing.

Murder Rate in Monroe County

As a resident of Monroe County, I want to point out that we live in a fairly safe place, and this book is not meant to portray the area as dangerous. Murder is not an everyday or even weekly occurrence here. If you were to Google "Murder Rate in Monroe County, Wisconsin," a colored map pops up showing its *Crime Grade*, giving the county a Violent Crime Grade of B-, Property Crime Grade of A-, Other Crime Grade of D-, Murder Crime Grade of A, and an overall crime grade of C+. What do we learn from this rating score? Your house may be broken into, and your car stolen, but your chances of being shot or stabbed are pretty low.

The A grade means the rate of murder is much lower than the average in other U.S. counties. There are 3,142 counties in the U.S. and 72 counties in Wisconsin. Monroe County is in the 88th percentile for safety, meaning 12 percent of counties are safer and 88 percent of counties are more dangerous. The rate of murder in Monroe County is 0.02 per 1,000 residents during a standard year. A crime occurs every 5 hours 28 minutes (on average) in Monroe County. Your chance of being a victim of murder in Monroe County may be as high as 1 in 50,600 in the northwest neighborhoods, or as low as 1 in 66,000 in the south part of the county.

The Murder

This was a crime unparalleled in its sheer brutality. A 260-pound, 6-foot, 4 inch, 36-year-old man pummels to death a small 3-year-old boy. So gruesome was the transgression, it prompted the UW-Madison forensic pathologist, Dr. Michael Stier, to exclaim, "Torture, Torture," during his testimony at the trial. Jury members were literally sobbing after seeing photos of the young victim.

This is a story of how a small city, well-trained police force apprehended the perpetrator, secured the crime scene, thoroughly assessed, and meticulously investigated the crime. It's an inside look at how that city police force worked together with a county police force and investigators, who question the killer and his relatives, friends, and contacts. It's also the story of an ambulance crew and a hospital trauma unit laboring feverishly to restore life.

It's an account of an award-winning District Attorney and an award-winning Assistant District Attorney who skillfully weaved together a prosecution that guaranteed a killer will never again walk freely, or buy, use, and sell drugs, and, to employ the informal colloquial term, never again "beat the crap" out of little kids.

It's a narrative of a mother who lost her only child and is not likely to have another, and of brutality, loss, shame, and families torn apart.

It's the story of an eight-day trial that cost tons of money, but in the words of the sentencing judge, "money well spent, and worth every penny." And finally, it is about our society that won by putting away a criminal who was totally bereft of feelings and empathy.

Chapter 1

Jessica Rice

Kyson Rice was a happy, fun-loving three-year-old boy in early March 2019 who would sadly be dead in 90 days. He was living with his mother, Jessica Rice, at the home of Jessica's aunt Jolene and uncle John Glynn. The Glynn family lived on the east edge of Tomah at the airport in a beautiful white house once owned by famed local aviator, Vic Bloyer. John is a Sales Manager at Cardinal IG in Tomah.

The airport was first known as the Tomah Army Airfield Technical School. It was established on November 30, 1942 to conduct technical training for United States Army Air Forces. The training included radio interception techniques and radio maintenance. The school was inactivated on April 1, 1944, and the airfield was eventually turned over to civil control. Vic Bloyer taught hundreds of people to fly, including this author. At this time, the single paved 3,900-foot runway sees an average traffic of ten operations per day. There are 12 aircraft based at Bloyer Field, including two multi-engine planes and two light sport planes. One light-sport aircraft is owned and operated by John Glynn and a frequent passenger was grandnephew, Kyson Rice.

Jessica's Parents

Jolene Glynn's sister Nancy Eckelberg married Greg Rice, and they had a baby girl, Jessica, born in La Crosse on February 4, 1993. Greg and Nancy divorced shortly after the birth of Jessica. Jessica was born with skeletal dysplasia, also known as dwarfism. The most common cause of dwarfism is growth hormone deficiency and there is a strong genetic component.

An early photo of Kyson Rice taken before his first birthday.

Raising such a child requires an extreme amount of medical attention and expense, and understandably strains the marriage. A child with special needs often causes parents to separate. Greg Rice had not been in the family picture since the divorce.

Nancy lived in Elroy for many years and had now moved back to Tomah. Nancy's cognitive and physical disabilities made her unable to work, and she was unable to raise Jessica. At the time of the tragic murder of Kyson Rice, John and Jolene Glynn maintained a busy household of six people, which included Jolene's parents Rueben and Pat Eckelberg as well as Jessica and her son, Kyson. It was a testament the John and Jolene Glynn's Christian faith and generosity.

In her early years before the tragic murder of Kyson Rice, Jessica grew up in the household of her grandparents, Rueben and Pat Eckelberg in the Tomah area. Jessica attended elementary schools, LaGrange and Camp Douglas, and high school in Tomah. As a small child, Jessica had the passageway for her spinal column in her neck enlarged to prevent pressure on the spinal cord that caused her breathing to stop. Prior to spinal surgery, she wore a monitor alarm in her sleep.

Jessica offers that she was generally treated well by students and teachers in both elementary and high school. Her first year at Tomah High School was somewhat difficult as it is for many freshmen, but it got easier after that.

When Jessica was a senior at Tomah High School, she underwent three painful medical procedures to essentially attain normal height. The doctors did extensive operations on the femur bones, then shins, and finally the upper arms. The technique involved fitting the skeleton with a spidery metal contraption of stainless steel threaded rods and braces, breaking the bones, and slowly pulling them apart, re-breaking the bones, and stretching them every day, followed by re-healing, to obtain normal height. The motor unit was on a timer that randomly, and without notice, would start up and stretch one-sixteenth of an inch each time.

It was a painful and long-term procedure requiring people to attend to her many needs. Jessica missed many days of school, but she did graduate on time in 2011. Jessica did not obtain a driver's license when she turned 16, did not have a car, and could not drive. However, she did acquire her Learners' Permit.

Jessica gets a job

John Glynn says Jessica always had a good work ethic. She worked several jobs after high school, including at Three Bears and Ocean Spray. She was hired at Taco Bell in 2014. After she was hired, Jessica met Marcus Anderson for the first time. They had a brief relationship.

Jessica took instruction to be brought into the Catholic faith through the Rite of Christian Initiation of Adults (RCIA), the program in which the Church directs and supports conversion and initiation into the Catholic Church. Instruction was given by Deacon Robert Reidl of St.

Mary's Catholic Church in Tomah. Jessica was confirmed at Eastertime in 2018.

Jessica dates and becomes pregnant

Jessica wanted what many young ladies want, a boyfriend and a serious relationship. She, like any number of young ladies, might be flattered that a guy would pay attention to her. Jessica, at age 25, became pregnant. The father was from Necedah and wanted the baby aborted. Jessica didn't know what to do. She did have a lot of medical issues, which could be fatal. Jessica informed John Glynn that some people were advising her that if she had the baby, she would be "selfish."

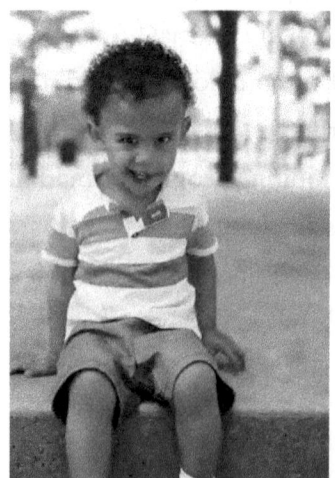

Kyson as a happy boy approaching age 2.

John Glynn said, "We were in a car, she asked me what she should do. I'm thinking, I got to answer very carefully, because what I say will be very important. I said a quick little prayer."

John relates, "I said to Jessica, 'If you bought a Christmas present for someone that you really, really loved, put a lot of care into that present, and on Christmas Day, that person opened the gift, and threw it on the ground, and said, I don't want it, would you call that person selfish?'" She says, "Well, yah."

John continued, "God's gift to you is a child. Do you want to throw it on the ground?" The father wants to kill it, who is being selfish?" Jessica smiled at this. The baby was born on September 3, 2015 and named Kyson Reid Morgan Rice. Reid was Jessica's brother and Morgan was the middle name of Jessica's other brother, Jayce.

John continued, "She had trouble with the delivery, had to have a Caesarean, and it was hard for her to get around. But she did it. She lived with us for three years before she moved out. Little Kyson would only grace us with his presence for three years and eight months."

Kyson was a fun-loving kid always looking for new adventures.

Kyson's biological father, a young man from Necedah, was court ordered to pay child support after a paternity test. Jessica applied for and received assistance from the Monroe County WIC (Women, Infants, and Children) program which provided milk formula.

In December 2018, Marcus Anderson, visited Jessica while she was working at Taco Bell in Tomah to rekindle their relationship. Jessica moved out of John and Jolene's house in March 2019 and was on her own for the first time in her life. It was her goal to be independent, to have her own place. She rented a house at 1009 Jodi Circle on the southwest side of Tomah.

The 1009 Jodi Circle is one of four streets named for daughters of the late John and Mabel Grumann. The house at 1009 Jodi Circle is one of a number that surrounds Grumann Park, the neighborhood area between Lake Tomah and Recreation Park. It has a playground area and an open-air shelter.

Jessica was happy with her independence. John Glynn gave Jessica a car in the hopes that she would get a license and drive. Later, Jessica loaned the car to someone, who was stopped for a traffic violation. The car was impounded and not returned to her. It eventually disappeared.

Chapter 2

Marcus Anderson

The Christian faith calls us to see the good in everyone. It's a doable undertaking for the vast majority of people that we come in contact within our everyday life. For a select few, it's a difficult struggle. Mass murderers, such as Stalin, Hitler, Mussolini, Pol Pot, Mao Zedong, and Saddam Hussein are in a category all their own. Mega murder comes to mind when their names are mentioned.

There are other, lesser-known figures, in which it's a stretch to find any redeeming value. One of those would be Marcus Wayne Anderson, a person so cruel, so lacking in empathy, so self-absorbed and selfish, that it's difficult to find any positive aspects to his character. We are reminded that "God doesn't make junk." Indeed, Psalm 139:14 says, "I will praise You Lord; for I am fearfully and wonderfully made: marvelous are Your works." But in the case of Marcus Anderson, one is left wondering if God didn't make a mistake.

Background Details

Marcus Anderson was born July 6, 1984, the son of Torry and Helen Anderson. A good account of Marcus and his behavior was provided by the person who knew him best, his one-time, live-in girlfriend, Julie Alvarez Alcala. Detectives Rob Walensky and Clayton Tester interviewed her in

Phoenix on August 12, 2019. She agreed to speak with the detectives if alone.

One of many mug shots of Marcus Anderson.

She recounts that she met Marcus Anderson in Bakersfield, California, when her car broke down at a club where she would party. Marcus pulled up and helped get her car going. He was under 18 at the time and she was 22. He told her he was 23 years old and he looked it. She learned his true age when he was put on probation as a juvenile for not going to school. Julie said she would hang out with Marcus as she was going through a divorce with Bobby Carolina Sr. at the time. In June of 2001, Marcus moved in with Julie and her five children. He was convicted of possession of narcotics in 2002.

In July 2003, Julie sold her house in Bakersfield and moved to Phoenix. Marcus moved with her. Julie received rent assistance and qualified for an apartment. Julie was pregnant with their first child. Her parents, Francisco and Frances Alcala, who reportedly did not like Marcus, moved to Phoenix in the fall of 2003. Julie and Marcus soon had two more children. She broke up with Marcus because he was beating her more frequently. Marcus became more violent toward her when she found out he was cheating on her in 2005. He was drinking and doing drugs at the time.

Marcus Anderson is a big guy, 6 feet, 4 inches tall, and weighing 240 pounds. When confronted, Marcus threw Julie through the door. She called her parents to come get her and the kids. Julie took him back. He'd be good for a week, then the drinking and drugs continued. Julie said that Marcus was a drug dealer his entire life and smoked marijuana all day. He was convicted of a marijuana violation in October 2006. She said that if Marcus wanted sex, he would get it, even after he beat her. She got burned with a hot spoon. She was punched in the face so hard she flew over the countertop. He often head-butted her. She stated that she and Marcus were fighting all the time, and he threatened to kill her several times. Julie said Marcus was never in the military.

Marcus Anderson often wore a Michael Vick #7 jersey which was seized after his arrest.

Julie reported that Marcus Anderson was good with the children while they lived in California, but the situation changed when they moved to Arizona. Her second child and oldest daughter, said that Marcus was nice to them when her mother was around, but became violent and evil when she was not present. Marcus became furious when any child cried.

Julie reported that Marcus "wanted to be out enjoying the single life, doing what he wanted to do. He would take his anger out on the children. Punishments included standing against the wall, sometimes hours at a time. The children stood facing the wall and could not look away or do anything or Marcus would hit them. Marcus also struck kids with his belt or used a paddle. One report stated, "When the defendant used the belt on the children, he grabbed them and hit them with the belt while holding onto their arms."

All of the children were physically abused by Marcus, except one. Two bore the brunt of the abuse. Marcus thought one was too light skinned to be his biological child, the other because he looked like his father and did not enjoy sports. If a child cried, moved, or made a noise, they were hit on the head. At times, the child's head was held under water in the bathtub.

The investigators wrote that it was a difficult interview, stretching over two days, and that Julie could go on and on about Marcus' behavior.

Interviewing Regina Carolina

None of Julie's kids, except for Regina Carolina, would talk to the detectives. Regina Carolina, Julie's daughter from her marriage to Bobbi Carolina talked with Investigators Walensky and Tester on August 14, 2019. She recounted that Marcus insisted all the kids call him Dad and got upset and angry if they did not. When Regina was in fifth or sixth grade, Marcus hit her so hard it left a handprint on her shoulder. He threw a remote, beat them with a belt, and slapped them around with his hands. Marcus was vicious when her mother was gone.

Marcus Anderson was a big man, 6 foot, 3 inches and weighing 240 pounds.

Regina Carolina stated that Marcus and her mother were always fighting. The children saw Marcus grab and hit their mother and threaten to kill their grandparents. Marcus brandished a gun several times. She said they moved around a lot both in California and Arizona. She explained how her mom would get beat up, Marcus would leave, but her mom always took him back. Regina also revealed that Marcus was always smoking marijuana.

By the time Regina Carolina was in eighth grade, she was back in California. All five children moved to live with their father, Bobby Carolina. She never saw Marcus again.

Robbery

Marcus and a friend committed an armed robbery at a Circle K Store. Julie Alcala's niece worked at the store and was involved in the planning. Julie drove the moving truck that Marcus borrowed from a relative of Anderson's business associate. She did not know of the robbery at the time.

Marcus and his friend were in the back of the truck. Cops pulled her over the two men were arrested. She was also arrested because to Marcus told the police that she planned it also, just to get even with her for her relationship with a new boyfriend. She was in prison from October 2010-2013. She told her mother if she knew this was going to happen, she would have killed Marcus. Her parents had guardianship of the kids while she was in prison.

On October 6, 2007, Marcus was found guilty in Maricopa County for armed robbery and began serving a seven-year sentence on January 5, 2008. He was released in 2014 after serving six years. In 2014, Marcus is released from prison. His father, Torry Anderson, picked him up as he walked out of the prison gates. The pair went to a restaurant to eat after which they went directly to the airport for a flight to Wisconsin.

Chapter 3

Marcus Comes to Wisconsin

In Wisconsin, Marcus Anderson lived in Sparta with his father, Torry Anderson and his wife Trulee Silver, and two stepchildren. He briefly met Jessica Rice at Taco Bell in Tomah.

That same year, 2014, Marcus met Shelby Anderson, who lived on Nakomis Avenue, a peninsula between French Island and La Crosse's north side. It's an area of upscale housing. Shelby was a nurse and they met while Marcus was in the hospital.

In early Spring 2015, when Marcus went to California to visit his mother and sister, Shelby traveled with him. He bought a large amount of marijuana. In March 2015 they started residing together. In the summer of 2016, the couple married in a ceremony at Alpine Inn up on Granddad Bluff in La Crosse. They had a son, Samir, together.

Marcus abused Shelby much as he did Julie, strangling and beating her. According to Shelby, Marcus believed that women were inferior to men, and he had a right to do whatever he wanted to her and his child. Marcus threatened to kill his wife and nearly did so several times. In Wisconsin, Marcus continued his almost daily marijuana habit and used methamphetamine on and off. He reportedly became very abusive when coming down from meth use.

Marcus traveled extensively during his marriage to Shelby. He connected with a girlfriend in Arizona, Regina Banks, and her mother, April Hall-Banks. From August 11 to August 16, 2016, April Hall-Banks,

Regina, and Marcus went on a cruise to Cancun, Mexico. Later in 2016, Regina Hall-Banks went to Chicago. Marcus drove Shelby's Camaro to see Regina, using Shelby's credit card along the way. When stopped by the police, Marcus denied he was married. It was the first time Regina heard that Marcus was married.

Shelby Anderson indicated that Marcus would hit her on the head, throw things at her, and pull her hair. At times, the injuries were not able to be covered, so she could not go to work. Marcus came up with excuses for her having marks on her body, telling her to say that she tripped getting out of the shower, or the floor was wet and she slipped, or her foot got caught on the rug, or the shower curtain rod fell and hit her. Shelby reported that Marcus was horrible with their infant. Any noise was inconvenient to Marcus.

On May 21, 2017, Marcus was upset because Shelby did not put the bills back and the Internet was not working. Marcus threw a syrup bottle at her, striking her in the stomach, then slapped the back of her head several times, and slammed her head into a wall mirror requiring removal of glass from the back of her head after the attack. On advice from a lawyer, Shelby began documenting the abuse. Shelby said that Marcus carried a gun. As a felon he was not legally able to carry a gun.

Another incident occurred on June 18, 2017. Marcus grabbed Shelby by the hair and flung her to the floor, kicked her, grabbed her neck, and cut off her breathing for 30 seconds. Another ugly incident occurred on June 20, 2017. Shelby made a report to La Crosse police about Marcus about these brutal attacks. In June 2017, Marcus was arrested for False Imprisonment and Battery. In July 2017, Shelby filed for divorce. After the divorce, she and her baby moved to Texas and built a new life for herself and her child.

During the next two years, Marcus Anderson was constantly in trouble with the law, with numerous offenses, many court dates, delays, and five changes of address. Using the Wisconsin Court System website and court records, I pieced together, hopefully with some accuracy, his life and whereabouts.

For several months in 2017 and 2018, Marcus' address was listed as 100 Avon Road, Sparta, where he stayed with Steven Douglas Ford and Theresa R. Severson. That did not work out well. The couple tried to help Marcus, but they end up losing a car and a considerable amount of money.

On December 4, 2017, Marcus was charged with stealing a car and fleeing Sparta Police. He was cited for ten traffic violations, including unreasonable speed, failure to stop at a stoplight, no vehicle insurance, following too close, operating left of center, and fleeing an officer. At the time, Marcus was living with his father at Avon Road in Sparta.

On March 14, 2018, Marcus was charged with stealing a vehicle and two counts of felony bail jumping. On July 11, 2018, Marcus was charged with resisting or obstructing an Officer, and a disorderly conduct charge thrown in.

But it's not until much later that he finally went to court for the previous three incidents and was sentenced to 16 months, to be served concurrently with his time for his one-year sentence for false imprisonment and battery domestic abuse of Shelby handed down on June 7, 2019 by La Crosse County Court Judge Gonzalez. Marcus gave Monroe County Circuit Judge Todd L. Ziegler a "tear-jerker story," claiming that he was a Marine in Afghanistan and lost a lot of men.

In the Fall of 2018, Marcus, who was now going by the name, Tank, lived in a duplex adjacent to Larry and Cheryl Quarles west of Tomah on Hwy CM. He is with a woman and her four children. When the woman and her children moved out, he had no place to go. Larry and Cheryl Quarles allowed him to stay in one of their rooms. The Quarles later told investigators that he was gone a lot, only coming back to shower and then leaving again. Marcus frequently goes to Madison. There was speculation that he picks up drugs. In December 2018, Marcus rekindled his relationship with

Jessica Rice, even though Regina flew up from Arizona and stayed about a week.

Eventually Marcus moved into Jessica Rice's rental house at 1009 Jodi Circle in Tomah in March 2019, becoming Kyson's daytime caretaker. By February 25, 2019, Kyson's last day attending his daycare center, Jessica owed them over $500.

Jessica Rice and Marcus Anderson lived in the left side unit. Jessica paid the rent.

On April 9, 2019, Marcus flew to California. When Marcus was gone, Jessica had Larry and Cheryl Quarles take care of Kyson while she worked at Taco Bell. Marcus returned on April 24, 2019 and was ill. He was admitted to Tomah Memorial Hospital on April 27.

On April 28, Larry and Cheryl Quarles visited Marcus Anderson at Tomah Memorial Hospital. Cheryl went to talk to the nurse, and Larry visited Marcus in his room. Marcus was acting crazy and talking weird, forming his hand and fingers into a gun and shooting out the window saying he is shooting cops. Marcus told Larry Quarles that he was expecting a shipment from Madison.

Both Larry and Cheryl later reported that Marcus was very changed since he came back from Arizona and California, and they were both embarrassed at his behavior in the hospital. They reported that Marcus got very jealous of other people. Marcus often talked to the Quarles about having "side" girls. Cheryl told Marcus he should not have side girls when involved with Jessica Rice, because Jessica has a child.

Marcus is released from the hospital on April 29. On Wednesday, May 1 he left the 1009 Jodi Circle residence between 5 p.m. and 6 p.m. to go to Alma Center. It will not be a good day for Jessica and her son, Kyson, when Marcus returned in the early morning hours of May 3.

Larry Quarles said he visited Marcus on Thursday, May 2, to see how he was doing after leaving the hospital, walking in on a loud argument between Marcus and Jessica. Marcus was upset, claiming that Jessica does nothing around the house and does nothing for him, and that she doesn't appreciate him.

***

Before Marcus Anderson went on trial for the murder of Kyson Rice, on March 28, 2022, Monroe County Investigator Rob Walensky completed an extensive background report on Marcus, following a trail that led from California, to Arizona, to La Crosse, Wisconsin, and finally Tomah, Wisconsin.

Brandon Crampes was one of the few friends Marcus Anderson made when arriving in Wisconsin after leaving prison in Arizona.

His accounts were used by Monroe County District Attorney Kevin Croninger and Assistant D.A. Sarah Skiles to file a Probative Report of Proffered Evidence. The legal term, probative value, refers to any evidence that serves the purpose of proving something during a trial. Probative value considers the evidence's usefulness in proving, or disproving, a particular fact in the case, with the court determining the actual value of such evidence according to its relevance to the case at hand. Proffered evidence is evidence in support of an argument.

It gets tricky. The State, meaning the D.A., is putting before the court, the crimes and witness testimony for the purpose of establishing motive, perpetrator identity, intent, opportunity, plan, knowledge, and absence of mistake or accident. Afterall, Kyson Rice cannot speak for himself. He lies in peace in Oak Grove Cemetery in Tomah.

The State must argue that this past history of Marcus Anderson's behavior toward other children is consistent with the treatment he meted out to Kyson Rice. The danger is that the judge may determine that the reports and proffered evidence may unfairly prejudice the defendant and could be grounds for appeal.

Chapter 4

Prelude to Murder

May 3, 2019, was a typical mid-spring day in Tomah, starting out at 38 degrees at dawn and climbing into the low 60s by mid-afternoon. The weather reports called for mostly sunny skies. The sound of lawnmowers could be heard anywhere in the City of Tomah.

A cyclone hit India, killing 33 people. The death toll was kept low as 1.2 million people evacuated in 24 hours. The French were cleaning up the Notre Dame Cathedral after the devastating April fire. Astronomers were fawning over the first photo of a Black Hole. In Wisconsin, Governor Tony Evers, inaugurated on January 7, continued to jaw with the Republican-controlled Senate and Assembly.

The ice had gone out of Lake Tomah on April 6 and the fishing was excellent, with a half dozen boats out on the lake every day and numerous anglers fishing from shore. The Amish came in, parked their buggies, unhitched their horses to graze, unloaded their long willow poles, and were trying the waters below the dam. Local Amish schools closed the previous Friday, April 26, ending with school picnics and graduation ceremonies.

The May 3, 2019, edition of 'The Tomah Journal' featured a full-color photo of trees being planted in Butts Park by the Tomah Middle School Science Club. Mayor Mike Murray spoke to the group. A second set of twins in eight days was born at Tomah Memorial Hospital. Columnist Tom Muench, the Old Rambler, discussed the turkey season. Hundreds of Army Reservists at Ft. McCoy were training under Operation Cold Steel, with four differ-

ent weapons systems. The Tomah Ho-Chunk movie theatre added the film 'Avengers Endgame' to their lineup of six movies.

The events of this dreadful day are recorded here based on police reports, court testimony, and interviews. Every measure was taken to ensure accuracy.

Marcus left for Alma Center on Wednesday night May 1, between 5 and 6 p.m. He was back in the house early Thursday morning. Jessica doesn't work until 11 a.m. on Thursday but has a medical appointment in the morning.

9:25 a.m. Jessica Rice was picked up at her 1009 Jodi Circle duplex by Amber Moseley. They drive to Dunkin Donuts on the north side of Tomah prior to going to work at Taco Bell. She is scheduled to work from 11 am to 8 pm. The neighbors heard loud yelling. Jessica later says the arguments started Wednesday evening after grocery shopping. Soda was spilled in Marcus' car. Marcus was upset because he claimed, in her words, "Marcus says I do nothing around the house." Larry Quarles was present. It's a strained relationship.

9:40 a.m. Kyson woke up. He has 7 hours and 30 minutes to live. Marcus and Kyson are alone in the house, but Marcus had visitors in the morning. Cody Harding lived in a house on the opposite side of the circular driveway from 1009 Jodi Circle. He was helping a friend prepare for a rummage sale. He later reported seeing a yellow Xterra Nissan SUV come and go several times that morning. The car belongs to Larry Quarles, and it will show up on Marcus' installed video system.

During the Day – The relationship between Marcus and Jessica was becoming very strained. The tension and stress had been building from April 24, the day Marcus returned from California. Marcus' acquaintances have noted the same friction and abrasiveness in Marcus' personality since his return to Wisconsin. He had hoped to obtain custody of his three children but was met with legal roadblocks. Marcus was in an angry, sour mood.

11:19 a.m. Marcus sent a text to Jessica, "Oh now u busy at work. I'm gona remember that shit so from now on don't ever call me or text me from work again so when u having bad days don't come to me when something go wrong don't call me anymore."

11:24 a.m. "So u need to find a permanent baby sitter."

11:34 a.m. "U don't need me no more if I die today I made the hood proud nigga. I thought you loved me I was wrong I'm sorry for coming back into your life."

Marcus guilt trips Jessica throughout the day with constant calls and text messages. Many of their text message exchanges will show up later in court.

Marcus' and Kyson's first stop in Sparta is Walgreens at the corner of Hwy 21 and Hwy 27. Marcus limps into Walgreens with his prescription.

12:33 p.m. Marcus: "Well Why don't u love me like I do u so u not give respond to me ok cool."

1:12 p.m. to 1:32 p.m. Phone records indicate that Jessica and Marcus talked to each other on their cell phones, taking up the entire time of Jessica's lunch break. (Cell phone text messages remain on the cell phone and can be subpoenaed and used in court. However, conversations on cell phones and land lines are not recorded and are private. However, there is a log of who called who and when.)

2:00 p.m. Marcus, "U need to call me now." (The call was dropped.)

Marcus' (Tank) phone log of calls.

2:05 p.m. – Outgoing call 1 minute.

2:07 p.m. – Outgoing call 2 seconds.

2:09 p.m. – Incoming call for 28 minutes

2:30 p.m. Marcus texted: "Call me," before he and Kyson drove to Sparta.

3:04 p.m. Camera surveillance showed Marcus entering Walgreens in Sparta at the corner of Highway 27 (S. Black River Rd) and Highway 21 (W. Wisconsin Ave) where Marcus dropped off a prescription. The footage showed Marcus struggling to move, limping badly, and dragging a leg.

3:09 p.m. Marcus texted, "Hey, I love you I want this to work out so you need to stop making me cry and feel like shit. I rather have u hitting me then doing what."

3:28 p.m. Marcus exited Walgreens and drove west on Wisconsin street, turned left, going south on Black River Street to McDonald's.

3:35 p.m. Video camera footage showed Marcus driving into McDonald's parking lot. Marcus parked the car and walked into McDonald's. Kyson is left secured in his car seat. Marcus put on an obnoxious act, waving his hands, talking loudly, backing away from the counter, then moving again up the counter. Management is so distraught and unnerved at the display, they give Marcus a free meal just to get rid of him. The McDonald's receipt, stamped with a time of 3:36 p.m., will be one of the exhibits at the trial.

3:42 p.m. Jessica, "I love you too and I want this too and we will and I feel like a piece of shit. I really do! We will get through this."

3:50 p.m. Video camera footage showed Marcus leaving McDonald's, limping, with a carryout bag, opening the front passenger door, leaning over the seat, apparently giving a meal to Kyson. Kyson was not shown due to tinted glass.

A demanding and belligerent Anderson puts on an exhibition in Sparta McDonald's. Camera footage is not the best quality.

3:51 p.m. Clerk from McDonald's comes out and hands Marcus a McFlurry.

3:52 p.m. Marcus pulls into the Cenex station in Sparta. Cenex does not have a camera surveillance system.

3:55 p.m. Marcus is back at Walgreens picking up the prescription through the drive-up lane. They drive back to Tomah.

4:01 p.m. Marcus texted, "I need help. I'm in pain you know. I'm suppose to be in bed rest."

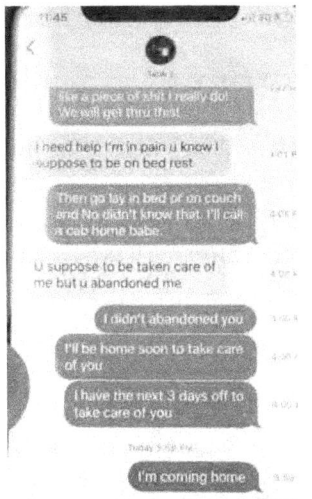

4:08 p.m. Jessica texted back, "Then go lay in bed or on couch and 'No" didn't know that. I'll call a cab home Babe."

4:08 p.m. Marcus, "U suppose to take care of me but you abandoned me."

4:09 p.m. Jessica, "I didn't abandon you. I'll be home soon to take care of you. I have the next three days off to take care of you."

4:35 p.m. Marcus and Kyson are back at 1009 Jodi Circle in Tomah.

Marcus guilt trips Jessica all afternoon with constant calls and text messages.

5:04 p.m. Surveillance cameras showed Kyson alive on a video of Marcus pulling Kyson into the house. Kyson has 50 minutes to live.

The last photo of Kyson alive, a few minutes after 5 p.m. on the day he was murdered.

Chapter 5

Murder on Jodi Circle

Every police officer, per standard operating procedure, writes a report about events that occur on their watch. It's fascinating reading as each officer has certain duties to perform and records the activities from his own perspective. The principal police officers involved in the Kyson murder case are Officers Furlano, Steinborn, Perkins, Scallon, Heckman, Sloan, Tester, and Walensky. Several more Tomah police officers were involved as were a number from the Monroe County Sheriff's Department.

The accounts of Officers Furlano, Steinborn, Perkins, Scallon, and Sloan are about five pages in length. Tester's is a bit longer and Heckman a bit shorter. During the investigation following May 3, officers wrote subsequent reports based on their findings. Many are quite extensive. For example, Robert Walensky's written summation of the surveillance cameras at 1009 Jodi Circle tallies 167 pages.

The ambulance crew report is written by the Ambulance Shift Supervisor Robarge. The EMTs on the ambulance call that fateful day of were Tanner Sutton, Thomas Colloton, and Andrew Rinehart. Each read the report and provided feedback to the Shift Supervisor Robarge. In a sense, it was a collaborative effort.

Author's Note: In this narrative, I borrowed, verbatim, from the written reports of several police officers. The progression of events may overlap. In other words, the exact same events are occurring but described differently by each police officer in his own report. These police reports reveal, in heart-wrenching detail, the desperate struggle that officers encounter in trying to save the life of a little boy.

Wil Steinborn was the first to arrive at the murder scene. The time stamp on Officer Steinborn's body camera reads 22:58 Zulu time, which is five hours ahead of CDT (17:58) or 5:58 p.m.

5:51:30 p.m. A call from Marcus Anderson's cell phone to 911 dispatcher Pat Deethardt. Witness #10

From Sergeant Furlano's Report

"I was on patrol on May 3, 2019, and assigned as the second shift supervisor. At approximately 1755 hours (5:55 pm), dispatch indicated there was a report of an unresponsive three-year-old at 1009 Jodi Circle. Officers Steinborn, Heckman, and I responded.

I arrived first, with Officer Steinborn arriving immediately behind me. I ran towards the residence and told Officer Steinborn to bring his AED in with him. I got to the door and located an adult male, later identified to me as Marcus Anderson, holding a small child, later identified to me as K.R.M.R (DOB 09/03/2015).

Sergeant Jarrod Fulano arrived at 1009 Jodi Circle at the same time as Officer Wil Steinborn.

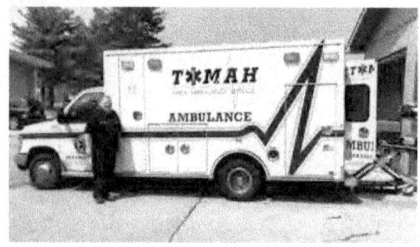

Tomah ambulance received the call at 5:56 pm and arrived at 1009 Jodi Circle at 6:00 p.m.

Kyson appeared to be unresponsive. Marcus was having an extremely difficult time controlling his emotions. I checked Kyson for a pulse and could not find one. It was around this time that Marcus made a comment regarding doing some form of CPR on Kyson, stating that he had been hitting Kyson hard. Marcus made motions with his hands as if he was holding Kyson and using an open hand to strike Kyson as a form of compressions.

We got Kyson to the floor so that we could begin life saving measures. I noted that Kyson and all of his clothing were completely wet. I initially thought it could have been excessive sweating due to a medical condition. I changed out the adult pads on the AED to pediatric pads and placed the pads on Kyson's chest and back. The AED advised that no shock was advised, and that we should begin CPR. Officer Steinborn began compressions on Kyson.

I noted that Officer Steinborn had not brought his medical bag into the residence, which contains our bag valve mask. I went out to Officer Steinborn's squad to retrieve his bag valve mask. The ambulance arrived around this time.

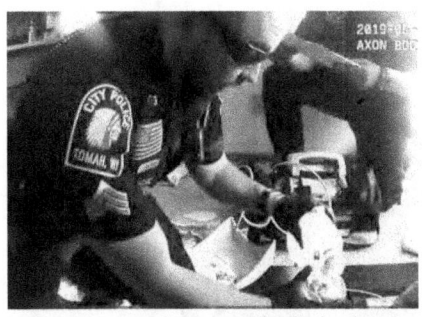

Sergeant Furlano applied the bag valve mask to Kyson to restore his breathing.

I returned to the residence and began providing Kyson with rescue breaths. The ambulance crew entered the residence and began working on Kyson as well. As the ambulance crew were working on Kyson, I began to notice that Kyson had significant bruising to several parts of his body. I noted that on almost every portion of exposed limb and on Kyson's face, there were multiple bruises. I began to suspect that the bruising may have been from physical abuse to a child, and that the medical emergency that we were currently assisting with was possibly a result of physical abuse."

End of Officer Furlano report segment.

5:56 p.m. The ambulance service received a call at 5:56 pm of an unresponsive boy at 1009 Jodi Circle. The ambulance arrives at Jodi Circle at 6:00 pm.

Officer Steinborn Report

"I was on patrol at approximately 5:55 pm in a marked City of Tomah patrol vehicle, Monroe County Communications Center advised of an ambulance call at 1009 Jodi Circle where there was a report of a 3-year-old male that was not breathing. I grabbed my AED and entered the residence to find an adult male, later identified as Marcus Anderson, holding a small male child. It appeared that Anderson was attempting to do an untrained version of mouth-to-mouth resuscitation. Sergeant Furlano and I ordered Anderson to hand over the boy. Anderson stated he was doing CPR on Kyson. He was sweating profusely, agitated, and not responding to the officer's commands to clear the area so we had room to work.

Officer Wil Steinborn's body camera captured a distraught Marcus Anderson in the garage.

Marcus Anderson continued to explain how he attempted to do CPR and then demonstrated it on a doll. Anderson was ordered to exit the living room area. He was screaming into his cell phone while calling someone."

6:05 p.m. Officer Steinborn gets an initial statement from Anderson while Kyson is being worked on.

"I could hear Anderson state, 'Hey, I was pounding pretty hard doing CPR, dog, I'm sorry.' I asked Anderson how he knew CPR. He said military. Sergeant Furlano instructed me to gather an initial statement from Anderson. Anderson was jumping around, pacing, and yelling. He was repeating statements. Anderson was instructed to sit down on a kitchen chair, but he could not, because he needed to look for a cigarette. He was unable to find any cigarettes.

Anderson stated he had just gotten back from the doctor because he had an infection. I observed a few prescription bottles in the house and one on the kitchen floor. Anderson stated they had just got back from the pharmacy, and he and Kyson were going to take a shower. Anderson stated he was in his room to get 'his stuff' and then he heard a 'boom' come from the bathroom. Anderson stated the shower gets slippery sometimes. Anderson stated he started his car, then called Jessica Rice, and then started CPR. I asked Anderson to show me how he performed CPR using a large toy for reference. Anderson picked up a large toy and began slapping it on the front, then turned it over and slapped it on the back. Anderson stated it was what the Internet had told him to do so the patient could get air.

Living room at 1009 Jodi Circle. The television screen shows the video from three surveillance cameras.

Anderson walked me into the bathroom to show me where this occurred. Anderson stated that when he came into the bathroom, Kyson was on the floor. The bathroom floor was wet.

Anderson stated there was no illicit or prescription drugs that Kyson could have gotten into. A record check provided information that Anderson is on felony bond out of Monroe County for case 2017CF727, 2018CF178, and case 2018CF423, which has a special condition of 'No acts or threats of violence.'"

Continuing from Furlano Report:

"I instructed Officer Steinborn to get an initial statement from Marcus on what had occurred. I also had Officer Steinborn use his Axon body camera to get close up footage of the visible bruising. Officer Steinborn took a statement from Marcus, and later advised me of some of the details. Officer Steinborn told me that Marcus said he was in the process of bathing Kyson. Marcus said he left the bathroom and heard a loud thud, followed by a groan. He said that Marcus found Kyson unresponsive in the bathroom. Officer Steinborn said that Marcus had told him that he put clothes on Kyson after discovering him unresponsive."

I had Officer Steinborn ask Marcus about any significant medical history for Kyson and Marcus made some mention of Kyson being born blind and with a nervous system issue. I was not close enough to the conversation to obtain good details on what his answer was for that, however.

Some things immediately stood out to me as abnormal from what Officer Steinborn told me that Marcus had said. It seemed odd that someone would try to put clothing on an unresponsive person. It struck me as odd that the clothing would be completely drenched, even after the child had been given a bath. It struck me as odd that Marcus had stated and demonstrated striking Kyson hard in order to provide CPR compressions, but that the bruising visible on Kyson was spread out over his entire body rather than localized to the spots that Marcus had stated he had contacted him.

Tomah Area Ambulance Service members worked on Kyson for an extended period of time at the residence, and at times were able to obtain a pulse from him. They decided to transport Kyson to Tomah Memorial Hospital for care there. I overheard one of the paramedics indicate they were already requesting MedLink (helicopter) for transportation beyond TMH. I offered to drive the ambulance so that the crew could focus on caring for Kyson. Around this time, Kyson's mother, Jessica Rice, arrived at the residence."

6:12 p.m. Jessica Rice arrives on scene. From Officer Steinborn's report, "Jessica Rice arrived on scene and entered the garage. Anderson met her there. I entered the garage to find the overhead door closed and a vehicle running in the garage. The garage was full of exhaust. I opened the overhead door to vent the fume. I asked Anderson why the vehicle was running, and he stated it was because he was going somewhere. I asked Jessica about punishment and that she was not aware of any physical discipline handed down by Anderson."

6:15 p.m. Sgt. Furlano, "I requested dispatch contact Investigator Sloan to respond to start an investigation, as I was aware he had just ended his shift and was likely still in or around Tomah. Dispatch indicated a short time later that Investigator Paul Sloan was responding and reporting to Tomah Memorial Hospital. It was assumed that Jessica and Marcus Anderson would be leaving for the Hospital."

6:19 p.m. The Tomah Ambulance leaves 1009 Jodi Circle, lights flashing and siren wailing, on a fast run to Tomah Memorial Hospital.

Chapter 6

Ambulance to Tomah Hospital

Jessica arrives at her house at 6:15 p.m. to find the garage door down, Marcus' car engine running, and Marcus in a frenzied, incoherent state.

6:19 p.m. The ambulance crew loaded Kyson in the ambulance. Sgt. Furlano drove the ambulance from 1009 Circle Drive to Tomah Memorial Hospital (TMH), a distance of about a half mile north. Kyson was brought into the trauma room and TMH staff began providing him with care. It was assumed that Jessica and Marcus would be leaving their residence and going to the Hospital.

6:21 p.m. Officers Steinborn and Heckman arrived at TMH. Hospital staff are in a desperate struggle to save Kyson's life. Jessica soon arrives at the hospital.

6:26 p.m. Furlano orders Officers Steinborn and Heckman to return to the residence and obtain their squad cars in case they were needed to respond to another call.

6:30 pm Investigator Paul Sloan arrived at Tomah Memorial Hospital. Sgt. Furlano gave him a brief rundown on what they had at that point. Sloan stated he would begin an interview with Jessica.

6:32 p.m. Sgt. Furlano received word from Officer Heckman that Marcus was still at the residence and was packing bags. Officer Heckman indicated that Marcus was taking an extended period of time packing, and that his mind was on things that seemed out of the ordinary for someone who was trying to get to a hospital to see someone having a serious medical crisis.

Officer Furlano asked Investigator Sloan if he was thinking a search warrant on the residence would be a route he would want to take at some point and Sloan agreed. Officer Furlano told Officer Heckman to secure the residence and remove Marcus if necessary.

Jessica confronts Marcus in the garage.

6:35 p.m. Officer Heckman reported to Officer Furlano that Marcus would not let him back into the residence. Officer Heckman reported that Marcus was confused as to why an investigation would be conducted. Marcus closed the door a second time. Heckman remained at the house until a search warrant was issued later in the evening.

Officer Steinborn had returned to Tomah Memorial Hospital and Officer Furlano sent him back a second time to 1009 Jodi Circle to assist Officer Heckman. Officer Steinborn arrived at 7 p.m., walked up to the residence and knocked on the patio sliding door. Steinborn tells Marcus that the police are securing the house and there will be an investigation of possible child abuse. Marcus bursts out, 'Oh hell no, I would never hurt a child. Please don't."

Marcus continues to talk non-stop. Officer Steinborn says, "Stop talking for a second." Marcus goes back to his room. At 7:07 p.m. Marcus drives away from the house. He will be circling the drive and coming back. Heckman backs his squad car into the driveway.

Sgt. Furlano briefed Lt. Scott Holum on what was transpiring and began calling in additional officers to assist. Furlano's shift was quickly becoming overwhelmed, personnel-wise.

A short time later, Officer Steinborn returned to Tomah Memorial Hospital and reported that Marcus had left the Jodi Circle address in his black Ford Fusion a couple of minutes prior and that Marcus had not shown up at TMH.

Amber Moseley was Jessica Rice's guardian angel on Earth, a true friend. Amber, with her daughter, arrives at the Rice house at 6:21 p.m.

Sgt. Furlano immediately began thinking that Marcus was attempting to flee the area and instructed Officer Steinborn to put out a statewide teletype requesting agencies to stop and hold Marcus for questioning should they contact him. Officer Steinborn contacted dispatch and a teletype was sent out.

Officer Steinborn also called the phone number that Marcus had provided him to see if he could be located. The number he called did not belong to Marcus. Officer Steinborn was quickly able to locate the correct number for Marcus, and it was grossly different from what he had provided Officer Steinborn initially. Officer Steinborn and Sgt. Furlano both agreed that it appeared that Marcus had provided police with a fictitious phone number.

7:00 p.m. The MedLink helicopter arrived at Tomah Memorial Hospital and began assisting with the care of Kyson. Sgt. Furlano spoke with Investigator Sloan, who suggested having Investigator Rob Walensky and Investigator Clayton Tester from the Monroe County Joint Investigative Task Force (MCJITF) respond to assist with the investigation, as they typically handle the major criminal investigations that occur in the area. The initial plan was to have MedLink transport Kyson to Gundersen Health in La Crosse.

Sgt. Furlano contacted Investigator Walensky who stated he would respond to Gundersen Health. Investigator Walensky also contacted Investigator Tester to assist with the investigation.

7:33 p.m. TMH staff, along with the help of the MedLink crew, continued to provide care for Kyson for a lengthy period of time. TMH staff indicated that they had done all they could for Kyson, and that would soon be pronouncing him deceased. They requested that Jessica be brought into the room. Jessica was being interviewed by Investigator Sloan in a private room. TMH staff made the death notification to Jessica.

7:35 p.m. Sgt. Furlano conferred with Investigator Sloan and Officer Steinborn. They determined that Marcus needed to be taken into custody. Officer Steinborn was tasked to locate Marcus. Investigator Sloan indicated to Sgt. Furlano that he was fine at TMH, and that Sgt. Furlano was free to join the search for Marcus as well.

May 4, 2019 12:44 a.m. Officers receive a warrant from Judge Mark L. Goodman to search 1009 Jodi Circle.

Chapter 7

Search for a Killer

The search is on for Marcus Anderson. Officer Heckman is left at the 1009 Jodi Circle house to maintain security and provide officers possible locations that Anderson might be. Several squad cars were on the hunt, scouring the city for a black Ford Fusion, Wisconsin license plate 39043DS.

Sgt. Perkins Report

"At approximately 7:00 p.m. on May 3, 2019, I was off duty when Sgt. Furlano contacted me and requested that I come to work to assist as they were dealing with an EMS call at 1009 Jodi Circle that turned into a severe child abuse investigation. I dressed in full police uniform and responded to work. I was serving as shift supervisor and operating marked patrol K-9 squad car #75. Viktor, my K9 police dog, was with me.

Anderson's Ford Fusion was spotted downtown at 7:52 p.m. parked in the 1100 block of Superior Avenue.

I was informed the child abuse investigation had turned into a homicide investigation as the child had succumbed to his injuries. I was advised that the father of the child, Marcus Anderson, was the main suspect at the time and needed to be taken into custody. I was further advised that Marcus was supposed to be at Tomah Memorial Hospital with family, but he never arrived. Marcus was reportedly operating a black Ford Fusion with WI Disabled Plate of 39043DS. His whereabouts were unknown. I was advised to use caution if I encountered Marcus due to the nature of the call for service and unknown information about possible weapons.

I was patrolling around the city and made contact with Deputy Geier to inform him of Marcus and Marcus' vehicle. (The time was 7:52 p.m.) I continued to scan for the vehicle and was in the downtown area when I observed a black Ford Fusion parked on Superior Avenue facing North. The vehicle was on the East side of the street and was parked in the first parking stall North of E Juneau St. I noticed the vehicle had its brake lights and right turn signal activated. I pulled up behind the vehicle and confirmed it was Marcus' vehicle. I advised dispatch I was out with the vehicle and provided my location.

Tomah Police and Monroe County Sheriff's vehicles box in Marcus' car. He has no where to run.

I parked behind the vehicle and activated forward and rear facing emergency lights. I was not immediately able to see anyone inside the vehicle. I approached the vehicle on the driver's side and obtained my duty pistol. I observed a black male slumped over in the driver's seat. I pointed my pistol at the backside of the male. The windows were at least partially open, so I yelled to the male to 'show me your hand.' I received no response from the male. I moved around to the passenger side, and I was able to see he was still breathing, and he had no visible weapon near his hands. I again gave more commands to the male and still did not receive any response. I backed away from the vehicle and went back to my squad."

Officer Scallon takes a position across the street from the Ford Fusion, providing cover with rifle ready.

Sgt. Furlano Report

"We had an influx of officers in and around Tomah, due to the personnel I had called in to work the road and the Monroe County Sherriff's Department, who all were trying to locate Marcus. Officer Heckman was doing research while maintaining security on the residence, providing possible locations for officers to check to locate Marcus. Around this time, Sgt. Perkins, who I had called to assist with road coverage, indicated that he had located Marcus' car parked in the 1100 block of Superior Avenue. Sgt. Perkins initially stated that he believed the vehicle was unoccupied. I was in the area and responded to that location to assist.

When I arrived, I saw Sgt. Perkins approaching the vehicle with his handgun drawn. Sgt. Perkins then advised me that there was a black male slumped over the steering wheel. I called Sgt. Perkins to back away from the suspect vehicle so that we could conduct a high-risk vehicle contact.

We quickly had several more officers respond to the area to assist. We closed the 1100 block of Superior Ave to vehicle traffic. Officer Scallon, who I had also called in to assist with road coverage, arrived and we had him begin telling people who were on the west sidewalk to get into buildings. I noted that Officer Scallon had a magnified optic (telescopic sight) on his rifle. I instructed him to take cover behind a vehicle and provide watch from that position directly to the west of the suspect vehicle. Since we had multiple agencies on scene, I requested dispatch to get all units on the Tomah PD main radio channel in order to improve communications abilities.

Officer Brennon Scallon arrived at the arrest site. He notices the windshield wipers are activated on Marcus' Ford Fusion. Perkins dog is barking. The loudspeaker is urging Marcus to come out of the car."

Sgt. Perkins Report

"Sgt. Lee (Monroe County Sherriff's Office) and Officer Steinborn arrived shortly after. Sgt. Lee parked near my squad and that allowed me to obtain my K-9 for a potential apprehension if Marcus decided to flee. Officer Steinborn parked his squad on Superior Avenue at Council Street and blocked all North bound traffic there.

Deputy Rice and Officer Scallon arrived to assist at this time. Officer Scallon blocked Westbound traffic on E Juneau St at Kilbourn Ave. and Deputy Rice blocked Southbound traffic on Superior Ave at Monowau St.

I confirmed with Sgt. Furlano that Marcus was a black male, as I had not met Marcus before. Sgt. Furlano stated he was a black male. I took position on the passenger side of my squad and focused my attention and my K9's attention to Marcus' vehicle. I gave my K-9 his bark command to let Marcus know a K-9 was on scene."

The Break Room Sports Bar and Grill is located directly across Superior Avenue from the suspect's Ford Fusion. Curious patrons are congregating on the sidewalks.

Officer Steinborn Report

"I approached the scene from the north, bypassed the locale and blocked northbound traffic on Superior Ave at E. Council St. I approached on foot and ordered vehicles to leave the area as I got to them. When I arrived on scene, Sergeant

Furlano instructed me to take over communications with Anderson, as I am a trained crisis negotiator.

I observed the brake lights were engaged and the right turn signal was engaged. The vehicle's engine was running. I was unable to see a person in the vehicle, but I did observe both the rear driver and passenger side window were partially rolled down. I used the PA system in patrol vehicle #50 to attempt contact. I spoke with Anderson for approximately seven minutes with no response."

Sgt. Perkins Report

"At that time, Sgt. Furlano and Deputy Geier arrived to assist. Sgt. Furlano pulled his squad up next to mine and we blocked off north bound traffic on Superior Ave. Due to the nature of the call and unknown mental state of Marcus or his intentions, we decided a high-risk contact would be the safest route to take Marcus into custody. I transitioned to my duty rifle and pointed it at Marcus' vehicle. Sgt. Furlano attempted numerous verbal commands to the male, but we received no response."

Sergeant Furlano makes the decision to use Tomah's Tactical Unit for a high-risk arrest.

Sgt. Furlano Report

"We tried several verbal commands and did not get a response from Marcus. We formed a team and approached the vehicle, sliding tire deflation spikes underneath the vehicle to hopefully prevent a lengthy pursuit should Marcus decide to flee in the vehicle. Officer Steinborn arrived and offered to do PA communications. Officer Steinborn is a trained Crisis Negotiator, so I had him begin communications with Marcus. Officer Steinborn also received no response.

The high-risk vehicle contact was occurring in the downtown bar area on a Friday night with nice weather. We were quickly drawing large crowds in the area. We did not have the personnel available to move them back to ensure their safety. I was aware that Marcus was now a suspect in a homicide.

I felt that Marcus being slumped over the steering wheel either meant that he had committed suicide or that he had ingested some type of substance causing his condition. I felt that Marcus needed to be taken into custody in as little time as was safely possible to minimize the potential for the crowd to grow or him to succumb to whatever was going on physically with him. I drove to the Police Department to retrieve the Tomah Police Department Combined Tactical Unit (CTU) truck, as I am a member of the CTU, and I felt that the equipment in the vehicle would open up more options for taking Marcus into custody. I also requested dispatch to have an ambulance stage near our location.

I returned to the area with the CTU truck. I formulated a plan to shoot out the passenger side rear window of the vehicle with a less lethal 12-gauge shotgun bean bag round. I felt that this would be used as a probing technique to solicit a response from Marcus. I also felt that this would create a sufficient opening for introducing chemical agents into the vehicle. I notified all units on scene via radio that we would be firing a 12-gauge beanbag round into the vehicle. Officer Steinborn obtained a shield and we got into a position about 20 yards perpendicular to the passenger side of the suspect vehicle. I then fired a 12-gauge beanbag round into the rear passenger side window. This was effective in shattering a portion of the rear passenger side window."

Sgt. Perkins Report

"We deployed a team of four officers, myself included, and we approached the vehicle to clear it of any other subjects. We utilized my K-9 and we cleared the vehicle. Sgt. Furlano and another officer approached on the passenger side of the vehicle and were standing in the empty lot to the east of the vehicle. Sgt. Furlano advised he would be using a beanbag shotgun round to break a rear window in Marcus' vehicle. The intent of the bean bag was to get Marcus' attention and get him to comply with us. Up to this point, all of our attempts to get Marcus' attention were futile.

Sgt. Furlano deployed the shotgun and it was effective in breaking the rear passenger side window. Immediately, I observed Marcus sit up and start looking around.

Officer Steinborn continued with PA announcements to Marcus. My K-9 and I moved to the driver's side of Sgt. Furlano's squad and we took up a position there. I again gave my K-9 his bark command to let Marcus know a K-9 was on scene.

Marcus followed instructions and exited the vehicle as he was directed. My K-9 barked a few times and Marcus turned and looked at him. Marcus complained that he was having a hard time hearing the commands when the dog barked. I did my best to keep my K-9 quiet. Marcus was slowly complying and at one point wanted to pull up his pants. With not knowing if Marcus had any weapons in his pants or waistband, Office Steinborn told him not to do that via the PA. I also told Marcus that if he did so, he would be bit. Marcus continued to comply, and he was taken into custody without further incident."

Officer Alex Brueggeman demonstrates the Remington 870 shotgun that Sgt. Furlano employed to shoot out the rear window of Marcus' car.

Author notes: *Marcus Anderson does not know, at this point, that he will be charged with homicide and a host of other crimes. He does not realize that* he will never be a free man again. When he is transported, he will be in handcuffs. If he goes to trial, he will have some kind of physical restraints. Anderson's life is changed forever but that is beyond his comprehension as he stands beside his Ford Fusion.

Officers confer on strategy: Perkins, Steinborn, Lee, Furlano.

"Almost immediately after the window shattered, Marcus began to respond. We set up an arrest team and Marcus was called out of the vehicle. Anderson took his foot off the brake and the vehicle lurched forward. (The time is 8:11 p.m.) Anderson placed the vehicle in park and extinguished the engine. Anderson was commanded back to officers while at gunpoint. Anderson was unsteady on his feet and was having difficulty understanding commands.

Marcus was taken into custody without incident. I pointed my firearm at Marcus during this time. We formed a team and cleared the vehicle, finding no one else inside."

Sgt. Perkins Report

"I then heard Officer Steinborn on a squad PA system talking to Marcus. The commands consisted of telling Marcus we were the Police and to surrender while showing us his hands. I did not observe any movement from Marcus.

I noted there was becoming in increasing amount of people on the sidewalks and in the streets watching what was going on. With the potential danger involved, I requested dispatch to contact the businesses on the 1100 block of Superior Avenue and had the citizens shelter in place or exit using the rear entrances.

Officer Steinborn continued with PA commands and at one point I had Officer Steinborn turn up the volume on the PA system. He did and the commands were louder and easier to understand. (8:07 p.m.) The loudspeaker blared out, "Take the keys out. Hands on your head. On your knees."

Law enforcement personnel are closing in on Marcus Anderson: Officer Perkins with police dog, Viktor, Monroe County Deputy Michael Geier, Sergeant Furlano with the shield, and Monroe County Sheriff's Captain Ryan Lee.

Sgt. Steinborn Report

"Once Anderson was in a position to be handcuffed, I holstered my firearm and handcuffed Anderson. I conducted a brief search of his person and secured him in the rear of Deputy Geier's patrol vehicle. Anderson's eyes were blood shot and watery and his pupils were extremely small.

The contents of Anderson's possession were not immediately searched. It was unknown to me if he was in possession of any contraband. Anderson's possessions were placed in a bag and put in Sergeant Furlano's patrol vehicle.

I remained on the scene until Larkin's Towing Service came and hauled the vehicle to the impound lot. I secured the vehicle in the impound lot.

Based on the events as they transpired it was clear that Anderson's blood may contain evidence of a Felony Murder, Aggravated Battery, Physical Abuse of a Child, Felony Bail Jumping, and/or Operating While Intoxicated. I completed a search warrant and affidavit for a sample of Anderson's blood and provided such to Investigator Walensky to present to a Circuit Court Judge.

Anderson was cited for Operating While Intoxicated, 1st Offense due to his lack of coordination, mental confusion, blood shot and glassy eyes, and extremely small pupils. The citation was faxed to the Monroe County Jail for service."

Sgt. Perkins Report

"Deputy Geier was searching Marcus' person and I asked Marcus for his middle initial and date of birth. He provided it to me, and I gave it to dispatch. Dispatch advised the information he provided matched the information they had.

I asked Marcus if he needed any medical attention as an ambulance was parked just behind us and I noticed Marcus complained earlier of not being able to walk easily. Marcus requested he be seen by EMS. Due to our location and blocking all North bound traffic, we decided EMS would check on Marcus at the Tomah PD. During this contact, Deputy Geier told me to look at Marcus' eyes and more specifically his pupils. I looked that Marcus' pupils and noticed they were constricted and very small. I have seen similar pupils on subject that have been abusing illegal drugs. Marcus was constantly talking and complaining."

Marcus Anderson is arrested and taken into custody. He will never be a free man from this moment forward.

Sgt. Furlano Report

"Marcus indicated that he wished to receive medical treatment for a previous medical condition. The ambulance was called from their staging location to the high-risk vehicle contact location. I advised officers on scene to transport Marcus via squad to the Police Department and the ambulance crew could check him out there, so that we could open the road to vehicle traffic. Marcus was transported via squad to the Police Department and the ambulance followed. I called Investigator Sloan and asked if he wished to have the vehicle Marcus was in, located in a secured impound. Investigator Sloan stated that he did wish for the vehicle to be impounded. Larkins was contacted to tow the vehicle to impound.

I went to the Police Department and met with the ambulance crew. They indicated that they believed that Marcus needed to be taken to a hospital. They stated that since Kyson had received care from the TMH staff and the TMH staff were not handling his death well, that Marcus be transported to a different hospital. The ambulance crew suggested Sparta Mayo and requested that an officer ride with them in the ambulance. I tasked Officer Scallon to ride in the ambulance to Sparta Mayo, not only to provide security for the ambulance crew but also to record all statements made by Marcus during the ride over. I also coordinated with Sgt. Lee of the Monroe County Sheriff's Department to follow the ambulance should another officer be needed to control Marcus. Marcus was then transported to Sparta Mayo Hospital via ambulance.

Following his arrest in downtown Tomah, Marcus Anderson was taken by ambulance to the Tomah Police Station.

Marcus was secured in Officer Scallon's squad and was transported to Tomah PD where he was seen by EMS. All traffic was transitioned back to normal, and I remained with the vehicle. I was advised the vehicle would be towed by Larkin's and taken to the Tomah PD impound lot. The plan was for a later search warrant to be completed for the vehicle."

At 8:25 p.m., Marcus is informed he is going to Sparta Mayo.

Officer Steinborn arrived back at my location and relieved me of my position. Officer Steinborn assisted Larkins' and followed them to the impound lot where he secured it.

At 8:44 p.m. Marcus was being seen by a new EMS staff that took over from the staff called to 1009 Jodi Circle earlier in the evening. It was decided he would be transported to the Sparta Hospital for further evaluation.

9:01 p.m. Ambulance leaves for Sparta. The ambulance crew tries to put an IV in his vein. Ambulance makes an ordered stop. Marcus' eyes are checked with a flashlight. Marcus babbled on about his routine that day. Scallon says, "Since you're in custody, don't talk about it." Marcus asked Scallon about his son. Scallon says he doesn't know. "I just came on duty." Marcus asked about his car and was told it was towed. Scallon asked Marcus if he knows his Social Security number. Marcus complains about his doctor and having to sit in an airport for seven or eight hours.

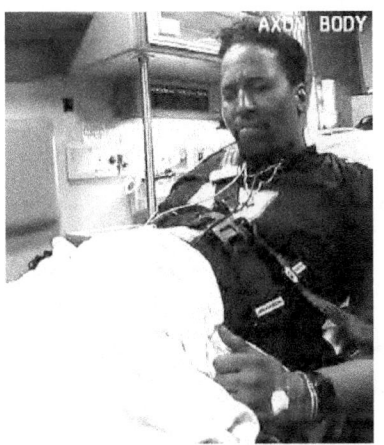

The decision was made by Tomah PD officers to transport Anderson to Sparta Mayo Hospital. The suspect was handcuffed to the railings of the gurney.

9:33 p.m. Scallon asks Marcus if he would consent to a blood draw and is informed if he does not consent, a warrant would be issued. "I don't do drugs" repeated several times. "All I want to know is if my son is alive."

Author notes: Some information was redacted from Sgt. Furlano's report. It was revealed later that the Tomah Memorial Hospital staff was distraught and angered that the perpetrator of Kyson's murder would be brought to their medical facility. Plus, they were exhausted by a valiant struggle to save a little boy's life.

Marcus Anderson was transported to Sparta Mayo Hospital with Officer Scallon riding along. Scallon had his body camera on the entire time, including the transfer to a Sparta Mayo hospital bed.

Chapter 8

Jessica Talks

May 3, 2019 6:15 p.m.

Detective Paul Sloan received a phone call from the Monroe County Communications Center (MCCC) advising that he needed to report for duty per Sergeant Furlano. Detective Sloan drives to Tomah Memorial Hospital (TMH) on Butts Avenue and is met by Sgt. Furlano at about 6:30 p.m. They are joined by Officer Steinborn a short time later.

In Sloan's own words, via his written report: "I observed medical staff performing CPR on Kyson Rice. He was unclothed and I examined Kyson's body and noted a large number of bruises covering his head, torso, arms, and legs. Bruises were in both circular and linear patterns and consistent with physical abuse of a child. I initially photographed Kyson using my department issued Apple iPhone."

The three Officers, Sloan, Furlano, and Steinborn discuss the situation. Steinborn informs Sloan that Kyson was in the care and custody of Marcus Anderson at 1009 Jodi Circle. Steinborn stated that Marcus was going to shower with Kyson. Marcus went to his bedroom. Soon, Marcus heard a thud in the bathroom and found Kyson lying unresponsive in the tub. Marcus attempted CPR and dressed Kyson before the police and EMS arrived. Steinborn described CPR as Marcus delivering chest compressions and back blows to Kyson. Officer Steinborn did note Marcus' vehicle parked and running in the garage at 1009 Jodi Circle.

Jessica Rice arrived at the TMH as staff were treating Kyson. Sloan conducted an audio-recorded interview with Jessica after hospital staff and EMT's talked to her. The interview was interrupted by occasional medical status updates and the evolving criminal investigation.

It was clear by this time that Marcus was not coming to the hospital. Detective Sloan was told that Marcus was looking for his wallet. Sloan told Sgt. Furlano to have the Jodi Circle residence secured pending an application for a search warrant.

Detective Sloan Report

"Marcus Anderson did not respond to Tomah Memorial Hospital at any point. Initially I was told Marcus needed to look for his wallet. In speaking with Sergeant Jarrod Furlano, I requested the residence of 1009 Jodi Circle be secured pending application for a search warrant. I later learned Marcus left 1009 Jodi Circle and was located in the 1100 block of Superior Avenue by Tomah Police Sergeant Adam Perkins. Sergeant Perkins observed Marcus slumped over inside his vehicle. Following a high-risk traffic stop, officers took Marcus into custody and processed him for OMVWI.

On Friday, May 3, 2019, at approximately 6:51 p.m., I conducted an audio-recorded interview with Jessica Rice in a private room at TMH. At the outset of the interview, Jessica was informed she was not under arrest and free to leave at any time, I shut the door for privacy; however, I told Jessica she could leave at any time to check on Kyson.

At the outset of the interview, I asked Jessica to explain what brought us to Tomah Memorial Hospital on this date. Jessica said she received a phone call from Marcus advising Kyson had taken a fall and was not breathing. Jessica told Marcus to call 911. Jessica left her place of employment, Taco Bell in Tomah, and went to her residence.

Jessica Rice slowly comes to terms that Marcus Anderson is a killer.

I asked Jessica to explain her morning. Jessica said on this date she left 1009 Jodi Circle between 9:20 a.m. and 9:30 a.m. Jessica went to Dunkin Donuts with Amber Moseley before arriving for work at Taco Bell. Jessica was scheduled to work until 8:00 p.m . Jessica stated her relationship with Marcus was 'rocky,' but Marcus was watching her son, Kyson. Jessica said Marcus called her around '5-ish', screaming, 'He's not breathing, he's not breathing,' so Jessica told Marcus to call 911. Marcus hung up the phone. Jessica tried calling back, but Marcus's phone went to voicemail. Jessica told her boss she needed to leave and she called Amber Moseley for a ride. Jessica stated Marcus was on the phone with her the entire way, but also it sounded as if Marcus was talking with the paramedics. Marcus related he tried performing CPR on Kyson.

I asked Jessica what Marcus and Kyson were doing leading up to this incident. Jessica stated it is common for Kyson to shower with Marcus. Jessica said Marcus takes many showers and bathes Kyson before bed. On this date, Marcus related to Jessica that he was getting Kyson out of the shower when Kyson slipped and fell. Marcus did not say what Kyson struck his head on, or what time Kyson hit his head. Marcus told Jessica he was in the shower with Kyson before Kyson struck his head. Jessica said she found it strange Marcus showered with Kyson at 5:00 p.m. on this date because usually Marcus and Kyson are not home.

I spoke with Jessica about Kyson's medical history. Jessica advised Kyson's primary doctors were at Mayo Health-Tomah, where he sees Doctor Cavaness. Kyson's only significant medical issue is that he was born without nerves on the left side of his face. This prevents Kyson from closing his left eye, which causes his eye to become dry. Treatment includes use of over-the-counter eye drops and ointment. Jessica related Kyson has never been to the emergency room prior to May 3, 2019.

Kyson learned to spell out "I love you" in sign language.

I asked Jessica if Kyson ever fell getting out of the tub, previously. Jessica said 'yes,' that Kyson was a 'pretty clumsy kid.' I told Jessica that Kyson has a large number of bruises on his body. Jessica said another officer told her that as well, but Jessica had not observed the bruises until today because of her work schedule. Jessica said Kyson is not awake when she leaves in the morning and in bed when she returns home in the evening. I asked Jessica who else would have watched Kyson on May 3, 2019. Jessica said just Marcus. Jessica did not know what Marcus and Kyson had planned on this date. I asked Jessica her thoughts on how Kyson sustained the bruises. Jessica said, 'I feel like he's done something, and I hate to admit.' Jessica said she was now going to leave Marcus. I advised Jessica that Kyson would require transport to a large trauma center. Jessica requested UW-Health in Madison, Wisconsin.

Mother and son at happier times.

Jessica and I spoke about methods of discipline used with Kyson. Jessica said she put Kyson on timeouts because she hates spanking. Jessica initially said she 'thought' Marcus put Kyson in a corner when Kyson misbehaved. Marcus uses no other forms of discipline. I asked Jessica the last time she used physical discipline with Kyson. Jessica advised this occurred in February 2019, at which time she spanked Kyson on his butt using her hand. I asked Jessica about the last time she witnessed Marcus spank Kyson. Jessica said. 'I couldn't even tell you.' Jessica said she never witnessed Marcus spank Kyson with his hand or any object. I told Jessica that Kyson has too many bruises for no one knowing. I asked if the abusive behavior has been ongoing and asked if she was afraid. Jessica indicated, yea and began crying. Jessica said, 'He's a good guy. I know he is, but I don't want him to get in trouble.'

I asked Jessica to tell me more about what was occurring. Jessica continued to cry and said, 'I love him, but I have to do this for myself. It's hard when you love a man but have to protect your son too.' Jessica then said, 'Yeah, it was him.' When Marcus punished or spanks, 'He just hits too hard and does not realize his own strength,' Jessica said."

7:15 p.m. *Sloan's interview with Jessica was interrupted for six minutes because Kyson was set for transport by medical helicopter.* "I stopped the recording at this point and allowed Jessica to see Kyson. The interview continued at 7:21 p.m. Upon return from the break, I asked Jessica to continue with her statement on how she knew Marcus caused the bruising to Kyson. Jessica said when Marcus gets mad and goes to punish, he does not know his own strength. Marcus needs to work on his anger, Jessica said.

I again spoke with Jessica about the bruises on Kyson's body and asked if she knew how Kyson sustained any of them. Jessica stated she did not. Jessica said she not only works all the time, but also that clothing covers those areas of Kyson's body. I asked Jessica the last time she bathed, dressed, or examined Kyson's body. Jessica estimated three weeks prior to this incident. Jessica said three weeks ago she gave Kyson a bath and helped dress Kyson, but never saw any bruises.

Kyson loved all things Spiderman.

Those that knew Kyson said he was very bright, affable, and eager to learn knew things.

I revisited my question about forms of discipline Marcus uses with Kyson. Jessica said Marcus had threatened with the belt before, therefore, he could have used the belt. Jessica again said she has never witnessed Marcus use physical discipline with Kyson. Jessica has observed Marcus use one hand to pick up Kyson by the arm and carry Kyson to his room.

I reminded Jessica that before the break she was worried and told me more was going on. I told Jessica she continues to tell me the same things. I told Jessica if more was going on, she needed to tell me for Kyson. Jessica then asked if I would tell Marcus. I assured Jessica I would not tell Marcus. Jessica took a deep breath, sighed and whispered, 'I got to protect....' Jessica knew Marcus has hit Kyson but had not witnessed 'with her own eyes.' Jessica said she did not see the incident but heard it. Jessica was in the kitchen cooking when Marcus was in Kyson's room yelling at him. Jessica heard noises of Marcus hitting something. 'Kyson was a trooper and did not cry,' Jessica said. Jessica later asked Marcus about the incident. Marcus told Jessica not to worry about it. After this incident, Marcus started bathing Kyson. Jessica said she knew the bruises on Kyson's back were from Marcus hitting Kyson with a belt. Jessica described the belt as a child's brown leather belt with a silver buckle.

Jessica did not know how Kyson sustained the bruising to his face. 'I was not there for that one,' Jessica said.

Jessica spoke in more detail about the bruising on Kyson's arms and demonstrated for me. Jessica had witnessed Marcus use his hand to pick up Kyson by his bicep. Jessica has noticed 'little fingers' on Kyson's arm."

7:33 p.m. TMH staff, along with the help of the MedLink crew, continued to provide care for Kyson for a lengthy period of time. TMH staff indicated that they had done all they could for Kyson and would be pronouncing him deceased soon. At 7:33 p.m. Sgt. Jarrod Furlano knocked on the door and advised Jessica that hospital staff wanted to see her. Sgt. Furlano wrote, "They requested that Jessica be brought into the room. I went to the room that Investigator Sloan was speaking with Jessica and told her she was needed in Kyson's room. TMH staff made the death notification to Jessica."

7:41 p.m. Kyson was pronounced dead. Sloan wrote, "I tried continuing the interview with Jessica, who requested some time. Detective Clayton Tester later interviewed Jessica Rice."

8:44 p.m. Investigator Paul Sloan photographed Kyson's body, "I initially photographed the body of Kyson using my department issued iPhone. I photographed Kyson's body using my Canon EOS Rebel T1i camera. After taking photographs, Kyson was moved to a different room in the Medical-Surgery unit of TMH. I remained with the body and allowed John Glynn to view the body." *Note: John Glynn requested to see Kyson and say a prayer for him.*

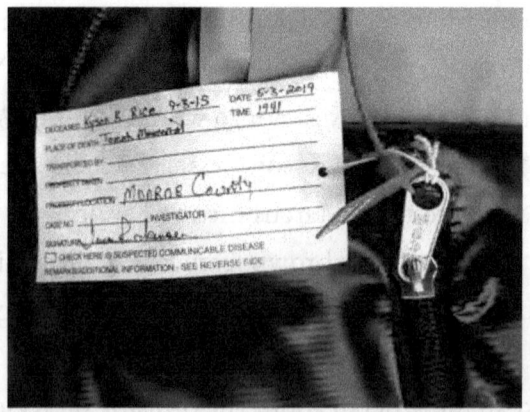

At 10:20 p.m. Kyson is placed in a body bag, sealed, and tagged.

8:56 p.m. Sloan's report continued at 8:56 p.m. "I turned Kyson's body over to Deputy Medical Examiner Theresa Isensee. Medical examiner Isensee examined and photographed Kyson's body before we placed him in a body bag at 9:52 p.m. with seal no. 2993296."

10:20 p.m. Lanham-Schanhofer Funeral Home removed the body of Kyson from Tomah Memorial Hospital. An autopsy was set for Saturday May 4, 2019, at UW-Health in Madison, Wisconsin.

Sloan report

"I uploaded the audio record of my interview with Jessica Rice to Evidence.com. I uploaded photographs of Kyson's body to the Omnigo records management system. I secured the clothes of Kyson provided to me by hospital staff and entered the items into evidence."

Chapter 9

Tomah PD, Ambulance, Sparta Mayo Hospital

The investigation into the murder of Kyson Rice began when Marcus Anderson fled 1009 Jodi Circle at about 7:30 p.m. on May 3, 2019. Everyone knew the name of the killer but proving it in court would be another matter. Thus far, there were no witnesses, no weapons, no physical evidence, and no motive. Investigators and the District Attorney's Office in Sparta, county seat of Monroe County, were tasked with proving that Marcus beat Kyson Rice to death on the late afternoon of Friday, May 3.

The majority of the investigation was carried out by the Monroe County Task Force of Robert Walensky, Paul Sloan with the Tomah Police Department, Clayton Tester, detective with Monroe County Sheriff's department, and Don Henry, Investigator from the Monroe County District Attorney's Office.

8:52 p.m. Officer Scallon's body camera was operating. Marcus makes statements such as, "I was gone two weeks. I don't do no drugs or nothing, I'm still wet from the shower."

Marcus was asked his Social Security number but does not respond. He was asked his address and he correctly responds, "1009 Jodi Circle." He added, "I got cramps, hurts really bad. My leg hurting."

Anderson is handcuffed to a Sparta Mayo Hospital bed. Local time is 9:39 p.m.

He was asked about his doctor. He replied, "Mayo." He talked about 16-hour flights and sitting in the airport for 8 hours. Marcus complained, "I'm in a lot of pain, man, where's my pain medication. I don't know what happened."

Marcus said he was just sleeping in his car on Superior Avenue and asked why he was pulled out of his car for just sleeping. Scallon answered, "We didn't know if you had weapons, we were just following protocol. Based on information that we had. Marcus asked, "Are you going to charge me with something just by sleeping in my car? I don't want to get into any trouble. I don't know what the hell is going on. Scallon asked if they can do a blood draw. He does not get a positive response. "I want to know if my son is alive." Scallon replied, "I don't know."

Several times Marcus said, "I don't want to get into any trouble." Asked again about his consent for a blood draw, Marcus responded, "I don't know. I don't drink, I don't do drugs. All I know is that I got opiates in my system from pain medication."

Marcus asked several times about the condition of his son. Scallon replied, "I don't know. He wasn't doing well. I will let you know as soon as I find out." Over and over, he said, "I don't know what's going on." When asked, Marcus gave Officer Scallon his phone number.

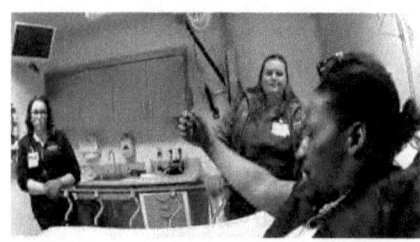

Marcus is uncooperative, argumentative, and otherwise obnoxious to hospital staff.

9:31 p.m. The Tomah Ambulance arrived at Sparta Mayo Hospital and Marcus was transferred to a hospital bed. He asked several times about a criminal investigation. Scallon replied, "I don't know all the details."

9:36 p.m. Two nurses were tending to Marcus. He was hooked up to monitors. His jersey was removed. Marcus complained about two broken ribs.

9:40 p.m. Dr. Kasten entered the hospital room and asked Marcus, "Tell me why you're here." She ordered labs. "Why did you get rhabdo? Doctor Kasten told Marcus, "You get that with extreme exertion, such as a marathon." Marcus complains again of lying on a hard floor in airports and doing lots of driving. Dr. Kasten tells Marcus, "We'll do a blood draw and see how bad it is."

Author's Note: Rhabdomyolysis (shortened as rhabdo) is a condition in which damaged skeletal muscle breaks down rapidly. Symptoms may include muscle pains, weakness, vomiting, and confusion. There may be tea-colored urine or an irregular heartbeat.

9:44 p.m. Investigator Robert Walensky arrived. He waited outside the hospital room.

9:52 p.m. Marcus was asked questions by the medical staff. "Have you been out of the country?" Marcus was vague. Are you a smoker? Marcus admits to a half pack a day. Do you use recreational drugs? The reply was "no." Do you have a pacemaker, and the answer was "no." Did you take your pain medication today? "No, the police have it. The doctor misled the administration, and that's why they took me off it for two weeks."

Marcus was handcuffed to the hospital bed. He thrashed around, moaning. A nurse, clad in a blue suit, said, "You have to hold still, I need to put this IV in." The nurse's demeanor was one of sternness.

Marcus moaned, "I don't know why I'm here. My wife works at Mayo. She says everyone gets the same treatment. I didn't do nothing wrong

The nurse was still trying to get an IV in. She checked the other arm. Marcus said, "They blew all my veins on my surgery."

10:00 p.m. Two nurses continued struggling to insert an IV into Marcus' arm. They used an ultrasound unit to locate a vein. Marcus asked Scallon, "What about Kyson?" Scallon replied, "I honestly don't know. I started at 7." Finally, they get an IV in the hand, not the arm. Marcus demanded, "I want my own medications. It's in my pocket, just got it today. You can read what's on the bottle." The nurse responded, "We can't give you what you brought in. People change pills in bottles all the time."

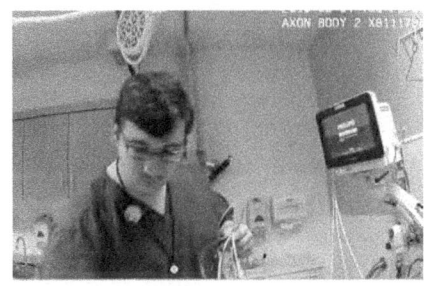

Marcus is sent to the X-ray unit. He had complained of falling and hurting himself.

10:18 p.m. Marcus was given a blanket. The nurse told Marcus he will go to x-ray. Marcus said, "I don't know what's going on. I was going to the hospital to see my girlfriend. At 4 this morning I fell on the porcelain in the bathroom, hurt my ribs."

10:23 p.m. Marcus was wheeled into the x-ray room. "Now I know why the police think I was drunk, 'cause I was parked by a bar.'"

10:28 p.m. The x-ray technician helped Marcus off the gurney to a chair. He constantly complained and moaned. They take 5 x-rays of left ribs. His upper body was covered with tattoos.

10:40 p.m. Marcus was wheeled out of the x-ray room back to hospital room ED4.

10:45 p.m. Marcus was constantly complaining. Scallon advised, "Take a snooze if you have to. Don't know what the charges are." Marcus says, "All I want to know is if my son is alive." Scallon texts for an answer.

Marcus said, "I was on my way to the hospital. Going to get some cigarettes. Later, Marcus asked, "Where's my girlfriend? He asked for pain medication. The nurse told him they need a urine sample before they can administer medication.

11:03 p.m. Marcus wanted to lay on his side so Scallon removed a handcuff. He received a water cup and straw and watched a news program on television.

11:18 p.m. A nurse informed Marcus that they must do a legal blood draw. Toni Halvorson, 17-year veteran nurse at Sparta Mayo Hospital, did a blood draw on Anderson per the Search Warrant. The blood-draw kits are from the State Crime Lab.

11:19 p.m. Marcus wanted relief from rhabdo. She said she can prescribe it but needs a blood draw.

11:24 p.m. Scallon showed Marcus the Search Warrant for a blood draw. He was lying on his side, reading the Search Warrant. He signed it and Investigator Walensky validated it.

11:25 p.m. Anderson screamed, "He's dying. They charging me with murder, what the fuck. He hit his head. What the fuck. My baby died." Marcus turned his head down into the pillow, wailing loudly, with a nearby nurse appearing unemotional. Another nurse prepared the labeling and paperwork for the blood sample before it is sent to the lab.

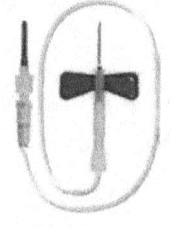

A butterfly needle is used to draw blood from a vein. A butterfly needle consists of a very thin needle, two flexible "wings," a flexible transparent tubing, and a connector.

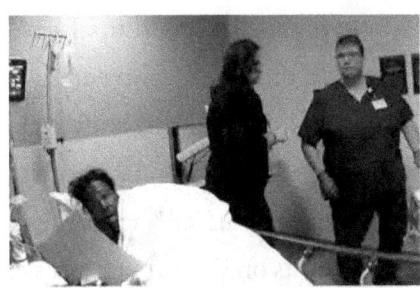

Marcus screams and goes into a total meltdown when he reads the search warrant for a blood sample.

11:29 p.m. Nurses and Scallon told Marcus he needs to lay flat on his back. "This can't be real," he wailed.

11:30 p.m. "I just picked up my pain medication from the pharmacy. It's in my pocket."

11:33 p.m. Marcus again read the Court-ordered Search Warrant. He wailed incoherently. "My life is over." He kept asking about his medication from the pharmacy.

11:36 p.m. Investigator Robert Walensky entered the room and pulls up a stool. Walensky had been at Sparta Mayo for some time and had handed a Search Warrant to Scallon, who passed it on to Anderson. Now, Investigator Walensky comes face to face with Anderson who will be his nemesis for over three years.

Walensky started with, "There's some questions I need to ask, and I will answer your questions. Also, you are in custody now, do you understand that?" Walensky read Anderson the Miranda rights.

Walensky asked questions about Marcus' whereabouts that day. His answers were rambling non-answers. Instead, Marcus mouthed several irrelevant statements, "Kyson always wanted to be with me." He was asked about McDonalds. Marcus damned his doctor, "That's why she's in my lawsuit." He rambled on about McDonalds and getting the American toy that they'd been trying to get.

11:55 p.m. Anderson appeared disheveled handcuffed to the hospital bed. Officer Scallon was with Walensky and had his body camera on the entire time. Hospital personnel were providing comfort, monitoring his vitals. Marcus provided answers to Walensky's questions but was evasive and frequently changed the subject.

Marcus explained to Walensky how Kyson hit his head and how he did CPR. Marcus was weeping. He explained how he went to help Jenna and her daughter with a flat tire. He said, "My days are all screwed up. I have nothing to hide." (Jenna was an acquaintance in the Alma Center area.)

Walensky told Marcus, "Kyson had bruises all over his arms, body, legs, where did that come from?" Marcus replied, "He is light-skinned, bruises easily, has a rash, born with something on his face, can't close one eye, has a blood disorder. I cut his hair. No physical restraints on Kyson. Did not see any bruises on Kyson. I was always there for her kid. Cops told me I have to get to the hospital. How do you unlock your phone?" Marcus often repeated the phrase "You know what I'm saying."

12:21 a.m. Walensky showed Marcus his iPhone. "This is a picture of Kyson's arm. How did this happen?" Marcus responded by saying three times, "What the fuck?" I said to Jessica. "You need to get him checked." Blood disorder. Marcus was in total denial. "If you are walking with Kyson and grab him, he will bruise." He is very light. Could be Jolene, she used to grab him like this."

12:30 a.m. Marcus added, "Last night I fell and hit the toilet and thought I broke my ribs."

Walensky asked Marcus, "Do you drink?" The answer was, "No." Walensky asked, "Do you do recreational drugs." Again, the answer was, "No." Marcus said Kyson was acting dizzy. Marcus was putting on quite an act of remorse, "What happened to my baby? What did they do to him?" He rolled around and back and forth. Marcus continued, "This is not true, man, not true. I'm trying to process this, man." There was plenty of thrashing about, wailing, and incoherence.

1:09 a.m. A nurse came into Marcus' hospital room and replaced an IV bag and said, "I want to give you Flexeril. It is a muscle relaxer." Marcus responded, "I can't take Flexeril. I know I will have an allergic reaction to it."

1:13 a.m. Walensky told Marcus, "I don't have any more information. But tomorrow, there will be an autopsy and I can give you more then." Marcus talked about the little red spots on Kyson. There were more outbursts from Marcus, "Why did they break my window. Can I talk to Brandon? The officer seen me limping. If I'm tired, I pull over. I would never drive if I can't drive safely."

1:36 a.m. Walensky left the hospital room. Marcus asked, "You mean right now, I can't go home?"

1:40 a.m. Nurses entered the room to get a urine sample. Scallon used two handcuffs on his left hand to lengthen his mobility. They have Marcus swing his feet off the side of the gurney bed. There were loud complaints, "My legs, my back, I'm in pain. Where's my prescription?"

1:44 a.m. Marcus protested, "I can't pee with all these people looking at my private parts."

Nurses replied, "Well, we can step back, step aside. But we cannot leave you alone in the room."

1:50 a.m. Nurses left the hospital room as Marcus was unwilling to cooperate getting a urine sample.

1:54 a.m. Scallon dimmed the lights in the room.

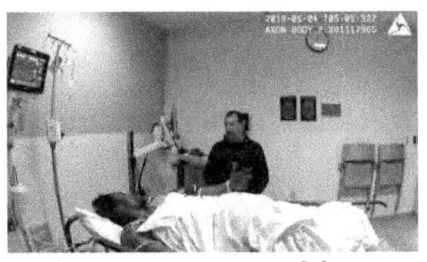

Anderson was evasive and frequently changed the subject when questioned by Investigator Walensky.

2:07 a.m. The nurse obtained a urine sample with a machine with a collection device that fits over the bladder area.

2:10 a.m. There was another blood draw.

3:09 a.m. Nurses were working in the room. Marcus asked about urine tests. The nurse said, "We want to know if you are having rhabdo, if the urine is brown, it's sometimes an indication a person is taking drugs." Even as the nurse was carrying the bottle with the urine sample, Marcus protests "I won't give you my urine sample."

3:10 a.m. The nurse left. Scallon told Marcus, "You're doing good so far. We appreciate it."

3:34 a.m. A wheelchair was brought in by Sparta Police Officer Kyle Erickson. The IVs and monitoring equipment were removed. Marcus sat up in bed, hands behind his back, and handcuffed. Marcus was transferred to the jail in the Monroe County Justice Center, wheeled by Perkins. It was a short distance of several hundred feet. Officer Perkins body camera filmed the journey. The audio portion of the video picked up the train whistle in the distance.

Officer Scallon stayed with Anderson the entire time, Scallon's body camera recorded both video and audio. In all, Officer Scallon was with Anderson for 16 hours straight.

Chapter 10

Crime Scene Search

May 4, 2019 12:44 a.m.

The day after Kyson Rice's murder, detectives from the Monroe County Sherriff's Department and the Tomah Police Department started an exhaustive and thorough investigation. On Saturday, May 4, 2019, after securing a search warrant, officers examined Jessica Rice and Marcus Anderson's house at 1009 Jodi Circle, starting in the dead of night at 12:44 a.m. It was some six hours after Kyson Rice has died, and authorities were thinking in terms of a homicide. Officer David Heckman had been on scene at 1009 Jodi Circle and kept containment on the residence.

Investigator Paul Sloan's Report

"On May 3, 2019, I drafted a search warrant for 1009 Jodi Circle while Officer David Heckman maintained security at the residence. I made application telephonically to the Honorable Mark Goodman, Monroe County Circuit Court Judge, Branch II. Judge Goodman found probable cause to issue the search warrant and granted me permission to sign his name to the warrant. I received the search warrant on May 4, 2019 at 12:02 a.m.

On Saturday, May 4, 2019 at approximately 12:44 a.m., Detective Clayton Tester, Officer David Heckman, and I executed the search warrant at 1009 Jodi Circle. Tomah Police Sergeant Adam Perkins and Investigator Robert Walensky later arrived at the residence.

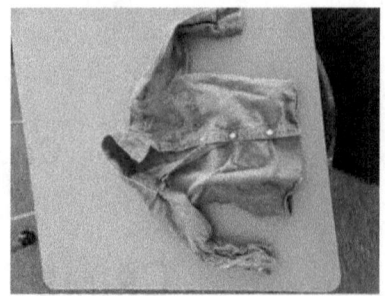

Kyson's shirt was found on the bathroom floor.

I initially took photographs of 1009 Jodi Circle. I also photographed evidentiary items found by officers during the search. The living room of 1009 Jodi Circle is located immediately upon entering the main door on the south side. The living room can also be accessed from a patio door west wall. I noted a sectional couch along part of the south and west walls. A small stand on the west wall contained a monitor (turned on) and digital video recorder for the surveillance system. I noted packaging and medical supplies scattered on the living room floor.

The living room/kitchen is an open concept. In walking through the kitchen, I noted the garbage can was empty (no bag). Officer Heckman related that the kitchen garbage can contained garbage when they initially responded. Marcus Anderson is believed to have taken the garbage, placing it in a can there.

To the east of the kitchen is a laundry room and half-bath all contained within one room. At the outset of the warrant execution, I observed a light illuminated on the washing machine. The light later turned off. I noted the clothes inside the washing machine were wet. Additionally, I located 46 rounds of .22 ammunition at the bottom of the washing machine. I examined the clothing within the washing machine and photographed the contents of the machine. I observed no obvious blood stains on the clothing. Positioned above the washing machine was detergent, including bleach.

The bedroom for Kyson is located in the northwest corner of the residence. I noted the strike plate to the bedroom door was falling off the frame and the bottom screw was missing. Inside the bedroom, behind the door, the doorknob had punched a hole in the drywall. Immediately upon entering the room, I observed a children's black/brown reversible leather belt on the floor. A child's bed was positioned along the west wall. The closet contained a minimal number of clothes and toys were on the floor near the closet.

Numerous items for drug use were found in the kitchen.

In the bathroom, I noted various hygiene and common bath products on top of the vanity. The top drawer of the vanity was open. Two bathmats covered portions of the bathroom floor, one at the base of the tub and a second at the base of the vanity. Scattered on the bathroom floor was two blue towels, adult Air Jordan tennis shoes, bath products, and a child's shirts (green and white shirts). I examined the green shirt and noted it was damp. I did not observe any blood on the green shirt.

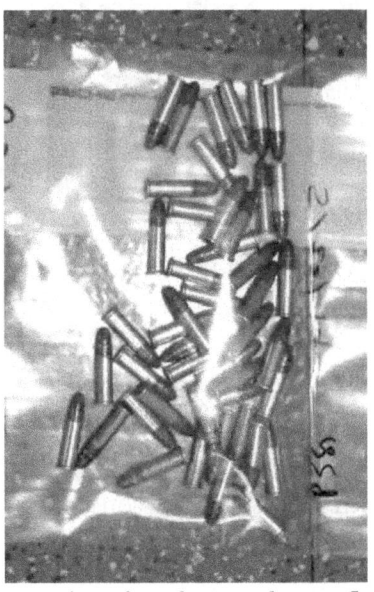

Searchers found 46 .22 long rifle bullets in the washing machine.

As previously mentioned, a 24-inch-long wall separated the vanity from the toilet. On the wall was the toilet paper holder. I observed the eastern arm of the toilet paper holder broken off from the wall and in the garbage can beneath it. The roll of toilet paper was lying on the floor next to the toilet.

The shower/bathroom tub is a cast iron tub. I noted no drain plug in the tub and a shower mat in the corner. A loofah sponge, with handle, and a piece of plastic was in the tub. Bath products lined the northeast corner of the tub surround. I examined the shower/tub, floor and walls in the bathroom observing no blood.

Police found a weapon hidden under blankets on a high closet shelf.

Detective Tester and Officer David Heckman searched the master bedroom of Marcus Anderson and Jessica Rice. I conducted a secondary search of the master bedroom closet and located nothing of evidentiary value.

Detective Tester, Officer Heckman and I all searched the kitchen. See evidence list for seized items, location, and locating officer. Officer David Heckman and I searched the garage. Located in the southeast corner of the garage was a large City of Tomah garbage can. Located in this garage can was a white garbage bag containing garbage. Officer Heckman and I searched the garbage bag locating four glass containers containing a wax substance and a McDonald's Happy Meal. Detective Tester later recovered a receipt for the Happy Meal pursuant to a consent search on 5/6/2019. Officer Heckman related this bag of garbage was previously in the kitchen as the contents contained medical supply packaging.

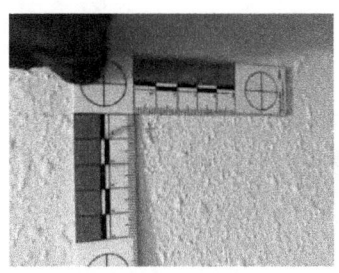

Several drops of blood were discovered on the walls by the bathroom.

While at 1009 Jodi Circle, I noted the residence did have a Swann video surveillance system monitoring the exterior of the residence. More specifically, I noted a camera monitoring the driveway, front door, and patio door on the west side of the residence. Cables ran through the living room and connected to the Swann digital video recorder in the living room, along the west wall. The video system was active and appeared to record after detecting motion. The DVR contained a SanDisk 32 GB SD card for storage purposes. Initially, I seized the Swann DVR and power cable.

During the search, a large safe was located in the bedroom of Marcus Anderson/Jessica Rice. Officer Heckman removed the safe to the garage, where a forced entry was used to gain access. Detective Tester and Officer Heckman searched the safe while I took photographs of its contents."

End of Sloan Report

Chapter 11

Marcus Anderson is Booked Into Prison

May 4, 2019 3:41 a.m.

Marcus was transported by wheelchair from the Sparta Mayo Hospital to the Monroe County Justice Center. It was a convenient journey of several hundred feet and ambulance or police transport was not necessary. The entourage entered the sally port of the Monroe County Justice Center for the processing procedures.

A defiant Marcus Anderson is booked in the Monroe County Justice Building, better known as the jail.

Sally ports are secure entrances to jails, prisons, and courthouses. It is within the closed sally port where all weapons are secured so they do not enter the facility. Newly arrested persons are usually driven in through a jail's sally port and the exterior doors closed. Once inside the sally port, arrestees are checked for weapons and officer weapons are stowed. Once all weapons are secured, the inner door is opened so that the prisoner and arresting officer may enter the jail. Sally ports are also used to transfer prisoners because they remain within a secured location to transfer from a building to a vehicle.

Surveillance cameras captured the video and audio. Marcus, seated in the wheelchair with handcuffs behind his back, was asked several questions by Monroe County Sheriff's officers.

Investigator Clayton Tester's Report

The following narrative is based on eight pages of reports by Investigator Clayton Tester aided by Sgt. Shasta Parker. It is 3:41 a.m. and Marcus was in a wheelchair, wearing a white shirt, blue jeans, white-topped shoes, and a white sheet wrapped around his upper body.

"Marcus asked Correctional Officer Jeff Schwanz, 'What's up man?' Schwanz was carrying Marcus' cane. Officer Todd Evers administered a PBT (Preliminary Breath Test). Anderson proclaimed, 'I don't drink or do no drugs.' Anderson asked about his shirt and was told it's been kept by the officers for now. Officers asked if he was sick or injured in any way. Marcus asked about his medication and complained about his leg. Officer Evers asked Marcus if he was withdrawing from drugs or alcohol. Parker asked the same question, to which Marcus replied, 'I just woke up, I've been sleeping for three hours.' Marcus said he was pulled out of his car at gunpoint and had been sleeping in his car.

His shoes and socks are removed. He was assisted to stand up and they walked him to the booking area. Anderson was then assisted with double handcuffs into Cell 6 by Schwanz, Jamal Wager and Shasta Parker. Officer Shasta Parker said to Marcus, 'I can smell pot. Do you have any on you?' Parker commented that the smell was even stronger in the cell.

During a search of 1009 Jodi Circle, officers found a scale used to weigh drugs.

What followed was a half hour marathon. Marcus Anderson became very confrontational constantly accusing Parker of being racist. Schwanz was continually talking to Marcus, trying to get him to exchange the clothes he was wearing for orange prison garb. Taking off the handcuffs, he repeatedly yelled and demanded a phone call to his family, talking about his baby and complaining about his back and leg. He was unhappy about having to give up his shirt. He complained that he was 'the only one treated like this.' Marcus reached into his pants and pulls out his penis. He reached down and pulls something white off the floor and had it in his hands. He walked to the toilet and used it. He took toilet paper and appeared to flush the object down. Jail attendees think he had hidden drugs in his butt crack. They began a search.

There was yelling, accusations, slamming of cell doors, and pounding on the mattress. Marcus yelled to the assembled that he has been to war and spent ten years in jails. He screamed about his nose bleeding. He acted like he's semiconscious and eyes closed."

Finally, the four Correctional Officers, Jeff Schwanz, Jamal Wagner, Todd Evers, and Kylia Frase, put Marcus in a wheelchair. An ambulance crew arrived, and Anderson was carted off to a hospital.

Chapter 12

The Investigation Switches into High Gear

May 4 Walensky and Tester.

The investigation into the death of Kyson Rice kicked into high gear the morning following the murder, led by Robert Walensky and Paul Sloan, both from the Tomah Police Department, and Clayton Tester, from the Monroe County Sheriff's Department.

While Tester and Sloan were busy interviewing people and gathering information and evidence in Tomah, Investigator Walensky was in Madison.

Walensky reported, "I attended the autopsy of Kyson Rice at the University of Wisconsin Department of Pathology on May 4, 2019. Forensic Pathologist Doctor Michael Stier performed the autopsy. Assistant Monroe County Medical Examiner Teresa Isensee also attended. Teresa Isensee and Lanham Schanhofer Funeral Home followed me to Madison for the autopsy, so we all arrived at the same time. The body bag was still sealed upon arrival. I took photographs throughout the autopsy. A DNA card was obtained from the autopsy as well.

At the conclusion of the autopsy, Doctor Michael Stier informed me that the death was a homicide. There were numerous injuries to Kyson that were counted and documented in this case. I am not going to try to describe them at this time. The body of Kyson had a constellation of injuries that will be described in more detail in Dr. Michael Stier's autopsy report.

At the conclusion of the autopsy, the body of Kyson remained at the University of Wisconsin Department of Pathology as Doctor Michael Stier wanted to view the body again. More injuries were noted at a later time on Kyson that Dr. Stier could explain in his report.

After meeting with investigators in this case, the Monroe County District Attorney and speaking with Monroe County Medical Examiner Bob Smith, it was also decided to proceed with a skeletal survey procedure on Kyson while he was still at the University of Wisconsin Department of Pathology. This was done by medical staff outside of the Pathology Department in Madison.

A copy of a preliminary autopsy report regarding Kyson, prepared by Doctor Michael Stier at the University of Wisconsin Anatomical Pathology Laboratory, had been reviewed. The report indicated the following conclusions among others; battered child, acute and extreme, head, face, limbs, chest, and back, 179 contusions focally patterned, 3 braded contusions, patterned contusions to the left leg, lacerated lips and frenulum, posterior right 4th rib fracture, and acute bilateral subdural hematoma.

A review of the treatment record of the defendant, Marcus Anderson, at Sparta Mayo Hospital, revealed his blood was positive for the following substances while being at Sparta Mayo on May 3, 2019; amphetamines, benzodiazepines, methamphetamines, opiates, oxycodone, and tetrahydrocannabinols."

Detective Tester Interviewed Jessica Rice on May 4, 2019

"On 5/4/19, I contacted Jessica Rice to arrange for her to bring her phone in so we could conduct a download of her phone. Jessica Rice came to the Sherriff's Office and met with Detective Walensky and myself.

While Detective Walensky was downloading the data from Jessica Rice's cellular phone, I went over a few additional questions as well as confirmed some answers from her first interview.

I asked Jessica to go over again the phone calls from that afternoon from Marcus Anderson. Jessica told me that the first call she got from Marcus was nothing about her son. Marcus called to tell her about a fire or smoke that was out in the garage. Jessica Rice told me that they have a small can out in the garage where they put out their cigarettes. Marcus was telling her that the can was smoking and on fire. She told me when she came back to the house that afternoon, she did not see anything that made her think that there was a fire in the can, so she does not know what that call from Marcus was really about.

Jessica told me she received the phone call from Marcus telling her that Kyson slipped and fell and hit his head and is not breathing. She told me he must have hung up because the line went dead. Jessica told me she tried calling him back and when he answered, it sounded like people in the background which she said sounded like the police and ambulance. She told me Marcus Andersson was freaking out saying that no one will tell him what was going on.

Jessica Rice told me she called her friend, Amber Moseley, to come pick her up from work and take her home because of what was going on. Jessica Rice told me Amber Moseley picked her up and took her home. She said when they got there, the Police and Ambulance were already there.

Jessica told me she tried getting in through the garage, but the garage door was locked. She told me she had to unlock the garage door to get in. She told me Marcus' car was running inside the garage when she entered the garage.

I asked Jessica again if Kyson had any medical issues that would cause him to bruise easily or any medical issue that related to anything with a blood disorder. Jessica Rice told me there was nothing like that.

I asked Jessica to tell me again what the dates were that Marcus had left for California and returned. She told me Marcus left on April 9 and came back April 24. I asked Jessica who took care of Kyson while Marcus was in California. She told me it was Larry and Cheryl Quarles.

I asked her if she worked while Marcus was in the hospital. Jessica Rice told me she did not work on Monday, April 29. She told me she worked 6 a.m. to 4 p.m. on Tuesday, April 30 and worked from 11 a.m. to 8 p.m. on Wednesday May 1.

I asked Jessica Rice when Marcus was discharged from the hospital. She told me she thought it was around 10 a.m. on Tuesday April 30, but she was not sure of the exact time. Jessica told me she dropped Kyson off at Larry and Cheryl Quarles' house so she could go to work. She told me Marcus Anderson picked Kyson up from Larry and Cheryl Quarles' house that morning after he was discharged from the hospital. I asked Jessica Rice if she was aware of any issues with Kyson while he stayed with the Quarles. She told me there were no issues.

I asked Jessica Rice about Marcus going to Alma Center. Jessica Rice told me he left to go to Alma Center after she got home from work. She told me Marcus told her there was a female friend of his that called him and wanted his help regarding some tire issues. I asked Jessica Rice what this female friend's name is. Jessica Rice told me she does not know that. She told me Marcus Anderson is secretive and does not tell her what he is doing.

I asked Jessica what she did on Thursday May 2. Jessica told me she worked that day from 1:00 p.m. to 8:00 p.m. She told me she had a doctor's appointment in the morning before she went to work, and Marcus was home before she left for her doctor's appointment. I asked her what time Marcus came home that morning. Jessica Rice told me he was home around 7:30 a.m. before she left. Jessica Rice told me she does not know what Marcus does during the day when she is at work.

Marcus Anderson delivered nearly 200 murderous blows to Kyson in this bathroom

I asked Jessica what they did on Friday, May 3. Jessica Rice told me she worked from 11:00 a.m. and was supposed to work until 8:00 p.m., but left work when she got a call from Marcus. I confirmed with Jessica that Marcus and Kyson showered together daily. She told me they do. I asked her if that was common for them to shower together. She told me Marcus and Kyson usually shower together and have done this ever since they moved in. I asked Jessica who Marcus hangs around with. She told me she only knows a guy by the name of Brandon and does not know his last name. I confirmed with Jessica about when she moved out of her uncle John Glynn's house. Jessica Rice told me she moved out on March 8 and into her apartment. She said Marcus moved in with her right away. I asked her about daycare. She told me she cancelled her day care because Marcus was laid off from his job and started watching Kyson while she worked.

I asked Jessica about Marcus going to Madison. She told me he goes to Madison on weekends and she and Kyson stay home. She told me she has not gone with him when he went to Madison. Jessica told me she doesn't know for sure that is where he goes because he does not tell her anything and always changes his story on things. She told me he would tell her something and then he would end up changing his story later. She told me she does not know what to believe.

Detective Walensky asked her what cellular phone plan Marcus had. She told us he has a Verizon prepaid plan and has an iPhone. I asked her if

Marcus has a lock code on his cell phone. She told me he does. I asked her if she knew what the code was. She told me it was 1014 but is not sure he has changed it because he is so secretive. She told me her unlock code and his were the same 1014, which is the date they met in October of 2014.

I asked Jessica Rice why they had a surveillance system and who owns it. Jessica Rice told me it is hers and she bought it, but Marcus had set it up. She told me she got it because Marcus wanted something for security when he is not at home. I asked her what the passcode was for the system. She told me she was not sure and assumed Marcus changed the password on it, but she would be able to get it by going through the company. She told me the system is hers so she can get information. She told me she would work on that when she gets back home.

I asked Jessica Rice again about the gun. Jessica Rice told me that Marcus brought it into the house after he moved in. She told me she told him to get rid of it, but he did not. She told me she last saw it in the closet up on the shelf under some blankets or clothing. She told me it was not registered to her, and she is sure it is not registered to Marcus because he is a convicted felon.

Detective Walensky asked Jessica Rice when the last time was that she spent any significant time with Kyson. She worked her way backward from Friday telling us that Kyson was still sleeping on Friday morning before she went to work. Detective Walensky asked her what time she went to work that morning. She told us she worked from 11:00 a.m. that morning. Detective Walensky asked her if that was unusual or odd that Kyson was still sleeping at that time. Jessica Rice told us that he sleeps in if he is up late the night before.

Detective Walensky asked her what time Kyson went to bed on Thursday night. Jessica Rice told us she was at home Thursday night. Marcus got Kyson ready for bed. She said she took a shower and then when she got out, Kyson was already in bed. She said she does not remember what time it was, but it was not late. She told us Kyson was in bed when she got out of the shower, so she went in and gave him a kiss. Jessica Rice told us she noticed the left side of Kyson's face was red and a little swollen and the left side ear was a little purple. She said she walked out of the bedroom and asked Marcus about the swelling on the side of Kyson's face. She said Marcus told her Kyson fell on a toy. Detective Walensky asked Jessica Rice if she noticed the swelling and bruising on the side of Kyson's face Thursday morning. She said she did not.

Detective Walensky finished downloading the data on her phone. This ended the interview with Jessica Rice."

Interview of Justin Harmon by Investigator Tester May 4, 2019

The day after the murder, Justin Harmon provided a statement to police: "I was advised by the officer I talked to, after calling in, to write a statement. I called in because I live in the other side of the duplex where the death took place on May 3, 2019. My wife and I decided to call the police station to share any info we have that may or may not be helpful in the case.

On May 3, we left our residence at around 5:05 p.m. to go to our daughter's art show at the high school. We returned home around 7 or so to a squad car in our neighbor's driveway. When we left, the neighbor's garage door was open, and we could hear some loud talking as we got in our car to leave.

The past several days, we could hear the man's voice several times. Sounded like he was yelling at the woman and calling her vulgar names such as 'bitch' and 'fucking bitch' and 'stupid bitch.' He sounded angry often the past several days. One night this past week at around 1 or 2 a.m., we could hear the same things. I also heard the man say something about 'why you looking at my phone, you stupid bitch' and things like, 'I'm tired of this shit' or 'I'm done with this shit.' This is basically all we could hear. The man yelling and the woman denying what he was saying.

We never heard anything that sounded like a threat or physical violence. We would have definitely called the authorities if we did. This was really nothing new for us as the previous neighbors used to get in even louder in their arguments.

The only other thing I can say is that we never saw the woman leave the apartment and the man was very private. We never actually spoke to either of them from the time they moved in a while ago. There were other vehicles that stopped by often for short visits. That is all the information we can think of. Thought it may be helpful in this matter."

Chapter 13

Tomah Detectives Seek Answers

Investigators Clayton Tester, Paul Sloan, and Don Henry were putting in some long days gathering information and evidence in the killing of Kyson Rice.

Detective Clayton Tester reported, "On May 6, 2019, detective Sloan and I made contact with Jessica Rice at her home for additional information. Jessica Rice told me she remembered something else. Jessica told me it was hard to remember everything, but when she stops and thinks about it, things come back to her. Jessica Rice told me that she had taken Kyson to see Marcus Anderson on Monday afternoon while he was in the hospital. Jessica Rice told me she stepped out of the room leaving Kyson with Marcus while she went to the snack machine. Jessica told me she walked back into the room and saw Marcus who was lying on the bed grab Kyson by the arms, pick him up, and set him on top of him, and then hit Kyson hard in the chest. Jessica said Marcus yelled at Kyson and said something about Kyson embarrassing him in front of the nurse and it's not going to happen again. Jessica told me she told Marcus to put him down, which he did. Jessica told me she took Kyson by the hand, and they left the hospital.

Jessica also told me that she and Marcus had gotten into an argument Thursday about how he was going to leave her and that she does nothing for him and does nothing around the house. Jessica told me Marcus said something about going back to Arizona.

Jessica also told me that Marcus had started accusing her of cheating and started confronting her about who she was with even when Amber Moseley would come and pick her up to take her to work."

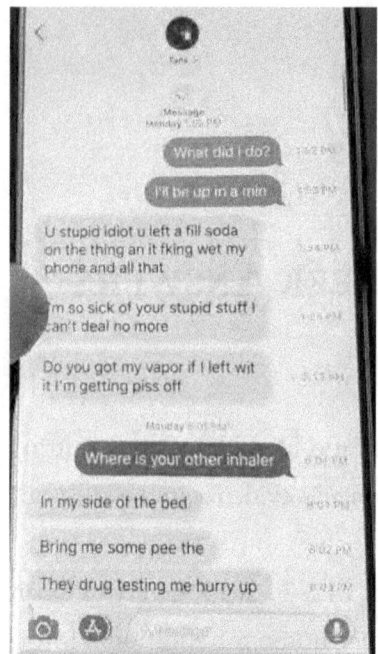

Marcus and Jessica texted each other many times each day. This text was from Tuesday April 30, the last day Marcus was in Tomah Memorial Hospital.

May 7 Tester interviews Cheryl and Larry Quarles

After interviewing their son Andrew Rowcliffe, Investigator Tester was called by Cheryl and Larry Quarles to their home. The interview took place around the dining room table.

"They met Tank about a year ago, living in the adjoining duplex with a lady and her four kids. The lady up and moved and Marcus needed a place to stay in one of their rooms. It was around September or October 2018, and Marcus was not around much and would be gone for days.

They said Marcus had a female friend, Regina, who Tank flew in from Arizona to stay a week. Tank was a person who would tell you something and change it a week later. He moved out and went to stay with Jessica. Before going to California, Marcus brought Jessica and Kyson out to the house to meet them and asked if Cheryl could take care of Kyson while Marcus was in California.

MURDER IN A SMALL TOWN

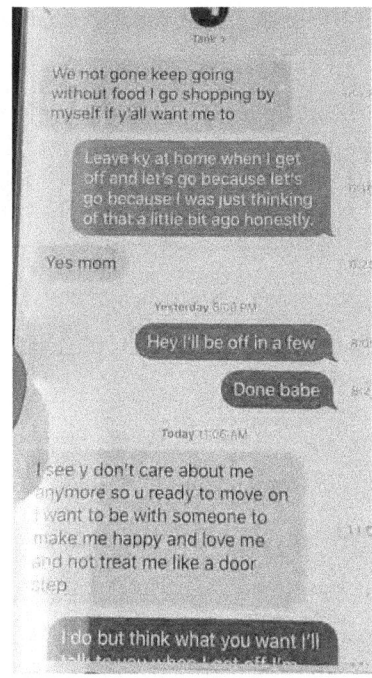

Text messages a couple of days prior to May indicates rising tensions between the couple.

When he got back, they visited him in the hospital. Cheryl talked to the nurse. Marcus was very upset, acting crazy, very defiant, and making a gesture with his hands as if shooting someone. There was no car seat in his car for Kyson, so Larry drove Jessica's car back to 1009 Jodi Circle.

Larry said he did not see Marcus on Wednesday, May 1, as Marcus needed to rest, but he visited Marcus on Thursday, May 2. Marcus complained that Jessica "doesn't do anything for me." Larry told Tester that Marcus was a drama queen. Larry told Tester he did not go see Marcus on Friday May 3."

May 7 Tester visited Sparta businesses

Detective Clayton Tester visited Walgreens Drug Store in Sparta on May 7, 2019, to retrieve any video footage from May 3, 2019. He talked to Elizabeth Wilde and Kristina Hitchcock.

Video surveillance cameras showed Marcus wearing a jersey with number 7 on front, and the name Vick and number 7 on the back. *Note: Michael Vick played quarterback for 13 seasons from 2001 to 2015 for four National Football teams, mainly for the Philadelphia Eagles and Atlanta Falcons.*

Marcus was wearing blue jeans, a doo rag on his head and sporting white sunglasses and wearing white-tipped tennis shoes. Camera footage shows Marcus going into Walgreens, limping badly, dragging a leg, and using a cane. Kyson was strapped in the child seat in the back seat. Back in the car, they moved a block to McDonald's for lunch.

McDonalds Visit

At McDonalds, Marcus parked the car and walked inside while Kyson waited in the car. McDonald's has two separate video systems, each covering a different area, one inside and the other aimed at the outside parking lot and entrance area. The general Manager, Eva Kline, provided Detective Clayton Tester with video footage from the camera systems. While Detective Tester was downloading the footage, Autumn Brandau steps forward and tells Tester that she was the one that waited on Marcus Anderson. She had recognized Anderson from the news release with the three-year-old that died. Autumn Brandau would later testify at the trial as Witness #39.

She was helping Todd Johnson with the cleaning of the McCafe Machine when this guy walked in. He asked about a Powerhouse meal. He was told that the Powerhouse was not something they have. Marcus then orders a Big Mac and a Happy Meal. He paid for it and then stepped back away from the register. And older male white subject stepped up and ordered a 2 for 5 meal. Anderson began to question the cashier in a loud voice as to why he did not get the 2 for 5 meal. This was when Autumn Brandau said she stepped in to help with the order.

Detective Tester continued in his report dated May 24, 2019, 'Autumn Brandau told me that she adjusted his order and gave him the 2 for 5 meal which was the Big Mac, Quarter Pounder with fries and the Happy Meal 4-piece McNuggets. Autumn Brandau said the black male subject mentioned something about a McFlurry which was not on the screen, but she gave him one anyway. He walked out to his car which was parked by the door before the McFlurry was done, so she walked it out to him.'

Marcus returned to Wisconsin in a foul mood.

Tester asked Brandau about the subject's demeanor and attitude during the encounter. She said Anderson was loud and bouncing around the place while he was waiting for his order. She said he even spun around in a circle and could not stand still.

Marcus put on an obnoxious act, waving his hands, talking loudly, backing away from the counter, then moving again up the counter. Management was so distraught and unnerved at the display, they gave Marcus and Kyson a free meal just to get rid of them. The McDonald's receipt will be one of the exhibits at the trial.

While Detective Tester was at McDonald's on May 24, 2019, he also interviewed Todd Johnson who confirmed much of what Brandau told him. He said he and Autumn Brandau were cleaning the McCafe Machine and overheard the conversation between Anderson and Neil, who was taking his order. He said he was very uncomfortable with the situation, and felt he could be on drugs, based on the way he was acting. He said Anderson was loud, dancing, and bouncing around, and other customers were staring to see what Anderson was doing.

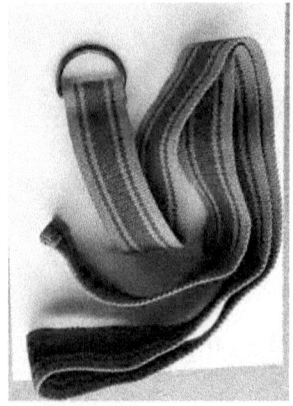

Marcus' belt was seized as evidence and later tested for DNA.

Walgreens—a return visit

Back at Walgreens to pick up the prescription, Marcus did not enter, instead using the drive-up lane. The time stamp on the prescription receipt was 4:07 p.m. When asked by Detective Tester if she saw anyone in the car besides Marcus Anderson, she replied, "I did not, but it was really strange. Most people always roll their window all the way down in order to talk and retrieve their medication. But Marcus Anderson rolled his window only half-way down. It made it hard for me to talk to him and he seemed to be in a hurry. He was very fidgety. The windows on his car were very dark, so I didn't see anyone else." He picked up one prescription with a time stamp of 3:14 p.m.

Cenex

Detective Clayton Tester visited Cenex in Sparta on May 7, 2019, the same day he visited Walgreens and McDonalds. He was looking to view any surveillance footage. No personnel were able to give any useful information to Tester, but he did view a video that showed Anderson putting gas in the car at pump #4, going inside to pay for the gas and buy some lottery tickets. Marcus pulled into Cenex at 3:52 p.m. and left at 4:00 p.m.

May 9 Investigator Don Henry Goes to Kids Kountry Learning Center

On Thursday May 9, 2019, Investigator Don Henry visited Kids Kountry Learning Center on Mark Avenue in Tomah. He talked to Josie O'Brien, whose mother, Vera Dechant, is the owner. Vera Dechant was on vacation in Arkansas with her husband, Steve Dechant.

Josie O'Brien revealed that Jessica owed Kids Kountry a bit over $500, and that Jessica had quit paying her bill. Josie related that it got weird at the end. Jessica added Marcus' name on the enrollment. There were a lot of bad vibes between the staff and Marcus. Vera, the owner, got very frustrated with Jessica. The staff related they thought Jessica was awesome until Jessica met Marcus.

Another staff member said that Marcus reeked of cigarettes and smelled bad and had bad body hygiene. Vera Dechant was interviewed by phone. She will be witness #3 at the trial.

Chapter 14

Evidence Seized

On May 10, 2019, Investigator Paul Sloan drafted a search warrant for the 2010 Ford Fusion. That afternoon, Sloan and Clayton Tester entered the compound, opened the vehicle and did a thorough search. Items of interest were bagged and taken to the police station: Car keys for Ford and Pontiac cars, Wisconsin Quest card issued to Jessica Rice, receipts from Kwik Trip and Love's BP, a cylindrical blue-white rubber container with residue, hotel keys from Wyndham and Super 8, Delta Airlines receipt, and $411 in currency. One of the $20 bills was rolled and contained a white powdery residue. Not surprising: a beanbag projectile, used on May 3 to shatter the right rear window to get Marcus' attention was also recovered.

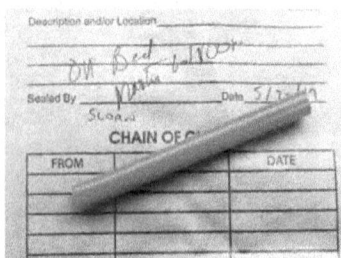

Straws found on the bed, under the bed, and on the kitchen floor were sent to the Wisconsin Crime Lab, testing positive for heroin and fentanyl.

Sloan obtained a search warrant from Judge Mark Goodman for the clothing Marcus was wearing when he was arrested and booked into Monroe County Jail. He received the following items from Monroe County Jail Lieutenant Ryan Hallman: black metal cane, Nike Air Jordan tennis shoes, four black socks, blue jeans, gray tank top, and belt. The items were taken to the Tomah Police Department, logged, photographed, and secured in the evidence room. All items were entered into the Omnigo records management system.

Video surveillance seized by Sloan

Investigator Sloan received a search warrant from Judge Goodman on May 10, for SD cards in the home surveillance system installed at 1009 Jodi Circle. It was a Swann digital video recorder. They tried to access the SD cards but were unsuccessful due to proprietary files. Swann technical support advised that the video recorder (DVR) had to be connected to the network at 1009 Jodi Circle and the MAC address acquired for a password reset.

Jessica Rice met with the investigators and consented to reconnecting the Swann DVR to her home network. Jessica provided investigators with both the network name and password. Walensky was able to read the SD card for one of the three cameras. An additional search warrant on May 14 revealed footage from the other two cameras.

Marcus' cane was sent to the State Crime Lab.

On May 10, 2019, Jessica Rice provided investigators with the remaining components, such as the monitor, remote and mouse. The storage device was searched pursuant to a search warrant issued on May 10, 2019, and a subsequent warrant issued on May 14, 2019.

There were three cameras on the external part of the residence. Camera 1 was a front door camera. Camera 2 was on the front corner of the garage. Camera 3 was a patio entrance view.

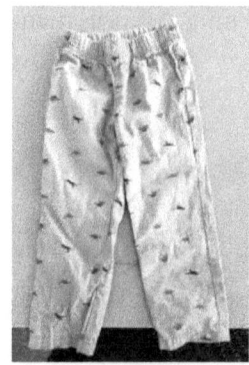

Using a search warrant, investigators found a great deal of possible evidence, including pants worn by Kyson Rice.

During the search warrant execution at 1009 Jodi Circle, the following evidentiary items were located and seized. Items from the Marcus Anderson and Jessica Rice bedroom include the Sig Sauer firearm located previously by Detective Tester on the master bedroom closet shelf.

On May 13, 2019, Investigator Clayton Tester ran a firearms trace on the Sig Sauer, model 522, .22 caliber rifle that was located as a result of the search warrant at 1009 Jodi Circle in the early morning hours of May 4. He received info back eight days later on May 21. The weapon was purchased at Moe's Hardware in Black River Falls on January 18, 2013, by Michael Ayala. Mike was a friend of Marcus and Larry Quarles. He will be witness #19 on Day 3 of the upcoming trial

Anderson had a Swann 3-camera surveillance system set up, paid for by Jessica.

Items seized include plastic straws with trace residue, plastic baggies with trace residue, Delta boarding pass, a black/tan children's belt discovered on the floor in Kyson's bedroom, red plastic straw with residue, Swann HD DVR with SD card in living room, monitor, remote, and mouse, 46 rounds of .22 ammunition in the washing machine with wet clothes, Triton T3 digital scale with white powdery residue, blue/white rubber pad in the safe, jeweler bags in the safe, blue/white rubber smoking device with glass pipe in the safe, marijuana grinder containing plant material in the safe.

(A grinder is a tool used to break down cannabis into smaller bits, so they are a similar size and consistency. Marijuana is commonly ground down for rolling joints, blunts, and spliffs, but this can also be done for packing bowls in pipes and bongs for a smoother, more consistent burn. A blunt is a cigar containing cannabis made by unrolling the cigar and replacing the tobacco with marijuana. The name comes from a Phillies brand. Blunts can also be called LP or L. A spliff is a large potent marijuana cigarette).

Four glass containers with wax substance were located in a garbage can in the garage. A black and orange one-hitter pipe, with burnt residue was located in the kitchen island drawer.

Sloan's report read, "Officers completed the search warrant at 3:13 a.m. and the residence was secured by Officer David Heckman. I transported all the seized evidence to the Tomah Police Department and locked it in a temporary evidence room."

Don Henry Interviewed Nancy Rice

On May 21, 2019, Investigator Don Henry interviewed Nancy Rice, Jessica's mother. The interview was at Nancy's request and not recorded. Nancy gave Henry an earful. Paraphrasing her comments to Mr. Henry, "Marcus didn't want anyone to know his real name and only by his nickname, 'Tank.' I figured out who he was, and I know he had prior domestic abuse cases. There were a lot of red flags, and I wished I had noticed them. Marcus didn't want Jessica associating with anyone in the family anymore. Jessica is shutting out the family and doesn't want any of them at any court proceedings. Jessica will not visit Marcus in jail. Jessica is upset because she heard that Marcus called a girlfriend in Arizona. Jessica lived with John and Jolene Glynn for three years until Jessica met Marcus. Jessica thought that Marcus had changed."

Chapter 15

The Final Farewell

Kyson Rice was laid to rest one week after his tragic death, on Friday May 10, 2019. It was a sunny day, with temperatures rising to 55 degrees. Life goes on. News of the day included Uber becoming a public company opening on the New York Stock Exchange. United States, led by President Donald Trump, began raising tariffs on Chinese imports after trade talks failed. People were watching *The Big Bang Theory*, *Rick and Morty*, and *Stranger Things*. Kids enjoyed television shows such as *Dora the Explorer*, *Horrid Henry*, *Henry Danger*, and *The Loud House*. Meanwhile, gamers were playing *Spider-Man*, *Red Dead Redemption 2*, *Resident Evil 2*, and *Kingdom Hearts III*. PlayStation 4 was popular. The number 1 song was *Old Town Road* with Lil Nas, featuring Billy Ray Cyrus.

Perhaps the biggest news was the college admissions scandal, in which *Desperate Housewives* actress, Felicity Huffman stood accused of paying big bucks to ensure her teenager gets into an elite university.

Famed American actress Doris Day was reported to be near death at age 97. She did pass away three days later, on May 13.

On the local scene, Anna Anderson was celebrating her 100th birthday with the help of her three daughters. She lived in a sod house her father built in Nebraska in her early years. The Tomah Timberwolves teams were in action. Ella Plueger was having an outstanding year pitching for the girls' softball team. The boy's golf team edged Holmen to move into first place in the MVC.

The memorial program at the Kyson Rice funeral.

A nearly full Church of parishioners and mourners attended the 11 a.m. Mass of Christian Burial at the Queen of the Apostles parish (St. Mary's Church) on Friday, May 10, 2019. It was one week after the hideous murder. It was time to remember Kyson, pray for him, and carry him to his final resting place. The previous night, Thursday, May 9, 2019, a visitation was held at Torkelson from 4:00 to 7:00 p.m. Rosary was recited at 3:30 p.m. The Torkelson people came up with a great idea. To ease the pain of loss for Kyson's many young cousins, Torkelson passed out superhero stickers and invited the young people to place the stickers on Kyson's casket. It was a grand gesture.

Kyson's cousins attached superhero stickers to his casket.

The Obituary for Kyson Rice

There is a new Saint in Heaven, Kyson Reid Morgan Rice, age 3, of Tomah, Wisconsin, died Friday, May 3, 2019. He was born September 3, 2015, the pride and joy of his mother, Jessica Rice. Kyson was a Super Hero in training. He celebrated the little things in life and gave to others unconditionally at such a young age. This sweet caring little boy, whose nickname was "Popeye" loved to fly with his uncle John and was fascinated by helicopters. Kyson's dream was to someday have a helicopter of his own. Although he was shy at first, he became fearless in no time. He loved a good peanut butter (not crunchy though) and jelly sandwich and his favorite colors were blue and green. Kyson had a special bond with his cousins, Declan and Garrett and was especially close to his "Nana" Jolene. Although his life was taken too soon, he has earned his Spiderman wings in Heaven. He is survived by his loving mother, Jessica, his grandma, Nancy Rice, aunts and uncles, Ashley (James) Smith, Jordan Rice, Tara Eckelberg, Reid (Kat) Rice and Jayce Newman, his great grandparents, Reuban and Pat Eckelberg, great aunts and great uncles, Rhonda (Dean) Burch, Jolene "Nana" (John) Glynn, Chip Eckelberg, Mindy (Chad) Gibson and Kelly Rice. He is further survived by many cousins, other relatives and friends. A Mass of Christian Burial will be held Friday, May 10, 2019, 11:00 a.m. at Queen of the Apostles Parish in Tomah., Monsignor Richard Gilles will officiate. Burial will follow in Oak Grove Cemetery, Tomah, Wisconsin. Family and friends are invited for visitation on Thursday, May 9, 2019, from 4:00 p.m. until 7:00 p.m. with a rosary at 3:30 p.m. at the Torkelson Funeral Home in Tomah. Family and friends are also invited for visitation on Friday from 10:00 a.m. until the time of service at the church. The Torkelson Funeral Home of Tomah is assisting the family with arrangements.

"She walks to school with the lunch she packed
Nobody knows what she's holdin' back
Wearin' the same dress she wore yesterday
She hides the bruises with linen and lace
The teacher wonders but she doesn't ask
It's hard to see the pain
Behind the mask bearing the burden of a secret storm
Sometimes she wishes she was never born
Through the wind and the rain, she stands hard as a stone
In her world that she can rise above
But her dreams give her wings and she flies to a place where
She's loved, concrete angel
Somebody cries in the middle of the night
The neighbors hear, but they turn out the lights
A fragile soul caught in the hands of fate
When morning comes It'll be too late
Through the wind and the rain, she stands hard as a stone
In her world that she can rise above
But her dreams give her wings and she flies to a place where
She's loved, concrete angel
A statue stands in a shaded place
An angel girl with an upturned face
A name is written on a polished rock
A broken heart that the world forgot
Through the wind and the rain, she stands hard as a stone
In her world that she can rise above but her dreams give her wings
And she flies to a place where
She's loved, concrete angel"

Poem appearing on the Memorial Program poem are the lyrics from the song Concrete Angel by Martina McBride.

The Guardians of the Children motorcycle group attended the funeral and provided an escort from St. Mary's Church to Oak Grove Cemetery.

Guardians of the Children is a nonprofit organization that recognizes and reacts to child abuse, serves as advocates to provide strength and stability to families in crisis, and be the answer to the prayers of an abused child or teen for courage, support, and protection.

Chapter 16

Surveillance Cameras Produce Evidence

On June 25, Investigator Robert Walensky reviewed the video segments from the three cameras at 1009 Jodi Circle. The videos Walensky scanned began on March 16, 2019, and continued to May 3, 2019, the day of the murder. Marcus Anderson had mounted three cameras, one on the front door, one on the garage, and one on the side door. It was tedious work for Investigator Walensky, requiring many hours of viewing and making notes. The videos were three hours behind, so the camera may say 6:24 a.m. but it was actually 9:24 a.m.

After Anderson's arrest, his Ford Fusion was towed to the Police Compound. The passenger rear window has been shattered by the bean bag.

A black Ford Fusion, registered to Marcus Anderson, went in and out of the garage several different days with Marcus as the driver and Jessica sometimes as the passenger.

Often shown was a 2006 gray Pontiac G6. This car belonged to Jessica Rice. Although she had a Learners Permit, she did not yet have a driver's license. Larry Quarles, driving a yellow Nissan SUV, visited Marcus many times, most often in the morning. A silver car, belonging to Brandon Crampes, parked in the garage and then backed out several times. A red GMC truck, owned by Amber Mosley, often brought Jessica to and from work. A silver truck delivered a safe on April 8, 2019. A dark SUV, registered to Jessica's cousin Beth Gerke, visited 1009 Jodi Circle on many occasions, bringing her small child with her. John Glynn visited the house on Easter Sunday to take Kyson for an Easter egg hunt at his cousins', dropping him back home at 5:15 p.m..

Marcus Anderson was in California from April 9-24, 2019. On April 30, 2019, at 5:49 a.m., Marcus pulled into the driveway, having been released from the hospital the previous day.

The Day of the Murder – May 3, 2019

(continuing with the summary of the video from the Swann Camera Surveillance System.)

9:24 a.m. Jessica Rice got in Amber Moseley's red truck.

1:38 p.m. Marcus Anderson was parked in the driveway.

5:58 p.m. Squad cars pulled up with their red and blue lights on, beginning a flurry of on-camera activity. Officer Steinborn ran towards the front door. Seconds later, Officer Furlano entered the front door with medical equipment. Officer Heckman was shown running to the front door as well.

6:00 p.m. EMT Tanner Sutton entered the front door, followed by two other ambulance workers.

6:01 p.m. Adam Robarge pulled the ambulance up to the driveway and removed a stretcher.

John Glynn took Kyson to the EAA Convention in Oshkosh.

6:14 p.m. Jessica Rice appeared with another female. They were trying to get in. Lots of people were shown going in and out of view on the video.

6:18 p.m. The ambulance crew brought out the stretcher carrying Kyson with Marcus attempting to follow but was being restrained by his left arm by Steinborn.

6:26 to 6:36 p.m. Many more people were seen coming and going. Amber Moseley's red pickup truck pulled into the driveway. Officer Steinborn arrived a second time. He met and talked to Officer Heckman. Marcus Anderson's car backed out of the garage and stopped. Anderson got out. He talked to the person in the red pickup truck, Amber Moseley. Anderson returned to the driver's side of his car.

6:42 p.m. Anderson got into his car and left. A squad car pulled away behind him. Anderson drove around the park and went back into the driveway. He talked to officers.

6:44 p.m. Anderson went into the side door of the house.

6:49 - 6:51 p.m. Anderson and Officer Heckman went in and out of doors. It's possible that Marcus was preventing Officer Heckman from entering.

6:57 p.m. Officer Heckman stood near the corner.

6:59 p.m. Officer Heckman was by the front door and Steinborn walked up the yard. Camera 3 showed Steinborn outside the side patio door and walking through the garage.

One of the first to arrive at 1009 Jodi Circle, Officer David Heckman provided support and surveillance for over 8 hours.

7:06 p.m. Anderson and Officer Steinborn talked on the front step. At this time, Anderson was holding clothing items. Anderson got in his car and left about 7:09 or 7:10 p.m. Officers Heckman and Steinborn remained.

On his return to Jodi Circle, Officer Steinborn tells Marcus to get to the hospital.

7:10 p.m. A squad car departed.

7:50 p.m. Investigator Paul Sloan was near the front door and met Heckman.

12:42 a.m. (next day May 4): Officer Perkins and Investigator Tester entered the front door.

Chapter 17

Anderson Works the Phones from Prison

May 4, 2019

Marcus Anderson was constantly making phone calls from the Monroe County Justice Center. The calls were limited to three minutes and recorded.

6:44 a.m. Marcus called Regina Hall, also known as Gina Rose Hall, or Gina, at 6:44 a.m., a three-minute call. Marcus told her the same story; he does not know what happened, says he called Kyson's mom, then he called 911. Regina told Marcus she was "pissed off" that he was "living with that bitch."

6:50 a.m. In another three-minute call, Marcus gave Regina a story about being shot at, but didn't see any bullets, forgetting his driver's license and trying to get to the hospital, how he fell asleep and broke his ribs. Marcus told Regina, "I must have passed out." He related how he woke up when police shattered his window with glass breaking over his neck. He woke up with a bunch of cops surrounding him and he didn't know why. Marcus tells Regina, "They're doing a blood test because they thought I was drunk, because I was parked by a bar." Regina told him the baby died and that they got him for murder. Marcus asked how she knew. Marcus repeated how he is just trying to figure it out. Regina said she has been talking to Larry, mom and "B." B is Brandon Crampes.

6:55 a.m. In a three-minute call, Marcus told Regina that he doesn't know what is going on. She read a press release from the Tomah Police Department to him. He said, "Wow." He wondered if Regina was going to leave him hanging, and that she should be worried about his safety.

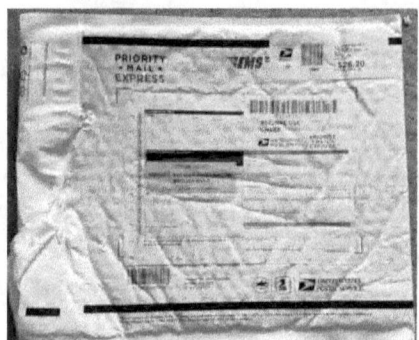

Regina Hall sent packages, letters, and money to Marcus Anderson.

Author note: Regina Hall had been sending letters and packages to Marcus Anderson on a regular basis. Regina mailed one large envelope via U.S. Postal Service from her home in Buckeye, Arizona on April 29, 2019. At that time, Marcus was just ready to get out of Tomah Memorial hospital. He received the envelope on May 1, 2019, two days before the killing of Kyson Rice. Marcus maintained a Postal Box at the Tomah Post Office.

6:59 a.m. Regina continued to read the press release. Marcus said that Amber told him to get some clothes for Jessica and that the police told him to hurry to the hospital. Then he realized he didn't have his wallet. He said he didn't know where the firearm charge came from. He said the Tomah Police set him up. The police said they would stay at the house and he said he needed to lock it up. Said he doesn't trust the police. Said at first he didn't have any charges and detectives told him they would be back in the morning to talk to him and that they took his $700 and all his skittles.

7:03 a.m. Marcus told Regina that he "would never harm no god damn baby." He said he is going to take CPR classes, because after Kyson, he knows they turn them over onto their stomach and pat their back. Anderson tells Regina he did nothing wrong. He told her that if he gets into trouble for this, he is going to end his life.

7:08 a.m. Marcus talked about his bail jumping charge and firearm charge and said he did not have a firearm. Marcus said that he told Jessica that if something happens to him, they would blame him because he is black. Marcus told Regina he loves her, and she responded the same, but not convincingly.

Oak Grove Cemetery, on the south side of Tomah, is the final resting place for Kyson Rice.

7:14 a.m. Marcus asked Regina why it matters if he was with another woman if there was nothing going on between them. Anderson professed his love for her and if he does not see her again, he would always love her. Anderson talked about passing out and going unconscious and they took blood test to check for alcohol and he said he does not drink alcohol.

7:19 a.m. Marcus told Regina that Larry Quarles was at his house earlier. Marcus said it happened so fast. He says they went to Walgreens, then McDonald's to get all the toys from McDonald's. He told her he walked out of the room to grab his underwear. Anderson was crying and denied any knowledge of a weapon.

May 6, 2019 2:28 p.m. Calls of 15 minutes are now allowed. When Regina accepted his call, Marcus was crying. He said he had been charged with a weapons violation. He told her he would never hurt a baby and was now being charged. Regina asked him what he was being charged for. He replied, "either for intentional homicide or reckless homicide for not paying attention and some shit." Regina cut him off. He said everyone loves him and he was going to fight this. He then talked about giving up and killing himself, but he can't do it because it would make him look like he did something wrong. "Four minutes and I would be dead," Marcus said.

He told Regina he was in court that morning. He talked about a judge sentencing him in La Crosse and they did not have any evidence and Shelby was going to commit perjury. He rambled on about the $700 he lost.

Marcus told Regina that he wanted her to come to him and do a face to face so he could talk to her about it and not over the phone. She told him she is not coming to see him. He asked her to text B'dag to take $250. He told her that detectives are coming back to talk to him. He said he was going to call Larry and Cheryl Quarles to ask them what they know.

May 6, 2019 3:44 p.m. In a 15-minute call, an angry Regina Hall told Marcus, "I hate you. You played me twice and make a fool out of me." She asked Marcus who Jessica Rice was. Marcus fed her a "cock and bull" story, about how Jessica was throwing money at him, how Jessica got pregnant by some guy by the name of Ricco. He said he stopped talking to Jessica for about four years. Regina asked about him going to Taco Bell, said he got free food, but Regina said it came out of Jessica's check. Regina told Marcus that he moved in with Jessica, which he denied and claimed that any number of women would have him. She asked him why he is playing stupid.

Jessica had informed Regina that they, Marcus and Jessica, have been together for six months. Marcus replied that he had not been "fucking that bitch." There seemed to be a misunderstanding about Marcus' trip to Arizona to get his kids. Marcus told Regina that Jessica is a habitual liar.

Regina asked Marcus what they (Marcus and Jessica) argued about that morning. He denied they argued. He said Jessica woke up screaming and he slept on the couch. He said he asked Larry Quarles "to get that bitch away from here." He asked Regina to put $20 on the books for phone calls.

Kyson's mother, Jessica Rice, spends a quiet moment at her son's grave.

May 6, 2019 4:01 p.m. In a three-minute call, Marcus told Regina that he did not put any women in front of her. He told her that he fucked up and that he was "getting money from that bitch. He asked her to have Bdog, who owes him $250, to put it on his books.

May 7, 2019 9:27 a.m. In a 15-minute call, Marcus told Regina that he talked to his lawyers who said they haven't filed any charges, and they don't know what to do. He said he did not kill that boy and he should not talk to the detectives, who were coming every day trying to get him to confess.

He told Regina how he disciplined Kyson, "When he is good, he buys him something to eat, when he is bad, he had to go to his room and no tv." Marcus rambled on about how he had not hurt any kids, and the reason he got a cash bond was so he couldn't get out and gather evidence. He said the jail people were trying to plant stuff in his cell. He talked about how everyone was turning their backs on him.

May 7, 2019 9:43 a.m. In a 15-minute call, Marcus told Regina how they were trying to pin it on him.

May 7, 2019 7:12 p.m. In a 5-minute call, Regina Hall was upset about his choices and being with Jessica. She was crying about it.

May 7, 2019 7:29 p.m. In a 15-minute call, Regina talked about how Marcus had hurt her and about how Marcus put himself in that situation. Marcus was crying and telling how women manipulate him. Marcus asked her to talk to Cheryl, but Regina said Cheryl was not on his side.

May 8, 2019 4:57 p.m. In a 15-minute call, Marcus told Regina he will fight this and as long as she was with him, he could keep going.

May 8, 2019 5:13 p.m. In a 14-minute call, Regina told Marcus that he was the one that did this and put himself in the predicament and made the same mistakes as before. She told him there was talk that he had been on drugs since he went back and that his picture in the paper made him look wild. She told him she didn't know that he moved in with her. He denied he was ever on drugs.

May 9, 2019 2:33 p.m. In a 15-minute call, Marcus told Regina that Trulee and Neveah came to see him yesterday and talked about how everyone is getting behind him. He talked about putting some good pictures of him on Facebook and starting "Go Fund Me" to get him out of jail. Regina connected a three-way phone conversation between her, Marcus, and Larry Quarles. Marcus told Larry about the shower incident, phone getting wet, how he called like nine people and called 911. She told him that Marcus was booked for the gun.

May 9, 2019 2:49 p.m. Again, in a 15-minute three-way call, Marcus talked about how he was in a white man's world and there was no one to speak for him where he is at. The male subject told (unknown) Marcus he would have been better killing the "bitch" because he was going to have a "green light" on him. The male subject told Marcus that he has known him for 34 years of his life and knows he has not hurt "any motherfucking kids" and that he had watched his kids a thousand times.

May 10, 2019 1:41 p.m. In a 13-minute call, Marcus tells Regina that his attorney told him that they didn't have a case and the DA was leaking info to the public. Marcus asked Regina to text Larry and have him step outside so he could talk to him. Marcus told Regina that Larry didn't do what Cheryl said. Marcus told Regina that his lawyer said to go ahead with the "Go Fund Me" and that Regina was to take care of the money.

May 10, 2019 2:24 p.m. In a 5-minute call, Marcus told Regina what he was "up otta here" he was gone. He said they were trying to hang him.

May 10, 2019 2:30 p.m. In a 15-minute call, Marcus told Regina what he was charged with now, which was bail jumping and a pistol charge.

He invoked Ashley Wankerl's name. Marcus got Larry on a three-way call. Marcus told Larry that was an accident and his lawyers said he should not talk about it. Marcus asked Larry if he got the money from Sam. Larry told Marcus that Sam was at his daughter's graduation and that he hadn't gotten ahold of him. Marcus told Sam that he needed a hundred thousand dollars to get him out.

Larry asked Marcus how he got his car and ended up in downtown Tomah. Marcus fed him a story about how he was headed to the hospital, but that he didn't want to drive and felt he was going to pass out because he was hysterical. Larry said they made it sound different and they had to smash his window out and pull him out of the vehicle. Marcus said he fell asleep. He said he had to pull over and passed out.

May 11, 2019 3:26 p.m. In a 14-minute call, Marcus asked Regina to call and ask about his money. The number to call was 608 374-7400 to the Monroe County Dispatch. He was told Tomah PD has his money. Marcus called Regina five times on May 12. He connected to Sgt. Furlano on May 13 and was told his car was in impound and he, Furlano, did not know where his money was. More phone calls were made to Regina asking for a three-way call between him, Regina, and Tomah PD. Regina was upset about Marcus' living with Jessica. Marcus insisted they are trying to frame him.

May 14, 2019 Marcus told Regina that they were trying to poison him. Regina told Marcus that she found out what she was looking for, that he, Marcus, was in a relationship with the mom (Jessica) and that there were charges of bail jumping and weapons possession.

May 16, 2019 More phone calls between Marcus and Regina. Marcus told Regina that his lawyer came to see him, that he wanted to kill himself, that he had a sexy dream about her last night, that he tried to kill himself and there are rope marks about his neck, and his vocals are all messed up.

May 17, 2019 Marcus told Regina he was on some kind of suicide watch and wears a "weird vest and gown" and eats with a wooden spoon. He told Regina he wished he had a shootout with police.

May 18, 2019 Marcus had visitors besides his lawyers. On May 18, 2019, some sixteen days after the murder, Trulee Ann Silver, wife of Marcus' father, Torry Anderson visited. All conversations are recorded, and Investigator Robert Walensky pieced together the conversation, which started at 6:18 p.m. Marcus' voice was loud and very much unintelligible.

Trulee Ann Silver asked Marcus what happened. He stuck to his well-rehearsed script. He told her he does not know. That they, Marcus and Kyson, had been home about a half hour after getting his prescriptions and eating, and that he had been getting Kyson ready for a shower. Minutes later he heard a thud, he came running, tried to revive Kyson, called 911, then called Jess, telling her to come home, and said he was freaking out. He told her he had nothing to hide. He told Trulee Ann Silver that he had not been charged with anything yet.

She told him he did: charges of reckless homicide, child abuse causing bodily harm, bail jumping and felony possession of a firearm. Marcus told her that they did not find a gun on him. She told him they tossed his house and found one. Marcus told Trulee Ann Silver, "That girl has totally flipped her fucking script on me." Ms. Silver asked him what he meant. He told her that Jessica had totally turned her back on him.

May 22, 2019 Regina told Marcus she was not doing well, and they upped her medication. She said she was under a lot of stress and that Marcus was to blame. There were more calls on May 24 and four calls on May 25. On May 25, Regina told Marcus that "she is done with him," but will take his calls.

May 26, 2019 On this late-night call, Marcus asked Regina what happened to all his stuff at the house. Regina told Marcus that the house was trashed, and that Larry Quarles helped Jessica move. She informed him that the police opened his safe. Marcus complained that the police took money from him, some $2,200. *Note: Larry and Cheryl Quarles, and Cheryl's son, Andrew Rowcliffe, found the 1009 Jodi Circle residence in disarray . Cheryl said, "There was trash and debris everywhere. Kyson's room was stuffed with junk, so there was hardly any living space."*

The following excerpt showed Marcus' frame of mind on the day Kyson was killed. Quoting directly from Walensky's report on the calls between Marcus and Regina Hall.

"Marcus Anderson told her that that day he should have told her he wasn't babysitting and 'that bitch' said she needed a ride to work. He told Regina Hall that he was already hot because when he came into the house, he said he had some business to take care of. He told her he was mad because it was supposed to be his day and he had a lot of 'shit' to do that day. He told her he was mad because he doesn't like people in his business. He told her he had someone meeting him at the house and it threw everything off. He told Regina that 'it pissed me the fuck off.' He told her he gave Larry 'some shit' and then Larry left. He told Regina it 'fucked up' his whole day."

Chapter 18

Shelby Anderson Reveals a Monster

Investigator Robert Walensky worked intensely on the Kyson Rice murder case. On August 16, 2019, he interviewed Shelby Anderson by telephone. Shelby is the former wife of Marcus Anderson and was his health care provider via Mayo Health Care. Her testimony as Witness #36 on Day 6 of the trial was powerful evidence as to the character of Marcus Anderson.

Shelby met Marcus in 2014. She was 23 years old and a nurse in the health care profession. Marcus was living with his father, Torry Anderson, his stepmother Trulee Anderson, and Marcus' two stepbrothers on Wisconsin Street in Sparta at the time.

Marcus told Shelby that he was stabbed in prison, had back problems, and needed prescription drugs. Shelby reported that Marcus was addicted to methamphetamine and opiates and played up the injury to get out of things and had an excuse for everything, including physical therapy to make his injury seem more than it really was, even trying to use it to his advantage in their divorce case.

Marcus would call Shelby to Sparta to treat him. She said Marcus told her he was in the military. However, the version of events related to the military would change depending on who he was talking to.

As to drug use, Shelby related that Marcus smoked marijuana every day and sold it to a lot of people in the area. In March 2015, when Marcus moved in with Shelby at her La Crosse house on Nakomis Ave on French

Island, he carried several locked duffel bags and satchel bags, wearing the keys to the locks around his neck.

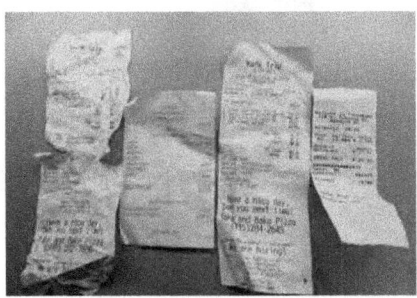

Receipts found at the crime scene indicated that Marcus was using Jessica's State-issued Quest card.

Before he moved in, he and Shelby went to California to visit his mother and sister. While there he bought a large amount of marijuana, and he and his brother packed it up and sent it to Wisconsin. The drugs would come packed in candles, or clothing, or shoes.

Shelby didn't know Marcus had kids, but she did know about Regina Hall and that Regina was sending Marcus drugs. Marcus would make Shelby wait for the mailman to receive a package from Regina and Shelby would see the oxycodone pills but was not allowed to touch them. She would be with Marcus when he sent money out from Walmart stores in La Crosse, Onalaska, Sparta, and Tomah to Regina Hall as payment for the pills.

Shelby said that Regina Hall had a lot of medical problems and would be prescribed oxycodone. Oxycodone is a prescription pain medication, an opioid drug, like morphine, codeine, and methadone. Marcus coached Regina on how to pass drug tests to show that she was taking her prescribed medication and not hiding or hoarding the pills.

Shelby told Investigator Walensky that she had not figured out Marcus was using methamphetamine until after they were married. Methamphetamine is a powerful upper. The speedy high is similar to cocaine, but unlike cocaine, the effects of this drug can last for up to 12 hours, depending on how it's used. Methamphetamine comes as a powder that can be swallowed, snorted, smoked, or injected. It also comes in crystal form, which is usually smoked. The crystal form is often called "crystal meth" or "tina." Other nicknames for methamphetamine include "speed" or "meth." People who use methamphetamine like it because it gives them energy and makes them feel confident, alert, and strong for many hours. Some like it because it makes them feel sexy. And some like it because it takes away their appetite and they feel like they don't need to eat.

Shelby told Walensky that meth made Marcus paranoid, and when he was coming "down," it was a horrible time for her and their child. He was abusive. Nothing she did was right, and anything, such as a noise, would set him off.

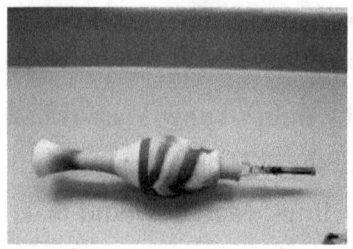

A smoking pipe was one of many possible pieces of evidence confiscated at the Rice-Anderson house.

Before they were married and she started working for Mayo in Rochester, Marcus would sometimes make them all stay in a hotel in Rochester for several days at a time because he thought people were following him at home in La Crosse. The behavior got worse after they were married. He put up cameras around the house and they were shown on television sets in the house, and he would constantly be watching them.

Shelby told Walensky that Marcus would go to Tomah, Sparta, and Wyeville to sell drugs most every day or every other day. And he was always bringing home money. He told her he had some kind of job.

There were people at three locations in Tomah and one in Sparta that he trusted to some extent. He would not reveal their real names. When Shelby went with Marcus, he would leave her with someone while he did his drug stuff. Shelby mentioned Brandon in Sparta and his girlfriend, Ashley, as people Marcus would deal with. There was a Mexican guy named Mickey in Tomah. He and his girlfriend attended Shelby and Marcus' wedding. Marcus stayed with them for a period of time after he was charged in La Crosse County with the crimes he committed related to assaulting Shelby.

Shelby said that Marcus had a gun and drugs in a lock box under the seat of his car that was impounded. She said Marcus got the gun from Mickey. She said she went with Marcus to a place where they were cooking methamphetamines. She stated that Marcus would travel to Chicago for meth, marijuana, and cocaine and bring the stuff back.

She said that Marcus would have her take him to various emergency rooms where he would play up his injuries to obtain pain medication for his own addiction. He often stated that she could not testify against him because they were married. When he got high, he would be very talkative about the illegal things he had done.

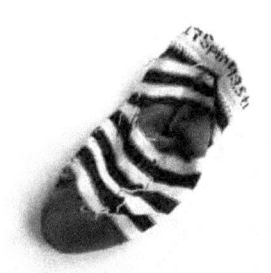

Tomah Police received Kyson Rice's socks from Tomah Hospital

Shelby said that people would use their food stamps or food cards to go shopping with him. Marcus would get food from them in exchange for drugs. He walked with a cane when he wanted people to believe he needed medication.

He talked to her several times about military training, claiming he was a sniper. She stated that Marcus got her fired from two jobs. He told her he was a Muslim and that women were inferior to men, and she was his property. He told her he killed two men when he was a juvenile. She stated that Marcus made her get pregnant and he beat her when he found her birth control pills.

Shelby finally went to the police in La Crosse on June 20, 2017. The police have all the documentation of her being beaten. She explained that Marcus had no rights to their child, as stated in the divorce decree.

She tried to get the courts in La Crosse to understand that Marcus would hurt someone, but the courts kept allowing him to push back his court cases, so he would be out of jail longer. She said if the court cases were handled properly, that kid in Tomah would not have died because Marcus Anderson would have been in jail.

Chapter 19

Anderson Continues Calling

By August 6, 2019, Marcus Anderson was in the Dodge County Correctional Institution on the southern edge of Waupun. He talked to his brother, Torry Jr., nicknamed "Toe." He told him that he had just been granted the ability to talk on the phone, and that his attorney's name was Russell Hammer. Torry told Marcus that Regina called him, and that some attorney had been trying to get a hold of her.

There followed a three-way call between Marcus, Torry, and Regina about a women private investigator who wanted to talk to Regina and Anderson.

Marcus told Regina that he needed the receipts from his rental car and plane to prove that he was out in California. And that Regina should pray for him that the charges against him would be dropped in two weeks.

On August 9, 2019, Marcus was moved to the Columbia Correctional Institution near Portage. He called Regina and told her he needed a television set and gave her specifics on ordering one. He called her three times, each ending on time limits.

On August 11, 2019, Marcus told Regina that his dad, Torry Anderson, called yesterday, asking about his lawyer and his divorce. There were two calls on August 11 and two calls on Aug 12. On the August 12, 2019, call, Marcus told Regina not to talk to any investigators without a lawyer.

A simple stone in Oak Grove Cemetery marks the final resting place of Kyson Rice.

Finally, Marcus got his lawyer on the phone. Marcus told Russell Hammer that two detectives were out in Arizona trying to talk to Regina, one was that "Walensky punk ass." Hammer told Marcus that he could not tell Regina that she should not talk to detectives. She said Walensky and a guy with red hair were there to see her and her mother, April. Repeatedly, Marcus told Regina not to talk to detectives unless there was a lawyer present, saying, "People are trying to send me up and they are trying to get her to turn her against him. They have no witnesses."

On August 16, 2019, there were more calls to Regina, asking about the detectives that came to see her. She said she told them nothing. Marcus told Regina that he was married to her and there was no one else except her. Later, he talked to his brother Torry Jr. about prison conditions.

On August 18, 2019, Marcus told Torry Jr. that those "bitch ass niggas went to Arizona to talk to people."

Note: Marcus Anderson was never married to Regina Hall.

Chapter 20

Interviews in Arizona

Needing information about Marcus Anderson's life in Arizona, Investigators Robert Walensky and Clayton Tester flew to Phoenix in August. The detectives had several long days ahead.

They interviewed Marcus' former girlfriend, Julie Alvarez Alcala, in Phoenix on August 12, 2019. She agreed to speak with the detectives, if alone.

She described how she met Marcus in Bakersfield, California when her car broke down at a club where she was at a party and Marcus pulled up to help get her car going. He was under 18 at the time and she was 22. He told her he was 23 years old, and he looked it, she said. She learned his true age when he was put on probation as a juvenile for not going to school. Julie said she would hang out with Marcus as she was going through a divorce with Bobby Carolina Sr. at the time.

In July 2003, Julie sold her house in Bakersfield and moved to Phoenix and Marcus moved with her. She qualified for an apartment. Her parents did not like Marcus. She learned she was pregnant with their first child. Her parents, Francisco and Frances Alcala moved to Phoenix in the Fall of 2003. She and Marcus soon had two more children.

She broke up with Marcus because he was beating her more frequently. Marcus became more violent toward her when she found out he was cheating on her in 2005. He was drinking and doing drugs at the time.

When confronted, Marcus threw her through the door. She called her parents to come get her and the kids. Marcus called Julie, and she took him back. He was good for a week, then the drinking and drugs continued. Julie told investigators that Marcus was basically a thug. She stated that she and Marcus were fighting all the time. He threatened to kill her several times.

Robbery

Julie recounted how Marcus dragged her into the Circle K Store robbery she had unwittingly aided by driving the truck. She was arrested for armed robbery in September 2009 and was in prison from October 2010-2013. Her parents had guardianship of the kids during the time she was in jail.

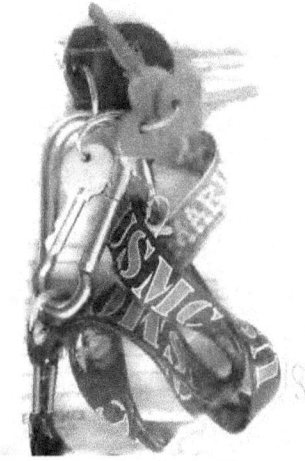

Marcus was fond of telling everyone that he was a Marine Corps veteran.

She stated that Marcus was very manipulative. He told his kids he was going to die.

When Marcus was in Phoenix in April 2019, Regina Carolina would not bring her children to her grandmother's house for an Easter party, knowing that Marcus was there.

Julie Alcala said that Marcus was a drug dealer his entire life and smoked marijuana all day. She said that if Marcus wanted sex, he would get it, even after he beat her. She got burned with a hot spoon and punched in the face so hard she flew over the countertop. He made the kids stand against a wall for long periods of time.

The investigators wrote that it was a difficult interview, stretching over two days, and that Julie could go on and on about Marcus' behavior.

Regina Hall Interview

Detectives Robert Walensky and Clayton Tester received an earful when they interviewed Regina Hall on August 13, 2019, at her home in Buckeye, Arizona, a suburb west of Phoenix. When the two investigators arrived at Regina Hall's home, her father, Marcus Hall, answered the door, and explained that Regina had taken her car to get it washed but would be back in an hour.

The detectives interviewed Regina at her kitchen table, with her mother, April Hall-Banks, on the phone during the interview. Regina explained that her mother had guardianship over her since she was an adult. Regina was now in her early 30s. She had a kidney transplant in April 2016 and has been in fragile health ever since.

She explained she met Marcus in 2014 through her brother, Marcus Hall Jr. The relationship started as friends, and they later dated. Regina stayed in contact with Marcus when he got out of jail and moved to Wisconsin to be with his father. Marcus told Regina that he was taking care of his father, who had cancer. He said he was painting houses and working as an electrician. He had a car, he told her and was "getting himself together." He divulged that he was stabbed in the back in prison and needed medication. Regina visited Marcus in Wisconsin in November 2015. Marcus told Regina he was in the military, with the Marines, and had PTSD.

In 2016, they took a six-month break from each other. Regina was told he had been in jail the last six months because Shelby pressed charges against him. He told her he was not married but she found out later that he had married Shelby. Later in 2016, Regina flew to Cleveland to visit a girlfriend. Marcus drove down to Cleveland from Wisconsin in Shelby's Camaro. While in Cleveland with Regina, Marcus cut through a parking lot of a gas station and police pulled him over. Police thought he was carrying drugs and tore the car apart but didn't find anything. Police told her the car belonged to Shelby Anderson and that Marcus had Shelby's credit card. Police told her Marcus was married to Shelby. This was the first she knew about it, but Marcus denied it. Regina was asked about a "Brandon" back in Wisconsin. Regina said he was Marcus' best friend and has a nickname "B'dag."

Tomah has a reputation of having a well-trained and competent Police Department.

Regina met up with Marcus again in Arizona in April 2019. Marcus flew to California and picked up his three kids. She met them off Highway 101. It was the only time she met his kids. Marcus was going to try to get custody of them.

Regina told the investigators that she had never been to the house on Jodi Circle in Tomah but had been to Larry and Cheryl's house. Marcus gave her an account of what happened on May 3, but the story was the same one he always told. He told her that Jessica was a friend of Brandon, and Brandon went to work, so Marcus stepped in to help. She did not know at the time that Marcus was Jessica's live-in boyfriend.

Marcus told Regina that he took the rap on those robbery charges for Julie, his former wife, so she would not go to prison, because Julie needed the money. She stated that Marcus called her all the time from prison.

Regina was asked about what she thought happened, and she replied, "I know for sure he is a liar, but didn't think he would harm a baby." She called him a crackhead.

Regina would be Witness #22 at Marcus' trial.

Chapter 21

Interviews Reveal Anderson's Character

Detectives Walensky and Tester interviewed April Hall Banks, Regina's mother, in Phoenix on August 14, 2019. She was Witness #21. The interview was at the dining room table, with daughter Regina Hall present as well as Marcus Hall, April Hall-Banks' son. Regina had been warned by Marcus Anderson not to talk to anyone without an attorney. April said she had nothing to hide, and detectives assured her that they only wanted to get background information about Marcus.

April explained why she is Regina's guardian. On March 15, 2010, Regina fell into a coma for a week. She was 22 years old. She could not make decisions or write, so she filed for guardianship. April said that Regina is intelligent and can remember things and speak but comes across as being a little slower than normal. April said that Marcus gave Regina a social life that she did not have before she met him. Regina would get very depressed when Marcus was absent for some time.

April Hall-Banks told the officers that she knew that Marcus lied many times. April and Regina worked in the healthcare field and wanted to see pictures of Kyson. Walensky reluctantly showed a couple photos of Kyson, after his beating, and April said, "There's a lot of anger focused here. That's not the result of falling down in a bathtub."

Clayton Tester was a tough, seasoned, and extremely competent investigator for the Tomah Police Department and Monroe County Sheriff's Department. Tester is now retired.

The first time April met Marcus was on a cruise to Cancun, Mexico from August 11-16, 2016 with Regina and others. Marcus was living in Wisconsin at the time and said he had joint custody of the kids. Marcus did not want to go back to Arizona because there was a warrant for him. Marcus told her he took the rap for a robbery committed by his wife, so she could stay out of jail and take care of the kids. Marcus told her his leg was messed up and he needed to go to court to get disability through the military for the injury to his leg.

April Hall-Banks told detectives that Marcus was always calling Regina. She was on dialysis and slept a lot. Regina went to Wisconsin to visit Marcus when he was living with his father at Sparta. She stayed about a week.

April talked about Regina going to Cleveland. Both confirmed the story about Marcus being stopped by police and the police confirming that Marcus was married. He denied it, saying Shelby Anderson was a friend and he co-signed for the car.

April said her mother passed away a few days after they returned from the cruise. Marcus still owed her money for the cruise and said he would pay it back, as the charges were on her credit card, but he never did. She called and called and Marcus wouldn't answer. He was living with his wife and baby in La Crosse. April called La Crosse police to do a welfare check on Marcus. After some delay the police called her and told her that Marcus and his wife were just fine and not to call again. The call confirmed to her that Marcus was married.

Police found a grinder, a tool used to break down cannabis into small bits so they are a similar size and consistency.

In June 2017, April received a collect call from Marcus, she picked it up thinking it was from her son, Marcus. He told her that he was in jail.

It gets complicated. Marcus wanted April to call his lawyer to find out the charges, and gave the name of Steve Ford, who with a friend, Theresa R. Severson, put up their house for the $10,000 bond money. Marcus said he couldn't go back home, so he was staying with Steve and Theresa. They had a falling out, so he moved in with a Mickey, (Mike Ayala) and Mickey lives downstairs from Larry and Cheryl Quarles.

April says Regina went to Wisconsin when Marcus was living with Larry and Cheryl and stayed about two weeks. It was the first time Regina met Larry and Cheryl Quarles. April said Regina went to California in April 2019 and met Marcus when he flew out there. Marcus was trying to get custody of the kids, so he got their birth certificates. While in California, Marcus rented a car and drove to Phoenix, riding around smoking marijuana. He got pulled over and Regina was with him. She rode back to California with him and then she flew back to Phoenix.

Marcus was in the hospital in Tomah in late April. April Hall-Banks called the hospital to try to get Marcus some medication. The nurse told her it would make things worse. Marcus had Regina believing that Jessica was just a friend.

April told detectives that Cheryl told her that other girls were sending money to Marcus. April, putting her hand over her face, said, "Marcus did not portray the monster he is in Wisconsin while he was down here."

Chapter 22

The Investigation Deepens

Cheryl Quarles called detectives to share new information since she had attended a hearing some months earlier. She told Investigator Tester that Jessica had a new boyfriend, Loren Mitchell Harris, and she did not have a good feeling about him.

Jessica moved out of her house and moved in with John Glynn for a week. Jessica was dealing with a child neglect case with Human Services. She was not to have any contact with children. The notice from Human Services is an indication that Jessica did not provide the necessary protection. Jessica had to move out of the Glynn house because they had a visiting foster child. Jessica moved to the duplex next to the Quarles. They helped move Jessica's stuff to their house

Jessica stayed a week and got better physically. Cheryl found out about Harris' domestic abuse problems. Harris had a "I don't care" attitude. The duplex next to the Quarles was occupied by a Marine Veteran, Jeffery. Cheryl and Larry helped Jessica move into a basement area of Jeffery's place.

During the week that Jessica and Harris stayed with Jeffery, the Quarles' son went over to visit and could smell marijuana. When confronted by Cheryl, Jeffery told Loren Harris to move out. When he moved out, Jessica moved out too and began staying at her Aunt Rhonda's place.

Jessica told Cheryl she didn't know why people were mad at her. She cried a lot, repeatedly saying she can't believe she didn't see this coming.

Mike Ayala Interview August 27, 2019

On August 27, 2019, Detective Walensky and Investigator Tester visited Michael (Mike) Anthony Ayala at the home of his sister, Angela Ayala in Tomah to talk with him about the gun found at the murder site. Mike purchased the Sig Sauer, model 522, .22 caliber weapon at Moe Hardware in Black River Falls.

Jessica and son Kyson share a quiet moment by Lake Tomah.

Mike was asked about a weapon that he reported was stolen on July 13, 2017. Mike said he heard about a gun found in the 1009 Jodi Circle address. When asked about Marcus Anderson, Mike responded that Marcus "was a piece of shit" and a very shady character. Mike said he sold the Sig Sauer to Brandon White (now Crampes).

Mike said he knew Marcus for five years. He met Marcus in La Crosse and attended his wedding to Shelby Anderson up on Grandad Bluff in La Crosse. After his divorce from Shelby, Marcus moved in with him for about two years in a duplex next to Larry and Cheryl Quarles west of Tomah. Mike told investigators that Marcus would not pay rent or help out around the house, or pay for food, did not work, but seemed to have a lot of money.

Mike said that Marcus brought a car home one day. The cops came to the house asking them about the car. The cops arrested Marcus because the car was stolen.

Marcus moved in to the duplex next to Larry and Cheryl. Mike said he moved to California but moved back to Wisconsin to take care of legal issues and moved in with his sister.

Mike said Marcus told him he was in the military as a sniper but said he didn't know much about guns. They used to smoke marijuana together. He noted that Marcus converted to Islam.

Interview with Larry Quarles

Investigator Clayton Tester interviewed Larry Quarles on September 24, 2019, at the Tomah Police Station. Also in attendance was Andrew Rowcliffe, the son of Cheryl Quarles.

Larry Quarles was asked about the time he and Cheryl Quarles visited Marcus in the hospital. Larry said that Marcus complained how the hospital staff were treating him wrong and bringing the wrong food. Marcus was acting rude to nurses. Larry told Marcus to calm down. Marcus called Larry when he was about to be released. Marcus got into Quarles' vehicle, and they went to 1009 Jodi Circle.

Larry Quarles arrives at 1009 Jodi Circle. Larry and Cheryl Quarles did all they could to help Jessica and Kyson.

On Thursday May 2, Larry was at Jessica's house and she and Marcus were arguing loudly. Marcus told Jessica she was being disrespectful in front of guests. Larry took Jessica to work, then went back to Marcus at the home on Jodi Circle. Marcus complained that Jessica was not cleaning the house and he was not taking much more and moving out of the house. Larry said the kitchen was messy. Quarles said Jessica knew about the girlfriend in Phoenix. Larry noted that when Marcus came back from his trip, he was very distant from Jessica.

On May 2, 2019, Larry took Jessica to work. Jessica was crying and didn't know what to do about Marcus. Larry went to the Post Office and then stopped to visit Marcus. Marcus came out of the house and moved the camera and said he didn't want people to know if he was home or in Madison. Marcus was angry at Larry for Larry taking Jessica to work the previous day. Marcus was very agitated, belligerent, and screaming that day.

Larry told Tester that he always took everything Marcus said with a grain of salt. Marcus told Larry he was in the military and was injured and needed to take medication. He lied about his divorce from Shelby. When he left town, he always took a wheelchair so he could get through TSA at the airport much quicker.

Larry originally thought the relationship between Jessica and Marcus was quite good. He got to know Jessica well. He thought Jessica was not very mature and was very naïve about relationships. Jessica did not act like she was 26 years old, lived a pretty sheltered life, and was not very worldly. She was very dependent on Marcus. Larry put her maturity level at about 16 years old. If he had realized earlier how Jessica was, he would have tried to help her.

He said after Kyson's death, Jessica showed him a letter from Human Services charging her with child neglect. Larry said Cheryl was very protective of Jessica and she stayed with them a couple of weeks. Jessica also stayed with a veteran next door named Jeffery until she got another job. Jeffery had extra room in the basement area. Jessica had her things in the basement of Jeffery's duplex house. She promised to pay rent but did not.

Larry thought Marcus just snapped. He felt that Marcus had some abuse in his life, his father's situation, not getting custody of his kids in California, and feels that he could not control others with lies, other woman, and problems between him and Jessica. Marcus' mind was not in a good state.

Chapter 23

The Investigation Continues

Detective Robert Walensky interviewed Theresa R. Severson by telephone on September 25, 2019. She said Marcus lived with her and Steven Ford for about 6 months in late 2017 or early 2018 after he was arrested in La Crosse. She said they tried to help Marcus out, but he wanted to do things the hard way. She liked him but he was a wild one. A good heart and a Muslim. She had no knowledge of his drug use. She was shocked by the murder. She talked to Shelby a few times and was surprised they broke up. She said that when Marcus and Shelby broke up, his life spun out of control.

Theresa said Marcus stole a car from them. After that, they parted ways. She said Marcus owed her and Steven Ford about $5,000. When his mom died, they gave Marcus money for fines, car payments, and expenses.

Walensky Interview with Brandon Crampes and Ashley Wankerl

Detective Walensky interviewed Brandon Crampes and Ashley Wankerl at the Tomah Police Department on October 21, 2020. They were living together. They knew Marcus for some time and also knew Shelby.

Brandon tried to see the good in Marcus. Ashley did not like him at all. He was always on drugs. Brandon said Marcus would sell his prescription drugs to get other drugs. Brandon said that Marcus did not have any friends. He said Marcus continually played the race card. Ashley told Investigator Walensky that she was close to Jessica and went to court with Jessica for hearings.

Kyson is thrilled with the huge Oshkosh army truck. His great uncle, John Glynn, took Kyson to the EAA Convention in Oshkosh.

Brandon said Marcus never gave Jessica a chance to do parenting things. He said Jessica believed everything Marcus told her about Shelby and Regina. Marcus would not let any members of Jessica's family come to the house, completely isolating them from her. Brandon and Ashley said that all the women seemed to believe that Marcus was needed by them, and they were nothing without him. Shelby told them that she lost her job as a nurse because Marcus had her stealing pills and fentanyl patches for him. Brandon was also using drugs at the time.

Brandon and Marcus spent several days in Madison and Regina came to visit them. He said Jeremy was a drug associate of Marcus, and that Jeremy was in and out of jail. Jeremy's wife, Christy Devine would be a witness in the upcoming trial.

Brandon said he got the gun from Mike Ayala and he and Marcus were going to go shooting but had no ammo. He left the gun in Marcus' car. Marcus took the gun into the house.

Marcus also said he was in the Marines, but knew nothing of Paris Island, which every Marine would know about.

Brandon said Marcus was totally different when he came back from out West. He was stressed, wanted to borrow money, couldn't hustle drugs, or meet people like he did before.

Walensky Interviews Jeremy Devine in New Lisbon

Detective Walensky interviewed Jeremy Devine at his house in New Lisbon on November 6, 2020. Devine knew Marcus as "Tank." Devine and his wife, Christy, met Marcus through Brandon Crampes and knew him for about six months. Marcus and Devine would smoke marijuana at times. Devine said Marcus was using heroin a lot.

Marcus called him on May 3, the day of the murder. Marcus told Devine he was on his way back from La Crosse and Marcus wanted a PlayStation 4 that Devine was selling and said he would be back in Tomah about 10:30 a.m.

Devine went to the parking lot of Festival Foods in Tomah, but Marcus did not show. Devine figures Marcus freaked out because two cop cars were around the Festival Foods lot. Devine said he left there and went to the casino at Wyeville to use the Wi-Fi. At the casino, Marcus called or texted Devine, and Devine hung up.

Devine told Walensky that later in the day, around supper time, he got a call from Marcus, Devine told him he was a "dumb fuck" and to call 911. Marcus wanted Devine to come to his house right away. Devine told Walensky that he didn't know where Marcus lived.

John Glynn and Kyson Rice watch the airshow at the EAA Convention in Oshkosh.

Jeremy Devine stated he has some difficulty remembering certain things because of an accident 10-12 years ago when he was ejected from a vehicle doing 100 mph and had to walk three miles for help.

Christy Devine interview at her house the same day.

Christy Devine met Marcus through Brandon Crampes. Christy had a falling out with Brandon's girlfriend, Ashley Wankerl. She said Marcus was vindictive and she would catch him in lies all the time. She said Marcus had a girlfriend in Madison.

Marcus came to their house on May 1 and made comments about getting Christy's kids to shut up. Christy told Marcus to leave her house because he was agitated and angry around the kids. She said the cops in Tomah were getting him every time he went there because he was a black man.

Chapter 24

A Jury Is Selected

On March 28, 2022, the long and intense murder trial began at the Monroe County Justice Center Courtroom Branch 2 in Sparta. It's a relatively new building, completed in 2017, and connected to the existing courthouse. The 103,000 square foot structure holds the jail, courts, sheriff's office, and dispatch services. It's set back a bit from four historic buildings in downtown Sparta.

The old Monroe County Courthouse is one of four buildings on the National Register of Historic Places.

On the southwest corner is the beautiful and original Romanesque-style Monroe County Courthouse completed in 1895 at a cost of $50,000. At the northwest corner is the 1923 Sparta Masonic Temple, a mixture of Classical Revival and Prairie School architecture, now the home to the Monroe County Local History Room and Museum and the Deke Slayton Memorial Space and Bicycle Museum. The 1902 Sparta Free Library is on the northeast corner, one of 64 libraries funded by steel magnate Andrew Carnegie. The 1915 Post Office is on the southeast corner. From 1982 to 1992, all four buildings were put on the National Register of Historic Places. Their grandeur stands in stark juxtaposition with the ugliness of the testimony about to be given.

The trial of Marcus Anderson took place nearly three years after the murder of Kyson Rice. Many people in Monroe County were of the mind, "What took so long?" There were many factors involved, but three primary reasons stood out. Marcus was incarcerated during that time for other crimes. Marcus fired his public defender lawyers on a regular basis. Marcus kept filing motion after delaying motion.

The transcript of the trial is 396,000 words, some 2,016 pages, four reams of paper that stack up ten inches. The transcript of Day 1 began with:

BRANCH 2, MONROE COUNTY CIRCUIT COURT
The Honorable MARK L. GOODMAN presiding
DATE: Monday, March 28, 2022
MONROE COUNTY JUSTICE CENTER
112 SOUTH COURT STREET, SPARTA, WI 54656
ON BEHALF OF THE STATE:
KEVIN CRONINGER, District Attorney and
SARAH SKILES, Assistant District Attorney, Monroe County
ON BEHALF OF THE DEFENSE:
PATRICK FLANAGAN, Attorney at Law, 759 N. Milwaukee Street, #215, Milwaukee, WI
MARCUS ANDERSON, appeared in person.
Tawni Kind, CCP, RMR (Court Recorder)

Judge Goodman addressed the Court, "We're ready to go on the record in 19-CF-353.

This is the State of Wisconsin versus Marcus Wayne Anderson. He's in the Courtroom. He's represented by defense counsel Patrick Flanagan. And we're joined by District Attorney Kevin Croninger and Assistant District Attorney Sarah Skiles. I always refer to this as a housekeeping type of meeting before we do the jury selection. We have the jury pool assembled next door in Branch 2. We're in Branch 1.

The potential jurors cannot hear us, what we're talking about. There will be a jury of 14 and because we'll have 14, each side will have six strikes. And what we hope to accomplish today is that we'll get the jury picked. We started today with 80. And I think we're going to probably lose two of those and hopefully we'll be able to pick a jury of 14 out of the remaining 78." (Note: The "19" designates the year of the crime, namely 2019. The "CF" indicates Circuit Court Felony. "353" is the number assigned to this case.)

Judge Goodman brought up a matter of "Mr. Anderson's Motion to Reconsider and Notice to Address." In this letter, Marcus stated that he doesn't think his lawyer, Patrick Flanagan, is well prepared and that Flanagan and DA Croninger "are in cahoots." Judge dismissed Anderson's motion by stating that it is not supported by a sworn affidavit. Goodman also assured the attendees that Mr. Flanagan is well-prepared to defend Mr. Anderson. Anderson also asked for a change of venue, which is also denied.

Judge Goodman talked about voir dire, which is French for "to speak the truth" the process through which potential jurors are questioned by either the judge or a lawyer to determine their suitability for jury service.

Courtroom #2 is where the judicial action will be for the next two weeks.

DA Croninger told the Court about another potential witness from Arizona who was subpoenaed to testify but can't be found. Croninger related that a number of potential witnesses are terrified to testify because Marcus' brother, Torry Anderson, Jr. travelled to Arizona from California and shots were fired at their house shortly after the Court made a ruling on the Other Acts Evidence. There were eight people from Arizona that were issued a subpoena, but only two came to Wisconsin to be witnesses. The two that DA Croninger really wanted were Julie Alvarez Alcala and Torry Anderson, Jr..

The following were issued a subpoena: Julie Alcala, Shelby Anderson, Mike Ayala, Katrin Behnke, Autumn Brandau, Regina Carolina, Dr. Jeffery Cavaness, Thomas Colloton, Brandon Crampes, Patrick Deethardt, Meghan DeFrang, Christy Devine, Jeremy Devine, Dr. Kevin Fitzgerald, Andrew Frei, Sgt. Jarrod Furlano, John Glynn, Aidalys Gonzalez Hernandez, Rachel Hahn, Regina Hall, April Hall-Banks, Lt. Ryan Hallman, Toni Halverson, Justin Harmon, Meaghan Harmon, David Heckman, Courtney Henshaw, Kristina Hitchcock, Scott Holum, Teresa Isensee, Todd Johnson, Steven Keller, Dr. Maude Kettenmann, Eva Kline, Catherine Kohl, Vera Kress-Dechant, Wil Limp, Dr. Jane Lyon, Tammy Maciosek, Dr. Wells Mangrum, Amanda Marshall, Joseph Merkel, Amber Mosely, Shasta Parker, Sgt. Adam Perkins, Dr. Heather Potter, Sgt. Mike Press, Cheryl Quarles, Lawrence Quarles, Andrew Rinehart, Jessica Rice, Adam Robarge, Andrew Rowcliffe, Olivia Sassman, Brennon Scallon, Jeff Schwans, Amber Sell, Inv. Paul Sloan, Sgt. Wilbert Steinborn, Dr. Mark Stevens, Dr. Michael Stier, Vaness Styx, Tanner Sutton, Clayton Tester, Meagan Vlasek, Inv. Robert Walensky, Ashley Wankerl, Danielle Warren, Kendall Wedemeier, Elizabeth Wilde, Elizabeth Fontaine, Jaiden Anderson, Bobby Carolina, Christopher Carolina, Serio Carolina, Kelly Goyette, Kelsey Jungbluth, Erica Murphy, Apryl Ravet, Investigator Brittany Westphal, Sandra Ringwell, and Torry Anderson, Jr.

Struck from the list of 80 prospective jurors is a nurse that worked at Tomah Memorial Hospital, the site where Kyson Rice was pronounced dead. At 9:18 a.m. Judge Goodman addressed the 78 persons called to jury duty. Twenty-six had been randomly picked by computer to sit in the jury boxes, with the remaining candidates in the gallery. Goodman asked a series of questions, first explaining, "The questions that we are going to ask are not intended to embarrass or humiliate you. I will first ask you lucky 26 some general questions about your qualifications to sit as jurors, and what I'll have you do, as I ask the question, I'll ask you to raise your hand."

Judge Goodman moved through a series of questions concerning understanding the English language, citizenship of the United States, resident of Monroe County, at least 18 years old, any felony convictions, and any mental or physical condition.

Through a series of questions about health issues and hardships, nine of the 26 are dismissed and each time a new perspective jury member is brought up from the gallery. Two have been dismissed because they were not able to sit for long periods of time. Three were let go because they followed the case on social media. One had ringing in the ears and was hard of hearing. One was on the Wisconsin State Patrol. The wife of one worked for the Tomah Police Department. One was on active military duty. One had a small family business to run. One had a prior record. One knew one of the witnesses. One had prohibitive child-care expenses. One didn't trust cops. One had a grandchild abused in school. One had no stomach for child abuse stories. One had a home invasion and couldn't let go of it. Another had a grandchild that was physically abused and could not be impartial. One was let go because their spouse was on the jury panel.

It is 10:28 a.m. when Bailiff Williams broke in with, "I think we can take a break." The prospective jurors exited the courtroom. Defense attorney Patrick Flanagan addressed the Court, "I just would say that Juror 15 is sleeping, like passing out sleeping." DA Croninger has noted the same and confirms, "I think he was even snoring."

At 10:43 a.m. the jury selection continued. A replacement is selected for the slumbering prospective jury member. Judge Goodman asked if any possible jury member had served on previous juries. Two said they served on drunk driving cases, one a theft case, and one on a child abuse case.

It is DA Croninger's turn to question the men and women who may be on the jury. He talked about how difficult this case could be, given it was the death of a three-year-old boy and there will be graphic autopsy photos that may be difficult to view. Some called up are dismissed upon questioning. One lady was let go because she does not believe she can deal with such possible vivid photos. Another prospective juror was dismissed due to religious beliefs. Another is let go because he knew many people in the law enforcement and medical field. One worked as a firefighter that dealt with children being mishandled. Another worked at Tomah Health and was quite familiar with the case. Croninger tells the panel that the State must prove intent but does not have to prove motive. Croninger discusses the concept of circumstantial evidence. He delves into issues of addiction, gun violence, and opinions toward the police.

Tawni Kind will be the court reporter for the trial of Marcus Anderson. Note the steno keyboard.

At 11:54 a.m. DA Croninger ended his questioning of the panel, and it was Defense attorney Flanagan's turn. It's close to lunch time but the decision was made to continue. Flanagan emphasized the concept of reasonable doubt and that the burden of proof being on the State, innocent until proven guilty, and that the defendant is not required to testify.

Judge Goodman told the Court that he has a checklist of 23 things he must do to run a jury trial. A list of the 26 prospective jurors was given to both the prosecuting attorney and the defense attorney. As the list is passed back and forth, each side had the opportunity to strike six names from the list, ending with a jury of 14 men and women.

While the list of 26 was passed back and forth, Judge Goodman talked about the responsibilities of being part of a jury and the rarity of being on a jury. Each stood up as their name was read: Cheryl Lakowske, Susan Baltich, Samantha Wagner, Mark Nelson, Jessica Clark, Mackenzie Pearson, Brian James, Jenna Keller, Sharon Monnahan, Penny Anderson, Wade Blackdeer, Isaiah Ohman, Adam Thompson, and Travis Benso.

Judge Goodman said, "OK, that's our jury." Those remaining are dismissed and told they could pick up a letter at the clerk's office if they needed one for their employer. He told the 14 that they should be back at 8:30 a.m. the next day for the start of the trial. Judge Goodman asked everyone to be seated as the Court had business to discuss.

The Court reconvened after lunch at 1:49 p.m. Dismissal of counsel, autopsy photos, admission of a letter by Mr. Anderson to the Court, and bond issues were debated by the State and Mr. Flanagan.

Judge Goodman pointed out the trial has been delayed by 993 days. The parties agreed to say in Court that Anderson was in possession of a firearm instead of a felon in possession a firearm and bail jumping instead of felony bail jumping.

There's a brouhaha over some 21 autopsy photos Croninger wished to show during the trial. The Defense objected to six or seven of them. The Court looked at them on the tv screens. DA Croninger pointed out the probative value of each and Flanagan stated his objections. Several of the 21 photos will not be shown during the trial.

Lawyers argued about one photo showing Kyson and Anderson with his pants worn very low. Croninger wanted the jury to note the huge size difference between Kyson and Marcus Anderson. Judge Goodman said he will rule on that photo later. The Court adjourned at 2:43 p.m. The trial will begin the following morning.

Chapter 25

The Trial Begins - Day 2: Morning Session

Tuesday, March 29, 2022 was the first full day of what was to be six or seven day trial.

It's a typical March day, with morning lows close to freezing with a promise of highs in the mid-40s along with blustery winds. Life in Monroe County went on with most people going to work and kids going to school. Russia and Ukraine were set to open peace talks in Turkey, this after Russia invaded Ukraine on February 24. In Mexico, 20 people were killed Sunday when gunmen opened fire on a crowd watching a cockfight in a small town in the western state of Michoacán. Some in Wisconsin were worried about the integrity of the upcoming Spring election. Monroe County High School students in Tomah, Sparta, Cashton, and Brookwood (Norwalk, Ontario, Wilton) were gearing up for the spring sports of baseball, softball, track, and tennis.

Judge Mark Goodman entered Branch 2 Courtroom. The bailiff chimed out, "All rise" and the Judge took his seat at the same time saying, "Please be seated."

Judge Goodman intoned, "We'll take up 19CF353, State versus Marcus Anderson." He acknowledged that counsel for the State and counsel for Mr. Anderson are present. "I've been told that all 14 jurors are sequestered in the jury room and they're ready to come into the courtroom. However, we have some housekeeping matters we'd like to take up."

DA Croninger presented the Judge with a document called Stipulated Facts. On April 29, 2019, Mr. Anderson was charged with a crime and released on bond. On March 3, 2019, Mr. Anderson was prohibited from possessing a firearm, and Mr. Anderson had previously been convicted of a drug offense.

DA Croninger brings up the fact that Marcus Anderson had made noises again about firing his attorney, Mr. Flanagan. Marcus Anderson addressed the Judge to that effect, but Judge Goodman cut him off, "We have 14 people that were told to be here at 8:30. It's now 8:43. So I would prefer you talk with your lawyer, but not do it while jurors are waiting."

Anderson said, "I have these documents that is new information to the Court. I have not previously added these documents to any of my motions." Judge Goodman sensed delaying tactics, the same technique Marcus had employed in the past, and part of the reason the trial was taking place three years after the crime was committed.

Judge Goodman admonished Anderson, "You haven't been to law school. You haven't been to college. You're not a member of the bar. Mr. Flanagan has done all those things. He's tried, many, many cases including many homicide cases and you are well served if you work with your attorney and not try to be your own attorney."

There was a brief exchange concerning using photo WW as an exhibit and the succession of witnesses. The protocol was that a witness is not allowed to be in the courtroom until after he or she has testified. They can sit through the opening statement, but they can't listen to other witnesses testifying before they themselves testify because that may affect their own sworn testimony.

The jury was brought in at 8:47 a.m. and sworn in by the clerk. The Court made a seating chart. Judge Goodman read a set of instructions and told them that a set of written instructions would be given to them in the deliberation room. The jury will not be sequestered, but Judge Goodman admonished the 14-person jury to not discuss the case, nor view any social media, or any news reports of the trial proceedings or any computer accounts of the trial. He said, "Do not speak to the lawyers, witnesses, or family members. Do not investigate the case or visit the scene of the crime. You can talk to anyone about the trial after the trial is over. You may take notes except during the opening and closing arguments, but don't let note taking distract you from carefully listening to and observing the witnesses. You may use the notes during deliberation. After the trial, the notes will be collected and destroyed. You will not have access to the transcript during deliberations, but you can ask to have portions of the testimony read back to you."

Judge's station at each of the four courtrooms at the Monroe County Justice Center.

Judge Goodman read the 16 Counts of Information which take up 17 pages of the transcript. Marcus Anderson had pleaded not guilty to all 16 Counts. Count 1 was the first-degree intentional homicide of Kyson Rice on or about Friday, May 3, 2019, in the City of Tomah.

Count 2 charged Anderson with physical abuse of a child, and intentionally causing great bodily harm on or about May 3, 2019. Count 3 dealt with the possession of a firearm. Counts 4, 5, 6, 7, 9, 10, 11, and 12, were bail jumping charges. Count 8 charged Marcus Anderson with physical abuse of a child on or about Monday, April 19, 2019, in the City of Tomah. Count 13 charged Anderson with operating a motor vehicle while under the influence on Friday, May 3, 2019, in the City of Tomah. Count 14 charged Anderson with the possession of narcotic drugs, heroin, and fentanyl on May 3, 2019. Count 15 charged Anderson with possession of THC on May 3, 2019. Count 16 charged Anderson with the intimidation of a Witness, Regina Hall, on or about March 4, 2022, in the City of Sparta.

Judge Goodman went on to describe what is meant by reasonable doubt. Instructions to the jury took about 45 minutes. At 9:30 a.m., Judge Goodman called on Assistant District Attorney Sarah Skiles to make the State's opening statement. It was a masterful 24-minute presentation.

Being a jury member or witness can be an extremely stressful event. Over the weeks and months following the trial, I heard numerous comments made by several of the trial participants concerning the extraordinary care Judge Goodman, DA Kevin Croninger, and Assistant DA Sarah Skiles took in making the jury panel and witnesses feel at ease.

Assistant DA Skiles Opening Statement for the State

After commending the jury on their attention to Judge Goodman's instruction, Assistant DA Skiles wished to talk to the jury about numbers: 200 bruises on Kyson Rice's body, 30 points of impact on Kyson Rice's skull, 46 minutes elapsed from the time Kyson Rice was last seen alive until he was not breathing, five minutes between the time Mr. Anderson called Kyson Rice's mother, Jessica, to say that Kyson wasn't breathing and the time he called 911, two teeth Anderson kicked out of Kyson's mouth two months before he died, five days before Kyson died Mr. Anderson was observed punching Kyson in the chest, four days before Kyson died he told a nurse he wasn't suicidal—he was homicidal, Kyson was three-years-old when he died. The evidence in this case will show you that one person, Mr. Anderson, the Defendant, caused Kyson Rice to die.

Ms. Skiles asked the Court technician to bring up Exhibit 2AA. It was a photo of Kyson Rice in his Spiderman outfit shortly before he was killed. She stated, "Kyson loved Spiderman. He loved helicopters. He loved peanut butter and jelly sandwiches."

Assistant DA Skiles introduced several people on the prosecution side of the courtroom: Investigator Paul Sloan, Investigator Rob Walensky, and several people from the DA's office. Assistant DA Skiles went on to lay out the process in which the State will prove that Marcus Anderson was the killer. She warned that some of the exhibits will be graphic, even gruesome.

Skiles did not provide a motive for this horrible crime but hinted at what set Marcus Anderson off on a murderous tirade. At approximately 11 a.m., on May 3, 2019, Marcus started contacting Jessica Rice at her place of employment, Taco Bell. He called her by cell phone, texting, and calling the Taco Bell phone. At 2 p.m., they talked on the phone for over a half hour. Anderson was trying to get Jessica to come home.

When Jessica was interviewed after the murder, she said she was trying to break off the relationship with Anderson. Skiles showed Exhibit 7D, a 1:11 minute video of the last image of Kyson alive, from the house surveillance system, the last portion showing Anderson roughly pulling Kyson into the house. She next showed Exhibit 7E, a two-minute video of police body camera flagged at 5:59 p.m., a video of Kyson on the floor of the 1009 Jodi Circle house.

Assistant DA Skiles told the courtroom that Marcus had many versions and multiple inconsistencies in his story. She concluded by asking the jury to return a verdict of guilty.

Opening Statement by Defense Attorney Flanagan

Defense Attorney Patrick Flanagan delivered a four-minute opening statement. Several times he issued a statement similar to, "my client is innocent until proven guilty. That burden is on the State."

Being a witness in a jury trial can be very intimidating and stressful. Judge Goodman was excellent at making a witness feel at ease. Each witness was not allowed to be in the courtroom until after he or she had testified. Even though the jury and those attending the trial hear the same mini sermon as each witness is being called to the stand, it is new stuff to the one testifying.

Judge Goodman delivered the same short speech to each of the 41 witnesses. Judge Goodman said, "Come around to the witness stand right over here. There's a couple of things I'd like to tell you about. We have a jury of 14. They are closely watching and listening to all of the witnesses and they, the jury, are paying very close attention. So, if you could draw the microphone close or get close to it, that will help them hear your testimony. I want to introduce you to my Court Reporter, Tawni. She's the lady that sits in front of the bench and she has a tough job. She has to write down everything that's said in this courtroom because we have to make a record. And so sometimes when the lawyers are asking questions and the witness wants to be helpful, the witness will start answering the question before the lawyer even finishes asking it. So, they're kind of stepping on the questions which makes it difficult for her to write down everything because she can only do one thing at a time. Sometimes people will ask you a yes or no question and you know this from your daily life that you'll say, uh-huh or hum-hum, meaning yes or no. So, it's easy to get into that habit. I do it myself. Everyone does it. So, if we hear an uh-huh or hum-hum. I'll say, do you mean yes or do you mean no? I'm not being mean to you. I'm just trying to make a good record."

John Glynn Direct Examination by Ms. Skiles

The State called its first witness, John Glynn. His testimony lasted a half hour and concentrated on his relationship with Kyson, and Kyson's mother, Jessica Rice. His background was established: He moved to Tomah in 1985 and worked his way up to sales manager at Cardinal Glass. His wife is Jolene, and they have two children, Sean and Desiree. Jessica Rice is his niece. John and Jolene had known Jessica since she was born. He met Marcus Anderson one time. He said Jessica had one boyfriend before

Marcus. Kyson was his grandnephew and lived in the Glynn household since he was born in 2015 to the time he and his mother, Jessica, moved out in March 2019

"He was young enough to be my grandson and about the same age, so I treated him like I did a grandson." Glynn described some of the things he and Kyson did together, such as working out in the hangar. John and Jolene's house is in the middle of the city-owned airport. They saw a lot of planes and helicopters come in and land. Glynn took Kyson to the EAA Airshow in Oshkosh.

John Glynn, Director of Technology Marketing for Cardinal Glass, took Kyson for rides in his Light Sport Weight shift Trike.

Glynn was asked to describe Kyson's personality. "He was wired to please, always asking to help. He wanted to work on stuff. He asked me twice to be his dad. I replied, I can't, but I'll be your Uncle John. I took him flying in my ultralight."

Assistant DA Skiles showed the Court a picture of Kyson. Glynn said, "Yes, that's him before he lost his two front teeth. He has that crooked little smile, as result of nerve damage. One eye won't close all the way. The photo was taken at the airport, as we had get-togethers in the hangar. He loved playing with his cousins. Declan is 6 months younger, and Garret is just a little bit older, Regan is a year younger, then there's Gabbie, and Mikey, and some I forgot. So, we had a lot of family. We were blessed.

"My wife, Jolene, and I, never had to discipline Kyson beyond an occasional time out for a few minutes. He loved to cuddle with Nana (Jolene) and watch television. I had to teach him to be careful around airplanes that came in.

"When he and his mother moved out, Kyson was reluctant to go, so I got him something special, a Spiderman poster and Jolene found him a Spiderman bedspread. When I took the poster to his new place, that's when I met Marcus for the first time. I saw Kyson on three separate visits from early March until he died."

Assistant DA Skiles probed Glynn's memory concerning Kyson's physical and medical condition. Glynn said, "On March 22, 2019, my wife texted me and it showed a picture of Kyson with two front teeth missing." Exhibit 2BB was pulled up.

Skiles asked about Easter Sunday 2019 (April 21), with an Easter Egg Hunt after church. Exhibits 2AA, 2BB, and 2CC are brought up on Courtroom screens. Glynn explained, "After finding out about the teeth, I wanted to find out if Kyson was intentionally hurt. His story about the teeth did not line up."

Glynn devised a scheme to look over or examine Kyson's body without really letting him know. Glynn explained. "With all the running around and the kids drinking water they would have to pee." When they used the bushes to pee, I told them to be careful to not get any on their pants. They pulled their pants down farther. When finished I helped Kyson pull his pants up, carefully looking him over and also pulled his shirt up looking over his chest, arms, and back. I did not see any bruising."

Defense Attorney Flanagan cross-examines John Glynn

Flanagan questioned Glynn about the nature of the play with his cousins. Next came a telling exchange, "Did you ask Kyson about the missing teeth?" Glynn replied, "He looked down and he said the words, 'On the carpet, in the bedroom,' that's it. It wasn't the story I heard." The back-and-forth exchange concerned the information John Glynn gave Investigator Tester about the place the teeth went missing; bedroom carpet vs. running on the concrete and tripping over a pipe. Defense Attorney

Flanagan suggested the missing two front teeth were caused by an accidental fall and not knocked out by an angry Marcus Anderson. During redirect, Assistant DA Skiles also questioned Glynn about the missing teeth.

Next Witness

At 10:30 a.m., Skiles called Witness #2, Dr. Jeffrey Cavaness, to the stand. The Q&A of each witness began by establishing name, with correct spelling, occupation, residence, and the relevance of the witness. In other words, why was this person on the witness stand.

Dr. Cavaness' background and credentials are probed and found quite extensive and competent. He was Kyson's primary care physician at Mayo Clinic in Tomah. Kyson's medical records, Exhibit 3, are produced and entail 178 pages, covering September 3, 2015 to May 29, 2019, from the first time Kyson came to the Mayo Clinic as a newborn baby.

The only medical condition of note was a left facial nerve palsy and a lengthy discussion, covering eight pages of the transcript, about the causes and manifestations of the condition. On the last visit, September 2018, before Kyson's death, Dr. Cavaness certified that Kyson was on track developmentally.

On cross-examination, Attorney Flanagan asked about a couple of spots found on Kyson, to which Dr. Cavaness said they are quite common. After any witness is finished with their testimony, Judge Goodman uses a quaint expression, "You may go about your business, sir. Thank you."

After a 15-minute break and before the third witness of the morning was called, District Attorney Kevin Croninger approached the bench (judge). "It has been brought to my attention that Mr. Anderson is displeased with the seating arrangements as far as where Investigator Sloan is seated." That happens to be two to three feet from Flanagan and behind him. Apparently, Anderson believed that Sloan could hear conversation between the defendant and his lawyer. Judge Goodman replied that if Flanagan needed some type of confidential conversation, he could get it.

The prosecution strategy was becoming quite evident. Subpoena all witnesses that could testify to Kyson's well-being and good health prior to his death.

Witnesses 3 and 4 were from the Kids Kountry Learning Center located on Mark Avenue in Tomah. Kids Kountry, licensed for 80 children, had eight classrooms serving children from ages six weeks to age 12. Vera Kress is the administrator and Aidlys Gonzalez was Kyson's 3-K classroom teacher.

Vera Kress described Kyson, "He was amazing. He was one of the most beautiful children we've ever had at Kids Kountry. He never caused any trouble. He was kind and gentle and a very soft-spoken little guy."

Kyson abruptly stopped attending on February 25, 2019. On cross examination, it was established that Jessica Rice was behind on her payments and owed Kids Kountry about $500.

Vera Kress was on the stand for five minutes and Aidlys Gonzalez was questioned for seven minutes.

Kyson was at Kids Kountry for about one year. Aidlys testified, "He was an awesome kid, very passive, a good listener, always willing to help. I think he was one of the best kids I had in that classroom of 13 kids." Both Ms. Kress and Ms. Gonzalez are asked if they saw any bruises, and both replied in the negative.

Witness #5 is April Ravet, a cousin to Kyson. Ms. Ravet has a son, Garret, who is about the same age as Kyson. Assistant DA Skiles asked Ravet about Kyson's front teeth and about a picture taken of Kyson on March 23 in Ravet's house where Garret and Kyson were playing. Kyson said that Tank had kicked him in his bedroom. (Tank was a nickname for Marcus Anderson). Kyson indicated to Ravet that he didn't want to go back to his house on Jodi Circle.

Next came a revelation that Jessica knew or did not really want to know what was happening to Kyson. On cross examination, Mr. Flanagan asked Ravet why she didn't report the missing teeth to any authority. Ravet said she told Kyson's mother, Jessica. A question from Mr. Flanagan, "Is there a reason why you didn't say anything until suddenly last month?"

April Ravet answered, "Because when I told Jessica, she said that's not what happened. That Tank wasn't home and that he fell in the garage."

Kyson lost two front teeth in March 2019, two months before his death.

The clock in the north wall of Courtroom 2 indicated it is close to noon. Judge Goodman observed there are several jurors from Sparta and some that live a distance away. He told the jury, "You can go home for lunch, but we have a number of restaurants here in Sparta. And if you go with another juror, do not discuss this case. If anyone tries to come up to you and talk about the case, tell them to stop it. Try to be back by 1:00. If you're late a little bit, don't worry. We're not going to yell at you, you won't be in trouble. When you get back, you can have the bailiff take you back to the jury room where you can be in private." It had been an intense and busy morning.

Chapter 26

Day 2: Afternoon Session

The Court reconvened at 1:02 p.m. Judge Goodman intoned, "We are back to case 19CF353, State vs. Marcus Anderson."

Sergeant Wilbert Steinborn was Witness #6 for the prosecution. His testimony was important, for he was one of the first officers on the murder scene. Steinborn testified for over two and a half hours.

Assistant DA Skiles did the questioning, initially asking Sergeant Steinborn about his background, training, and certifications. Skiles asked him about the weather on May 3, 2019, "It was a sunny day in the low to mid-60s, comfortable, I was wearing a short-sleeved duty shirt."

Steinborn explained how he knew the time that he received a call to aid an unresponsive child at 1009 Jodi Circle, "When we are called to a scene, the Monroe County Communications Center would log that on the CAD, Computer Aided Dispatching. The confirming initial call was 5:55 p.m. and I was on-scene at 5:58 p.m."

Skiles asked about the body camera. Officer Steinborn answered, "The camera captures an incident, and when finished with our duty day, we place it in on a docking station, which then connects to the server that is maintained by evidence.com and it's automatically uploaded into that server. There is an audio component."

Skiles asked Steinborn how the camera is activated. "One of three ways, one is through a Wi-Fi or Bluetooth burst from either the squad car or when you activate your emergency lights or from a Taser when you activate it. The third is by manually depressing the center button twice."

Skiles asked Steinborn if he was aware that 1009 Jodi Circle residence had an exterior security camera. Exhibit 7A showed Steinborn and Furlano arriving and Steinborn carrying an AED. Steinborn was asked what he saw when he first arrived, "Anderson was seated on the couch holding Kyson in his arms and appeared to be doing some sort of untrained mouth-to-mouth breathing technique."

Officer Wilbert Steinborn was on the witness stand for 2.5 hours and articulately covered all aspects of the arrest of Anderson.

Steinborn described the proper method of CPR and how he took Kyson from Anderson and proceeded to attempt to restore life to Kyson. Utilizing the AED, Steinborn said he was getting a faint pulse, and noticed significant bruising on Kyson,

Steinborn described how they attached the AED to Kyson with the two pads to analyze the patient and if a shock sequence was called for. Skiles asked Steinborn if Anderson was present and what was his demeanor. Steinborn answered, "He was directly in front of me, hysterical, and at one point attempted to demonstrate how he did CPR and slapped Kyson on the chest. He had to be instructed several times to back away from us so that we could work."

Steinborn related that Officer David Heckman arrived on the scene and was instructed to keep Marcus Anderson away from Steinborn and Furlano. Soon Tomah Ambulance came and took over the efforts to resuscitate Kyson.

Skiles asked that another portion of Exhibit 7E, body cam video, be played. She asked Steinborn about the video, "It's hard for me to watch. I really don't like to witness this." Steinborn was asked about a mask over Kyson's face, and he explained, "It is a bag valve mask." It created a seal, so the air is coming from the bag directly into the lungs and expanding the lungs.

Marcus was walking about, apologizing, standing by the large television, and calling Jessica. Skiles played another segment of the body cam video. Steinborn was asked by Furlano to get a statement from Anderson.

From the transcript:

Q. Where did this occur?

A. In the residence inside the ...we kind of traveled around the back part of the residence.

Q. What was his demeanor?

A. Again, he was just very hyper, animated, uhm, had to keep kind of directing him to stay on task.

Q. Did you ask him what had happened to Kyson?

A. I did.

Q. What did he tell you?

A. He told me that he and Kyson were taking a shower and that he had exited the shower to retrieve, I believe he said a towel from another room, and he heard a bang.

Q. Did you ask Mr. Anderson why Kyson was wearing clothes if he had been in the shower?

A. I did.

Q. What did he tell you?

A. He told me that he was going to take Kyson to the hospital so that he got him dressed.

Q. You said that as you were talking to him, you were kind of moving around. Did he take you into Kyson's bedroom?

A. He did.

Q. Why did he do that?

A. He showed me where he got the clothes from to dress Kyson.

Q. Did you ask him to demonstrate how he had been administering CPR which he had told you he was doing?

A. I did.

Q. How did he do that?

A. I requested that he demonstrate on a large stuffed animal. I believe it was like a Spiderman or something like that. And he began slapping it on the back and then slapped it on the front. It was more consistent with a toddler infant-like Heimlich maneuver or fixing a choking problem than it was appropriate CPR.

Q. Did you ask him why that was the method that he believed was appropriate to administer CPR?

A. He told me that's what he found on the Internet.

Q. Did Mr. Anderson take you into the bathroom where he alleged that Kyson fell?

A. Yes.

Q. Did he show you where he found Kyson?

A. He just motioned in the general area of the tub.

Q. Did you make an observation about the bathroom floor?

A. It was wet.

Q. At some point did you ask Mr. Anderson if he had drugs in the house?

A. I did.

Q. What did he tell you?

A. He informed me there was no illicit drugs in the house.

Q. The statements that you told us he made, were those captured on your body camera?

Skiles asked the Court to play another segment of Exhibit 7E.

In the video clip, Marcus Anderson went into the master bedroom, the bedroom he and Jessica shared, and closed the door. Steinborn, when questioned, said that he found it very unusual, like he was trying to hide something. Anderson was profusely sweating but showed no tears.

Anderson is urged to get to the hospital. Time stamp is 6:49 pm local time. Note the "1" is missing from the 1009 Jodi Circle address.

Jessica Rice arrived at her house at 6:12 p.m. Steinborn met and greeted her in the attached garage. The overhead door was closed or down, but the pedestrian door was partly ajar. The car was running. Anderson was present. When Steinborn asked Marcus why the car was running, he replied that he was going to drive them to the hospital. The car exhaust fumes were heavy.

Steinborn told Jessica that he was one of the first people on the scene and that the medical personnel were doing the best job that they could. Exhibit E, body cam video, and Exhibit 7F, exterior surveillance video, are alternately pulled up on the two large flat screens as well as the small screen in front of each juror. The video showed Marcus in the driveway as the ambulance crew was taking Kyson on a gurney to the ambulance. Marcus was excited, hysterical, and tried to approach the gurney, only to be pulled away by the officers. Sergeant Furlano drove the ambulance to allow the EMTs to provide care for Kyson. The time is 6:19 p.m. A squad vehicle was left behind. Steinborn drove his own squad car, and Officer Heckman drove the supervisor's (Furlano) car.

At Tomah Memorial Hospital, both Furlano and Steinborn were surprised that Marcus Anderson had not arrived. Steinborn and Heckman took Steinborn's squad car and went back to 1009 Jodi Circle. When they got there, it was close to dark and they could see Marcus in the garage but could not determine what he was doing. There was a vehicle in the garage, and it was not running.

In a bit, Steinborn did talk to Marcus and told him that when he got to the hospital, he should go to the waiting room. Steinborn instructed

Officer Heckman to follow Marcus to the hospital when he left. Marcus got in his car, got out of his car, got in again and backed the vehicle into the driveway. He got in and out several more times. Steinborn drove back to the hospital, and Officer Heckman remained on the scene.

Anderson drove around the circle and back into his driveway and parked his car and went back into the house. This was all captured on the surveillance video. This was not a person anxious to get to the hospital and check on the welfare of Kyson Rice.

While Heckman and Steinborn were talking, Amber Moseley (Day 3 Witness #11) pulled up. Her red 1996 GMC Sierra truck was captured on a house surveillance camera. Marcus Anderson talked to Amber, and he did not show any signs of immobility.

Anderson drove around the circle again and Officer Heckman followed him in his squad car. Marcus backed into the driveway. Heckman pulled into the driveway. Anderson questioned Heckman as to why he was being followed. Anderson went back into the house. It was 6:44 p.m. and the ambulance had left at 6:21 and yet Anderson has not made it to the hospital.

Assistant DA Skiles questioned Steinborn concerning the distance from 1009 Jodi Circle to the Tomah Memorial Hospital. Steinborn replied that it is a two-minute drive, and the hospital is about 8 blocks north of the Rice residence.

Steinborn said the EMTs wanted to get back into the house to retrieve some equipment they may have left behind. Heckman informed Steinborn that Anderson would not allow anyone back into the house. Steinborn went back a third time to the Rice house and was told to lock down the house as a crime scene as they were proceeding to get a search warrant.

When Steinborn arrived at the house, he told Anderson, who answered the front door, to leave. At the end of their conversation, Marcus told Steinborn that he was in pain. He appeared hunched over. Skiles pulled up a video 7L for when Steinborn arrived a third time. It is 6:58 p.m. Anderson left the 1009 Jodi Circle residence in his car at 7:07 p.m. Steinborn believed Anderson was going to the hospital to catch the helicopter that will be transporting Kyson.

The Court took a 10-minute break. Judge Goodman announces, "We're back on the record in 19CF353. The appearances are the same and the jury has returned from recess. And, Ms. Skiles, you were in the midst of questioning the Sergeant."

Steinborn told the Court that he left the house scene to return to Tomah Memorial Hospital and left Officer Heckman to secure the house. He told the Court that shortly after he arrived, Jessica was talking to various members of the staff, and soon Kyson was pronounced dead.

Now the search was on for Marcus Anderson. On the witness stand, Steinborn explained that messages were sent out over the TTY system, an internal secure network for surrounding agencies to also be looking for Mr. Anderson and his vehicle.

Steinborn explained a high risk stop to the Court: "The vehicles create a "V" pattern. Most of these take place at night so we call it the cone of darkness in which we're able to get numerous points of advantage on the squad cars, using them for cover and concealment. And then using either your PA system or your voice, to give commands to the driver and the occupants of the vehicle, to remove them safely and direct them back so that they could be taken into custody."

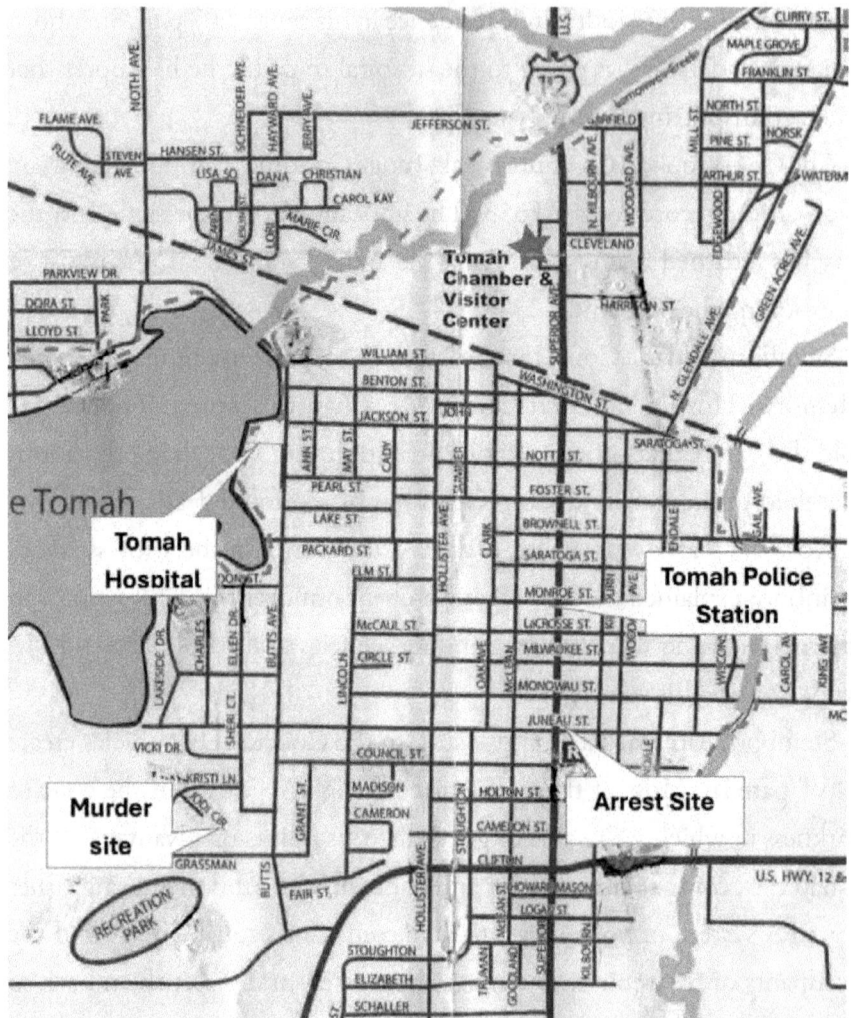

The tragic events of May 3, 2019 play out in less that one square mile.

Officers were able to hear Anderson's vehicle running. The right-turn signal was blinking, and the brake lamps were illuminated. The action was captured on Sgt. Perkin's squad car camera. It was a body cam modified for squad car use. When the squad car blue and red lights are turned on, it activated the Wi-Fi burst so the squad car camera and body camera come on simultaneously. Later, it was uploaded to evidence.com.

Steinborn testified that Anderson was complaining of medical issues. Officers took a blood test. Skiles asked Steinborn how police do a sobriety test for somebody suspected of operating while intoxicated. "We start with a test called horizontal gaze nystagmus. It checks for certain involuntary movement of the eyes usually attributed to depressants or alcohol. I would move on to a walk-and-turn test, which is a divided-attention-task test. And then I would move on to a one leg stand test, which again is a divided attention test. I am also trained ARIDE so I would have performed a modified Romberg Balance Test and a Lack-of-Convergence Test. I'm also a certified drug recognition expert so I probably would have put him through the 12-step drug influence evaluation process."

Anderson claimed he needed medical attention, so none of those tests were performed. Police handcuffed Anderson and did a pat-down search on Anderson and emptied his pockets. He was put in the rear of Deputy Geyer's patrol vehicle. His property was placed in a bag.

Witness # 7

Erica Murray was questioned by D.A. Croninger. Ms. Murray worked at Tomah Health and was currently enrolled in a doctorate program to be a nurse practitioner at UW-Madison. She was being questioned about Marcus Anderson's stay as a patient at TMS from April 27 to April 30, 2019.

Erica Murray described Anderson's behavior as angry and aggressive. She described for the Court the day she went to give him a medication, called Cymbalta, which treats depression and nerve pain.

Ms. Murray said, "Like every patient, I tell them what the medication is and what it's used for in their care, that I have Cymbalta, it's an anti-depressant. He knocked it out of my hand and said, 'I am not suicidal. I'd rather be homicidal than suicidal.'" Murray reported the comment to the Physician's Assistant.

Anderson was being treated at TMH for rhabdomyolysis or simply rhabdo, a massive release of creatinine to the kidneys, usually caused by a prolonged period of immobility most often seen in elderly patients who have fallen. It is treated with IV fluids.

There were a series of questions about the police having been called to the hospital the night before. Mr. Flanagan objects. The jury was out for 13 minutes while attorneys argue about a line of questions. Erica Murray was on the stand for 26 minutes.

Witness # 8

Christy Devine is questioned by Croninger. Ms. Devine lived in New Lisbon and met Marcus Anderson through a friend, Brandon Crampes, who occasionally went by the name of Bdawg. DA Croninger asked about her relationship with Marcus Anderson. She explained that they would hang out together, go to McDonald's and he would come to her house and usually bring Brandon Crampes with him, and sometimes Kyson Rice, but she never met his mother, Jessica Rice.

Croninger asked, "At some point in time, did you become aware that Kyson was deceased?" She answered, "Yes." She explains that Anderson brought Kyson to her house a couple days before his death and Anderson also came by himself. When asked to describe his demeanor, she said that Marcus was mean and agitated. She testified, "I had two small children at the time, that were one and two and he was agitated with them and wanted them to be very quiet or shut up. I was asking him to leave. And that was two days before Kyson died." Christy Devine was on the witness stand for seven minutes.

The jury was excused, and the Court was adjourned for the day at 4:23 p.m. The Court was very respectful of the jury. Everyone in the courtroom rises as the jury exits. After the jurors leave the room, Judge Goodman had some business with the two lawyers. The admissibility of a photograph, WW, is brought up by DA Croninger. Marcus had an issue with his attorney. There's a discussion about a witness on the fourth amended witness list, Torry Anderson. Croninger asks the Court to seal some of Kyson Rice's medical records. Judge Goodman agreed to the sealing of those records.

Chapter 27

Day 3: Five Witnesses in the Morning

The trial's third day was again a typical March day in Monroe County, starting at 23 degrees and edging up to 43 by mid-afternoon.

The United Nations said that more than 4 million refugees had now fled Ukraine as Russia's invasion nears its sixth week. The media was still abuzz about actor Will Smith slapping comedian Chris Rock at the Sunday night March 27 Oscars. Chris Rock made a joke about Smith's wife's short haircut, who was bald, and suffering from a hair loss condition of alopecia.

A fire broke out in an unoccupied house in the 1200 block of Kilbourn Avenue a bit before 2:00 a.m. The house was near Gillett Park and was completely destroyed. Tomah Police asked the public to stay away from the area.

Marcus Anderson, sporting a yellow shirt, with blue tie, was escorted to the defense table by two officers of the Court. Before the jury was brought into the courtroom, Judge Goodman addressed the issue of Photo WW being admissible. Photo WW is of Mr. Anderson, and it was taken from behind. The photo showed Mr. Anderson with his pants below his buttocks. The question concerned it being prejudicial. Croninger argued it is probative, which meant it had value to the State's case.

Croninger also argued that the photo showed the huge difference in size between Anderson and Kyson Rice. Judge Goodman said there are other photos that show the large difference in size between Anderson and Kyson, plus the photo did not show Kyson missing some teeth, but autopsy photos clearly indicate teeth are missing. Judge Goodman did not allow Photo WW to be shown to the jury.

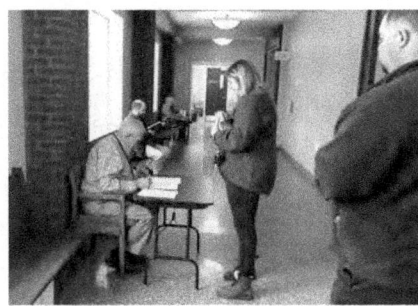

Bailiff Dale Kanable has the duty of checking in prospective jurors when they approach one of four courtrooms.

Croninger raised the issue of Marcus Anderson wanting to address the issue of dismissing his lawyer, Mr. Flanagan. Anderson reminded Judge Goodman that he sent an eight-page motion to that effect. Judge Goodman had denied the motion because it did not have an affidavit attached to the motion. Anderson then said that Flanagan will represent him at the trial.

The jury came in at 8:32 a.m. Judge Goodman announced, "Welcome back, everyone. The jury has returned, and we are ready to proceed. Mr. Croninger, call your next witness." Assistant DA Sarah Skiles said, "Judge, the State calls Deputy David Heckman to the stand."

Deputy David Heckman Testimony

Skiles asked several questions about his background, training, and current employment, which is the Monroe County Sheriff's Department.

Heckman explained that when he arrived at the Rice residence at approximately 5:55 p.m., Sergeant Furlano and Officer Steinborn were already performing CPR on Kyson Rice and Anderson was coming out from where the bedrooms were located. When Skiles asked Heckman about Anderson's demeanor, Heckman replied, "Frantic." Anderson says Kyson had slipped in the shower and hit his head and became unresponsive. Heckman testified that Anderson was sweating profusely.

Officer Heckman went on to explain that when the ambulance arrived, he drove one of the patrol vehicles to the hospital. Then he returned to the residence to ensure that Anderson would make it to the hospital.

Officer Heckman testified that on his return to 1009 Jodi Circle, Anderson was packing belongings. With Exhibit 7BB, a total of 3 minutes and 27 seconds, Heckman's body camera and radio conversations indicated that the ambulance crew wanted to go back to the residence to retrieve some medical equipment.

Skiles asked Officer Heckman about the conversation between him and Anderson. Anderson said he was packing things for himself and Jessica. Heckman was asked if he found that strange. Heckman answered, "The child was at the hospital. It seems that a parent would go directly to the hospital. If supplies were needed later, then they could be obtained at that time."

Heckman was ordered by Steinborn to secure the residence as it had now become a potential crime scene. Heckman told Anderson that he was to take control of the house. Anderson was agitated and asked why.

Exhibit 7CC was played, showing the front of the residence. Anderson was uncooperative. Officer Heckman called for Steinborn to come to the residence, which he did. Skiles played Exhibit 7CC from about 2:20 to 13:51. The video showed Anderson leaving in his black Ford Fusion at 7:07 p.m.

Heckman said that investigators were applying for a search warrant. When Skiles finished her direct examination, she told Officer Heckman, "Good luck on your deployment." Officer Heckman had previously been deployed to Iraq and Afghanistan and was now headed to Jordan. Officer Heckman was in the witness chair for 40 minutes.

Under cross examination by Flanagan, Heckman revealed nothing new. Under redirect, Skiles played a part of Exhibit 7AA to help Heckman recall Anderson's telling the officers how he applied CPR.

Dispatcher Patrick Deethardt Testimony

It was Officer Heckman's body camera that caught the chaos at 1009 Jodi Circle on the early evening of May 3. Note the television screen.

The next witness was Patrick Deethardt, Dispatcher with the Monroe County 911 Communications Center. The Dispatch Call Center handles all 911, Monroe County Sheriff, Sparta Police, Tomah Police, and ambulance services calls. Deethardt explained how the CAD (Computer Aided Dispatching) system works. The 9-page CAD document was Exhibit 6.

One of the calls at 6:00 p.m. "92 has a pulse" indicated that Officer 92 had found a pulse in the subject. On the second page, Mr. Anderson told the Dispatch officer, "I'm trying to do CPR. I'm patting him on the back, trying to get him to breathe."

Another call at 6:56 p.m. "Marcus is unwilling to let officers back into the house." Anderson left the residence at 7:07 p.m. Deethardt was on the witness stand for 20 minutes.

Amber Moseley Testimony

The next witness is Amber Moseley, Jessica's coworker at Taco Bell. She was the shift lead manager and had been at Taco Bell for over three years, but at the time of the killing, she was a crew member. She met Jessica Rice in 2012 when she moved from Illinois to Tomah. She told the Court how Kyson and her daughter were really close and enjoyed many play dates, cookouts, and Easter egg hunts.

Amber described the relationship between Kyson and Anderson as father and son, and Anderson would often bring Kyson into Taco Bell at the same time dropping Jessica off to work. Jessica would converse with both of them and ask Kyson what he was doing that day. That cordial relationship changed two or three weeks before Kyson's murder. Anderson and Kyson would no longer come into the restaurant. Kyson seemed sad.

On May 3, 2019, the day of the murder, Amber picked up Jessica at about 9:30 a.m. Amber was scheduled to work at 10 a.m. and Jessica at 11 a.m. Amber tells the Court that Jessica seemed upset when she was picked up, coming out of the side door of the garage. Jessica told Amber that she and Anderson had argued and fought all night.

Amber told the Court that she left work at about 3:30 p.m. She said that Marcus called Taco Bell to speak to Jessica. Jessica told Marcus that they were busy, and that Jessica would call Marcus back when they weren't busy. Jessica was scheduled to work until 8 p.m.

Amber Moseley was home and got a call about 6 p.m. from Jessica to come pick her up at Taco Bell, driving her red 1996 GMC Sierra pickup. "I had my three-year-old daughter with me. It takes about 15 minutes to get from Taco Bell to Jessica's house. When we got to the house, there were lots of EMTs and police officers and I never got into the house. I tried to get through the garage but there were a lot of people there. I stayed on the lawn."

Amber told the Court that Anderson came up to her:

Skiles: Did you make an observation about his face?
Amber: I did.

Skiles: What did you see?
Amber: He looked like he was under the influence. His eyes were yellow.

Skiles: And what did he talk to you about?
Amber: He just kept saying: My son, my son, my son.

Skiles: And did he talk to you about what had happened to Kyson?
Amber: He told me that he was giving him a shower and he fell in the shower.

Amber Moseley tells the Court that she saw Kyson being put into an ambulance and that she and her three-year-old daughter went to the hospital. She said that she asked Marcus if he wanted to ride with them, but he declined. He said he would be coming on his own.

Amber was at the hospital with Jessica for half an hour, comforting her. Jessica asked Amber to retrieve some things for her: shoes, slippers, a pair of pants, as she was still in her work clothes. Amber returned to the residence at 1009 Jodi Circle. Marcus was there and Amber asked him to help her find some clothes and shoes. She described the house inside as a mess. She did not get the clothing items requested. Instead, Marcus said he would bring them to the hospital.

Amber Moseley was asked by Anderson to remove the Sig Sauer Model 522 .22 caliber rifle from the Jodi Circle residence. She refused.

Marcus asked Amber to take the gun out of the residence. She refused. Amber left and took her daughter to her grandma's house and went back to the hospital. Amber is asked by Assistant DA Skiles when was the last time she saw Kyson and what was his condition. Amber said it was May 1 or May 2 and Kyson appeared normal. At 10:21 a.m. the Court takes a brief recess. Amber endured 35 minutes on the witness stand.

Cheryl Quarles Testimony

After a 20-minute break, Cheryl Quarles was the next witness, taking the oath at 10:42 a.m.. Assistant DA Sarah Skiles asked the questions. Quarles tells the Court that she works at online sales with a home office. She tells the Court that she has a son, Andrew Rowcliffe, who will also be a witness in this case. Cheryl Quarles testified that Marcus Anderson was her neighbor for some time, via a side-by-side duplex. Marcus eventually moved in with her and her husband and rented a room from them. Anderson moved out in the spring of 2019 to live with his girlfriend, Jessica Rice.

A question arose about Marcus Anderson's military service.

Q: Did Mr. Anderson ever tell you that he had served in the United States military?

A. The Marine Corps.

Mr. Flanagan: Objection: relevance.

Skiles: May we be heard?

The jury is escorted out of the room. There is an exchange between Croninger, Flanagan, and Judge Goodman about the admissibility of Skiles line of questioning concerning Anderson's military service. Croninger pointed out that Anderson lied to both law enforcement officers and Judge Ziegler in another case, about his military service. Judge Goodman allows the line of questioning by Skiles and the jury is brought back into the room.

Skiles questions Cheryl Quarles about how she got to know Kyson Rice, "Anderson and Jessica would bring him by occasionally. Anderson asked me if I would babysit Kyson for a couple of weeks while he was out of town, which she did in April 2019. Kyson revealed to Cheryl that Anderson punched him in the chest. After Anderson returned, Cheryl also took care of Kyson while Anderson was in the hospital. Cheryl tells the Court that she visited Anderson one time in the hospital and when asked about his demeanor, she says that he was "all over the place, angry, acting like a child, and disrespectful to the nursing staff."

Cheryl said she was watching Kyson for a few hours on the day Anderson was released and did not notice any bruises on his face or neck. Assistant DA Skiles asked Cheryl if she knew a woman by the name of Regina Hall, to which she replied, "Yes."

Under cross examination by Mr. Flanagan, Cheryl revealed that Detective Tester came to her house to interview her on May 7, 2019, four days after Kyson's murder. Four months later, September 24, 2019, Detective

Tester interviewed her again at the her home. Cheryl told Detective Tester about the conversation Cheryl had with Kyson concerning Anderson hitting him in the chest. Cheryl Quarles was on the witness stand for 45 minutes.

Witness Andrew Rowcliffe

Seated next in the witness chair is Andrew Rowcliffe, age 21, native of Warrens, Wisconsin, and son of Cheryl Quarles and stepson of Larry Quarles. He moved out of the duplex on County Highway CM at the beginning of 2019.

Rowcliffe was asked about Marcus Anderson's demeanor when he came back from Arizona and California on April 24. He responded by saying Anderson was extremely aggressive, a totally different personality than before he left. Rowcliffe's testimony was consistent with the testimony of several witnesses. Rowcliffe's testimony took eight minutes.

Judge Goodman glanced at the clock on the north wall, reading 11:36 a.m., and declared it was a good time to break for lunch.

Chapter 28

Jessica Takes the Stand

The trial is back in session at 12:41 p.m. The next witness is Kyson Rice's mother, Jessica Rice. She will be on the witness stand for a grueling hour. Assistant DA Sarah Skiles questions her.

Jessica Rice provided her name, with spelling, and provides her age, 29. At the time of the trial, she worked at McDonald's as shift manager. She worked there for two years. Jessica was not tall, barely four feet, six inches.

Jessica explained that she first met Marcus Anderson in October 2014, a short romance that fizzled. She was asked about her son, Kyson, born on September 3, 2015. His biological father was from the Necedah area, and never in Kyson's life, except when the father was in court for paternity issues.

The discussion was directed to Kyson's left facial palsy, something that Kyson was born with, causing trouble with Kyson closing his left eye and necessitating eyedrops. Jessica described Kyson: outgoing, fun loving, loves peanut butter (not crunchy) and jelly sandwiches, superheroes, dinosaurs, and airplanes.

Jessica said she reconnected with Marcus at the end of 2018 and Kyson called him "Tank" and later started calling him Dad. At the time they re-established a relationship, Marcus was living with Larry and Cheryl Quarles. Marcus told Jessica he was laid off, and she supplied him with money from time to time.

Kyson was born with left facial palsy, necessitating frequent eye drops.

Jessica was asked about what happened to Kyson's teeth. She volunteered, "I got a call from Marcus saying that Kyson fell in the garage over a pole, like the shower pole that we took out of the bathroom because we put up a new one and he bashed his face, and he said one tooth fell out and there was another one hanging."

She said she met the Quarles couple in April 2019 because they were going to take care of Kyson while she worked. Jessica related the story of when Marcus went to the hospital after he came back from his trip to Arizona and California. She saw Kyson sitting on Marcus' lap who was sitting up in bed. Marcus was punching Kyson in the chest because he said Kyson was embarrassing him in front of the nurses and doctors. She said it was a closed fist, and he was hit twice, and then we left.

Assistant DA Skiles asked Jessica about a gun in the house shortly after he moved in. "He brought it in, and I didn't want it there. Marcus said he would take it out, but he never did."

Q. On May 2, the day before Kyson died, did you and Mr. Anderson get in an argument?

A. Yes.

Q. When did that argument start on that day?

A. That one happened after I got off work and he picked me up and we started fighting in the car.

Q. What were you fighting about?

A. Just random stuff and then a soda spilled onto his floorboard, and he called me a worthless fat piece of shit.

Q. How did you respond?

A. I was quiet and then we got home we fought and then we said it was over.

Q. Were you going to remain living together?

A. No. He was going to move out that following weekend.

Jessica was asked about Kyson's face before he went to bed. She replied that his face was fine and there were no injuries. Skiles then proceeded to ask questions about Jessica's entire day, starting with the early morning. She said, "I woke up about 8:00 to get ready for work. I was supposed to work at 11. Marcus was sleeping on the couch. Before I left, I told Marcus I just need to get out of the house. Amber picked me up about 9. Marcus called me at work on the store phone, I had my cell phone shut off. About 11, he called about a fire in the garage. I said I would notify the landlord."

Marcus said that the fire was out. To her, it sounded like Marcus wanted her to come home and Jessica said she would not be coming home. Jessica said she returned to her house on Sunday, two days after Kyson's death and did not see there had been a fire in the garage.

Exhibit 2EE is pulled up. A photo of Jessica's cell phone, a phone contact showing, with Tank, Marcus' nickname and a picture of his two kids. When asked about the kids and if she was aware of them, she replied, "Yes, they reside in Arizona."

Jessica had provided law enforcement with her phone at the hospital on the night of Kyson's death. Phone conversations are not recorded or saved on a cell phone, but text messages are. A series of telling and perhaps embarrassing text messages are shown on the courtroom screens and Jessica was asked to read them.

A text message Marcus sent to Jessica, timestamped 11:06 a.m., "I see you don't care about me anymore so you ready to move on and want to be with someone who makes happy and love me and not treat me like a doorstop."

Remember that Jessica's phone was in the Taco Bell safe, turned off, so she cannot read these in real time. Text message at 11:19 a.m. "Now you busy at work. I'm going to remember that shit. So from now on and don't ever call me or text me from work again. So when you having a bad day don't come to me when something goes wrong. Don't call me anymore." Several text messages follow at 11:24, 11:36, and 12:14.

The Monroe County Justice Center, completed in 2017, is connected to the old historic courthouse, and the site of the Anderson homicide trial.

There are text messages and phone calls at 2:00 p.m. from Marcus to Jessica. Exhibit 2GG. "You need to call me now," was a plea from Marcus. There were further messages sent at 3:00 p.m. and 3:09 p.m. On Jessica's break, she talked with Marcus by cell phone for over a half hour. At about 4:09 p.m., Marcus told Jessica that she is supposed to take care of him, that he was in pain, and she has abandoned him. When Assistant DA Skiles asked Jessica if she still planned to get out of the relationship she replied, "yes." Kyson was to have one more day with Marcus and then Marcus would leave.

Skiles has the technician bring up Exhibit 2KK, a call log starting at 5:52 p.m. with a series of calls back and forth between Jessica and Marcus. Exhibit 2LL is put up on all the television monitors. It displays a series of missed calls from Marcus to Jessica.

At 5:55 p.m., Jessica got that dreadful call from Marcus on the Taco Bell store phone, "Kyson is not breathing," to which she responds, "call 911." Marcus told Jessica that Kyson slipped and fell and hit his head in the shower.

Jessica called Amber Moseley for a ride home. While waiting for Amber and during the approximate 15-minute ride to her 1009 Jodi Circle house, Jessica called Marcus several times. She heard background noises of EMT's working. Marcus was frantic. She heard one EMT say, "Sir, we don't care if there's drugs in this house. We're here about Kyson."

The following is a condensed version of Jessica's answers, from many Assistant DA Skiles' questions.

"I tried to get in the front door, but the EMTs told me I couldn't because they were working on Kyson. When I went to the garage, Marcus' car was running. The overhead garage door was closed. Marcus was not there, but Officer Heckman or Officer Steinborn came into the garage. The Officer asked me if Marcus was in the hospital for a brain injury. They told me that Kyson was being taken to Tomah Memorial Hospital and helicoptered to La Crosse. I told Marcus to change his clothes, because they were wet, and meet me at the hospital. Amber drove me to the hospital, and when I got there, I saw Kyson, they were working on him, and he was hooked up to all kinds of machines. Just looking at him, I knew it wasn't a slip or fall. Kyson was bruised from head to toe. Then they notified me that Kyson was not going to make it. They gave me an opportunity to say goodbye."

Exhibit 2HH Skiles brought up the last text message Marcus to Jessica at 6:53 p.m. It asked her to call him ASAP. She did not.

Exhibit 2QQ phone log showed that Marcus tried to call Jessica at 6:46 p.m. again at 6:48, 6:51, 6:52, 6:53, 6:54, and a final call attempt at 6:57. Jessica did not return any of those calls. Those calls were made by Marcus to Jessica when he was essentially missing in action and between the time he left 1009 Jodi Circle and until he was spotted at 7:52 p.m. sitting in his Ford Fusion parked in downtown Tomah.

After an hour of direct examination by Assistant DA Skiles, Attorney Flanagan has an opportunity for cross examination. Jessica revealed that she met Marcus in October 2014, but just as friends, as he had to have back surgery. A romantic relationship started in December 2018. She signed a lease in the first week of March 2019. She and Marcus painted for a week and Marcus moved in on the second week.

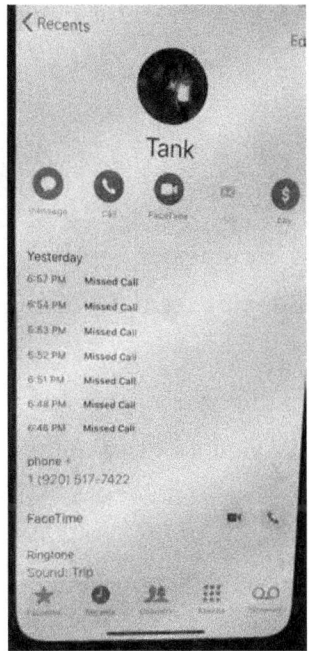
Cell phone calls from Marcus to Jessica.

Flanagan asked about Kyson's teeth. There is no new information here as Flanagan is going over old ground. It's the same with Marcus hitting Kyson as Kyson sat on Marcus' lap in Tomah Memorial Hospital. He was there because the nerves were breaking down in his legs. Jessica did not report Marcus striking Kyson because she said she was scared but she said she started planning to get out of the relationship.

Defense Attorney Flanagan zeroed in on the belt hitting incident, casting doubts, because Jessica heard, but did not see the incident. Flanagan's cross examination lasted about 15 minutes. Frankly, an observer might have determined that he did not have much to work on.

Redirect by Assistant DA Skiles

Jessica related that when Marcus returned from his trip to Arizona and California, he was a lot angrier. She said, "Just little things would set him off. He would yell. One time he used a belt to strike Kyson. I could hear it. I was in the kitchen and Kyson and Marcus were in his room. Kyson did not cry. He was a real trooper. They did not talk about it, because Marcus left the house angry that day. We never talked about it after, it was just his way."

Jessica was asked about being interviewed by Detective Sloan and Detective Tester several times. She answered the questions as best she could, being distressed.

Q. Miss Rice, did you love Marcus Anderson?
A. Yeah.

Q. Did you see yourself being together with him for quite a long time?

A. That's what we talked about, yes.

Q. Did you love your son?

A. More than anything.

Q. When you were first questioned by law enforcement and you were processing this situation, did you feel to some extent defensive or protective of Marcus?

A. At first, until I found out the extent of how bad everything really was.

After nearly an hour in the witness chair, Flanagan does a two minute recross.

Witness #15 Larry Quarles

Larry Quarles, husband of a previous witness, Cheryl Quarles, and stepfather of witness, Andrew Rowcliffe, takes the stand. DA Croninger executes the direct examination. Larry states that they have been married for 19 years and live in a duplex on Highway CM, west of Tomah.

Larry said that Marcus and Mike Ayala lived there, and that Mike Ayala's girlfriend lived there also. The Quarles rented one of their rooms to Marcus.

DA Croninger asked Quarles his general impression and demeanor of Jessica Rice. Marcus knew the Quarles, and Jessica was looking to have someone take care of her son while he was out of town.

Larry said that he knew Marcus planned to go to Arizona and that Marcus had a girlfriend, Regina Hall, in Arizona. Regina Hall had come to Wisconsin to be with Marcus at his place on Highway CM.

Larry described Kyson as above-average intelligence, very verbal, with a good depth of knowledge and vocabulary. Larry received a phone call that Marcus came back to Tomah on April 24 and that Marcus went to the hospital on April 27.

When the Quarles visited Marcus in the hospital, he seemed stressed, confused, and belligerent. Quarles said, "It seemed Marcus had a really rough trip or something out of town and he was just stressed."

Larry Quarles picked up Marcus at the hospital on April 30 and took him to the house at 1009 Jodi Circle. Marcus wanted Quarles to pick up Kyson at the Quarles house and take him to 1009 Jodi Circle. Larry hesitated because he did not have a car seat for Kyson. Switching car seats and cars, Kyson was transported back to his mother's house. Kyson seemed nervous and not too happy about leaving the Quarles' home.

Larry went to the 1009 Jodi Circle address on the May 2, the day before Kyson died. There was confusion and arguments about how Jessica was getting to work that day, as she indicated she was running late. Larry did take her to work as he had to go daily to the Post Office. The Quarles run a business from home. After dropping off Jessica at Taco Bell, Larry returns to see Marcus. He said he did not see Kyson.

On May 3, the day of the killing, Larry visited Marcus on his way to the Post Office. The surveillance video shows it is about 10:04 a.m. Larry tells the Court, "I gathered there was some tension between Marcus and Jessica, about housekeeping, division of labor, organization, and because of her job, a lot of that was falling onto Marcus."

After dropping off material at the Post Office, Larry visited Marcus for a second time that day. The camera video showed 11:13 a.m. and a visit for 20-40 minutes. Kyson was in his room.

Q. How would you describe his demeanor on that day?

A. Frustrated, more of the continuation of the day before. Building up, the frustration about the house and the logistics and washing clothes and cleaning dishes and that sort of domestic stuff. Belligerent and confrontational, and he seemed to be angry with me. Also, manipulative. Claiming a medical condition that would prohibit him from doing a job.

After 45 minutes in the witness chair, Croninger says, "Thank you Mr. Quarles, I have no further questions. Flanagan has no cross examination.

Kyson is helping his mother dye Easter eggs on April 21, 2019. Kyson has 12 days to live.

Witness #16 Justin Harmon

Justin Harmon was called to the witness stand at mid-afternoon. Justin Harmon, his wife Meaghan, and 11-year-old daughter live at 1011 Jodi Circle, the right-hand side of the duplex, sharing a wall with 1009 Jodi Circle, the residence of Marcus Anderson and Jessica Rice.

Harmon revealed that they did not know Anderson and Rice but were aware of Marcus after the Kyson murder. They did not know Kyson but saw him entering and leaving the residence. Mr. Harmon said, "On May 3, 2019, we left about 5:05 p.m. to attend an art show. Before leaving, I could hear Mr. Anderson scolding someone. Other times we could hear arguing going on, as the master bedroom is right on the other side of the wall. He was using vulgarity to her, Ms. Rice, calling her 'fucking bitch, mother-fucking bitch.'"

Witness #17 Meaghan Harmon

Justin Harmon was on the stand for ten minutes and his wife, Meaghan Harmon was sworn in and confirmed the statements her husband, Justin, made to police and in the courtroom. She added that the garage door was open or nearly open and Anderson's car was running. Meaghan Harmon was on the stand for nine minutes.

Witness #18 Courtney Henshaw

Courtney Henshaw took the oath and was seated in the witness chair. Ms. Henshaw was the general manager at Taco Bell and hence Jessica's boss. Assistant DA Skiles asked her about Jessica's work schedule, her interactions with Kyson and Marcus, whose name she remembered as Tank. Exhibit 10 was brought up on the large television screens, a three-page work schedule. It confirmed that Jessica was scheduled to work from 11:00 a.m. to 8:00 p.m. on May 3. Courtney also confirmed the phone calls that Jessica received from Marcus, both her cell phone and the store phone. Flanagan does not cross examine.

Witness #19 Mike Ayala

Next up on this busy day is Mike Ayala with direct examination from DA Croninger. Ayala lived in the duplex opposite Larry and Cheryl Quarles, and Marcus Anderson lived with him for a short time. Also living with Ayala was his girlfriend, Kiera, and her kids. Ayala's kids were there, part time.

Q. Was there a reason he (Marcus Anderson) no longer lived with you or what happened with that?

A. We started having a falling out. Not so much that we hated each other, it's just he wasn't really paying the bills like he said he was. I started noticing that he had a change in behavior, and I noticed that he was slowly taking stuff out of the house and going next door. Mike Ayala also told the Court that Marcus told him that he was a Marine special forces sniper.

Q. Was there a reason why you didn't believe that?

A. I handed him a gun one day and he didn't know how to use it.

Mike Ayala said he bought the gun at Moe's in Black River Falls in 2013. He later sold it to Brandon Crampes in 2018. Brandon also goes by the name Bdawg. It was a .22 caliber.

Under cross examination by lawyer John Flanagan, Ayala said he was a friend of Brandon, and he bought the gun for cash, and the bill of sale is in California where he used to live. Ayala told the Court he had some legal issues and that is the reason he got rid of all his guns.

Mike Ayala was the last of 11 witnesses that day. The jury is excused at 3:54 p.m. The Court briefly discussed the witness line up for Day 4.

Chapter 29

Five Witnesses Testify

The temperature dropped to 16 degrees in the early morning of March 31, with rain and the potential for icing conditions. The projected high is only 32 degrees, unseasonably cold for late March. There was concern that witnesses from Madison may not make it to Sparta or perhaps be late.

Yesterday, two Russian cosmonauts and one American NASA astronaut had returned from the International Space Station amid rising tension between Russia and the United States over the invasion of Ukraine. Biden ordered a massive release from our oil reserves to bring down gas prices. Bruce Willis was diagnosed with aphasia and will retire from acting. In Monroe County, the closing of the Cataract Elementary School was a hot topic of discussion and community anguish. The Sports Page of the Monroe County Herald touted a baseball headline, "Tomah Boys Top BRF 6-2 in Season Opener."

Eight witnesses will take the stand today. But the "big gun" is Dr. Michael Stier, a pathologist from UW-Madison, whose testimony will take over three hours.

Witness #20 Dr. Heather Potter

First up to the witness chair was ophthalmologist Dr. Heather Potter from the University of Wisconsin Hospital in Madison. She was questioned by DA Croninger. Dr. Potter related her years of education, experience in eye care, surgery, and research. She detailed how sections of the eye are viewed under a microscope. After her examination of Kyson Rice, Dr. Potter came to a diagnosis of preretinal hemorrhage, blood on the surface of the retina. An eye model showed how preretinal hemorrhage can be caused by trauma or diabetes. She went on to demonstrate Kyson's intraretinal hemorrhage, or blood within the layers of the retina, also caused by trauma. She also described his subretinal hemorrhaging or blood pooling underneath the retina, also caused by trauma. She discussed a macular fold, caused by trauma. Then to choroidal congestion. The choroid is a spongy vascular layer that supplies blood to the retina. "There's too much blood there," says Dr. Potter. Next was the topic of nerve head or optic disc edema, describing the swelling present.

Dr. Heather Potter was one of four experts from the Wisconsin State Crime Lab to testify.

Dr. Potter described subdural hemorrhage, hemorrhaging between the optic nerve and the covering of the optic nerve as well as subarachnoid hemorrhage. Dr. Potter explained seven different types of hemorrhages, all pointing to brutal head trauma, during her one hour on the witness stand. Her testimony was powerful and defense Attorney Patrick Flanagan rehashed her testimony in cross-examination.

At 9:16 a.m. the jury was dismissed. Croninger asked the Court to have Detective Sloan take pictures of the eye model that was used by Dr. Potter.

Witnesses #20 and #21 April Hall-Banks and Regina Hall

The mother and daughter were the next two witnesses. They were subpoenaed from Buckeye, Arizona on the west side of Phoenix. With the jury in the next room, Croninger, Flanagan, and Judge Goodman wrestled with who should testify first and about Fifth Amendment rights and procedures that might throw the case to the Appellate Courts later on. Regina Hall was Marcus Anderson's girlfriend in Arizona. She was recognized to have some intellectual difficulties. The mother, April, wanted to be in the courtroom when her daughter, Regina, testified. That can only occur if April testified first.

April Hall-Banks, in her early 50s, was questioned by DA Croninger for 11 minutes. She told the Court about medical difficulties of her daughter, Regina: lupus, kidney shut-down, flat-lined twice, a coma, and memory issues due to anoxia.

Asked about Regina's relationship with Marcus Anderson, April said that Regina met Marcus through her son, Marcus Hall, Jr. She talked about how Regina was in an off and on relationship with Marcus from 2015 to 2019. Marcus stayed at the home of April and Regina when he came out to Arizona from April 9-April 24. During part of that two-week period, Marcus and Regina went to California.

Marcus told April that he was once in the military. The testimony from other witnesses indicated that Marcus told everyone that he served in the military.

The jury is excused, and the lawyers argued about the upcoming testimony of Regina Hall and what kinds of questions could be asked.

At 9:45 a.m., the questioning of Regina Hall began, again by DA Croninger. He elicited a "yes" response from Regina Hall when she was asked if she intended to use her Fifth Amendment Rights to not answer certain questions. Regina was assured by Croninger that whatever she would say cannot be used against her in any court of law.

It's getting testy between DA Croninger and defense attorney Patrick Flanagan. Flanagan raised the impeachment issue. Impeachment is the process of attacking the accuracy of a witnesses' testimony, in this case, in terms of any possible prior criminal record. The jury was excused, the lawyers argued, the jury was brought back in, and questioning resumed. Detective Walensky was sent to check CCAP (Consolidated Court Automation Programs) for any prior convictions of Regina and found none. CCAP is operated by the Wisconsin Court System and is a database of court and criminal records.

Regina was asked about the time she spent with Marcus in Arizona. She stated they both flew separately to Los Angeles, spent a week together, and both returned to Buckeye, Arizona by rental car.

Several items found in Marcus' Ford Fusion were sent to the State Crime Lab for testing.

Regina testified that after Marcus returned to Wisconsin on April 24, they texted and FaceTimed quite often, and she saw Kyson with Marcus when they FaceTimed. Marcus told Regina that his friend, Brandon (Bdawg) went back to work, so Marcus was taking care of Kyson. She told the Court that after Kyson's death, she communicated with Marcus from his jail cell, and all calls were recorded. More than a few will be played in Court.

We learned that Marcus told Regina that Brandon (Bdawg) turned on him, and he (Marcus) needed to beat him up. When asked about what business Marcus was in, she replied, "Narcotics, he's a street pharmacist." The jury was excused amid more arguments between lawyers about what was admissible and the relevance of testimony.

Additional phone calls on March 4, 2022, between Marcus Anderson and Regina Hall are played in which Marcus tells Regina to not answer questions and to plead the Fifth. Regina said several times that she did not want to be in Court.

At 10:17 a.m., Attorney Flanagan began his cross examination. Several times, the reluctant witness, Regina Hall, said, "I didn't want to be involved. I still don't want to be involved." She was adamant that Marcus did not threaten her if she testified.

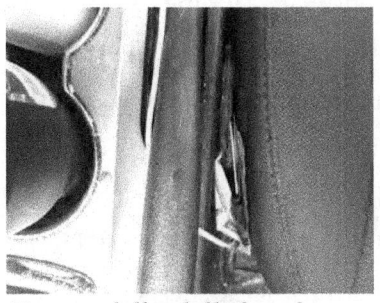

Twenty-dollar bills found in Anderson's car were found contaminated with illegal drugs.

Witness #23 Rachael Hahn

Ms. Hahn is a Controlled Substance Analyst at the Wisconsin State Crime Lab in Madison and testified in past criminal cases. She related her training and employment status and told the Court of the procedures, chain of retention, evidence chain of custody, and the review processes.

Ms. Hahn detailed the various tests she performed on controlled substances, mostly involving gas chromatography and mass spectrometry. She said, "I identified both heroin and fentanyl." She added, "Fentanyl is so dangerous, we don't bring it into the courtroom."

Ms. Hahn removed Exhibit 28, a marijuana grinder, from its case. The green plant material in the grinder was identified as tetrahydrocannabinols (THC). THC is the most active form of cannabinoid in marijuana, the one that produces intoxicating results. She showed the Court a cut red plastic straw with white residue that tested positive for the presence of heroin and fentanyl. Ms. Hahn showed several $20 bills that tested for fentanyl and a pipe with THC residue.

Under cross examination by Flanagan, Rachel Hahn described gas chromatography as a fancy oven that separates out different chemicals based on their properties. No new information is discovered, and Ms. Hahn is excused after being on the witness stand for some 40 minutes.

Heroin and fentanyl were found on this bill.

Witness #24 Kelsey Jungbluth

The next four witnesses are from the Wisconsin State Crime Lab in Madison. Kelsey Jungbluth is a six-year toxicology employee, and her job was to analyze biological samples for the presence or absence of drugs and alcohol. Exhibit 26, a two-page document, indicated her tests detected opiates, benzodiazepines, cannabinoids, fentanyl, and THC in a blood sample of Marcus Anderson taken at 23:31(11:31 p.m.) on May 3. Under questioning by Skiles, Ms. Jungbluth told the jury of the effects each of the detected drugs have on the human body. After five witnesses, it is 11:54 a.m. and time for lunch.

Chapter 30

The State Pushes Its Case

Witness #25 Venessa Styx

Immediately after lunch, the first witness was also from the Wisconsin Crime Lab. Venessa Styx was a nine-year veteran forensic fingerprint and footwear examiner. Her 17 minutes on the witness stand, questioned by DA Croninger, explained how fingerprints are processed. She talked about Exhibit 15, a large white box, with a tag that indicated it was a Sig Sauer SIG522 rifle. Ms. Styx held up the rifle and was asked to remove any other items in the box, which were an optical sight. The SIG522 retailed for around $495. It fired .22 long rifle bullets.

Ms. Styx explained the various tests she used to pick up any fingerprints on the SIG522 weapon. She could not find any prints.

Croninger then moved on it Exhibit 16, a brown and black leather belt. Then attention is turned to Exhibit 33, a small belt.

Ms. Styx told the Court, "I only examined the buckle portion because the belt had been examined for DNA. I began with the visual exams

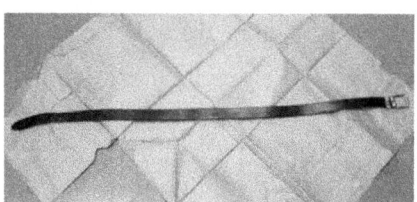

Kyson's black brown reversible belt was tested positive for DNA from both Kyson and Marcus.

using white light, alternating that light source with laser light. Then I did superglue fuming, a florescent dye stain, and I did black fingerprint powder on this. I did not find anything suitable for comparison, but DNA testing was done on this item before I received it." Vanessa Styx was on the stand for 17 minutes.

Witness #26 Catherine Kohl

Ms. Styx was followed by another expert from the Wisconsin Crime Lab, Catherine Kohl, Senior Forensic Scientist in the DNA Analysis Unit. A crime lab veteran, Ms. Kohl had worked on over 1,000 cases in her 15 years at the Wisconsin State Crime Lab. Her testimony dealt with 13 Exhibits provided by the State, taking about an hour.

There was a long Q&A exchange between Croninger and Ms. Kohl concerning her background, evidence handling, evidence security, and lab reports. She told the Court that DNA can be left on surfaces and the lab can do a Short Tandem Repeats (STR) DNA profile.

Ms. Kohl removed Item A, the SIG522 rifle, from its long white carton and demonstrated how she swabbed the grip area, textured areas along the grip, and the trigger. She said, "I extracted DNA from the swabbing. I determined there was a three-person mixture with at least two males along the textured areas. From another textured area, there was a low-level partial four-person mixture with at least two males."

She added, "With newer equipment allowing greater accuracy in quantifying that I obtained in March 2022, I retested and found Marcus Anderson's DNA to be at least one quadrillion times more likely than the original testing."

Ms. Kohl also tested a swab from a hallway in the Rice-Anderson house and Kyson Rice's blood was found on the opposite hallway wall. Also tested was a dried blood sample taken from Kyson at the autopsy.

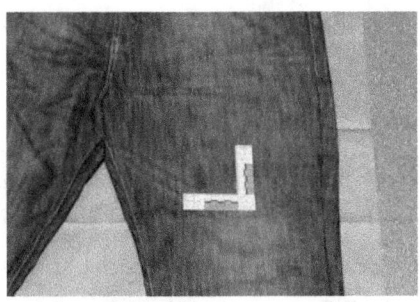

Anderson's pants were seized at Sparta Mayo Hospital. Kyson's blood was found on the pants.

A test was made on the sweatpants of Marcus Anderson. Kyson Rice's blood was found on several areas of the sweatpants. Attention was turned to Kyson's brown and black belt. DNA from Kyson Rice and Marcus Anderson was found on that belt. A black belt with a silver-type buckle belonging to Marcus Anderson yielded DNA from Kyson Rice.

Ms. Kohl told the Court that she tested a buccal sample that had been taken from Marcus Anderson. A buccal sample is swab taken along the interior side of the mouth.

On cross-examination, defense attorney Patrick Flanagan asked Ms. Kohl questions about who did the swabs in the Rice-Anderson house, what kind of swabs, how the swabs were transported, questions about the sweatpants, and the accuracy of DNA testing. He tried to create doubt about how and when the DNA was transferred to the items tested.

There is a short redirect by DA Croninger.

After a 15-minute break, the Court was back in session and the State's star witness entered the courtroom.

Witness #27 Dr. Michael Stier

Dr. Michael Stier, now retired, was with the University of Wisconsin School of Medicine and Public Health. He told the Court that a spinal disease forced him into retirement. He had shoulder problems and prostate cancer and was undergoing radiation treatments.

The State's star witness produced powerful testimony.

His mentor in forensic pathology was the renowned Dr. Robert Huntington III with 17 years of training. He performed between 4,000 and 5,000 autopsies. Croninger handed Dr. Stier the autopsy report so he might refer to it.

The report started with a summary and diagnoses with further explanations, beginning with, "Battered child, acute and extreme. We have 200 individual bruises, acute, and they're not old bruises to the body of Kyson Rice."

Q. The number of autopsies, between 4,000 and 5,000, have you ever seen that many bruises on a child?
A. Not even close.

Dr. Stier explained to the Court about contusions (bruises), focally patterned, abraded contusions, plus patterned lesions. He told the Court that a lesion is a tear and explains lacerated lips and lacerated frenulum (inner upper lip). A tear or laceration is caused by tissue being either stretched or compressed.

Dr. Stier described that the tears or lacerations on Kyson's lips are created from pressure from outside the mouth in contact with the inner part of the mouth, namely the teeth and bone of the jaw. He said, "That type of injury cannot be caused by a fall because it is protected by the nose and chin. A right fourth rib fracture, in pediatrics, is regarded as a child-abuse type. It's not something that is created by chest compression because one can have rib fractures from resuscitative chests when EMTs come to resuscitate an individual who has lost their ability to breathe, but this is not one of those. This is in the back, and it implies, again, a fair amount of force because children's ribs in particular are soft, softer than adult ribs, so they tend to bend before they break. So, when you have a fracture, it implies a significant degree of force."

The next description of injuries to Kyson was subdural hematoma caused by a direct blow to the skull. A 100 cc of blood had collected in a space where there should be none. It could also be caused by severe shaking of the head or movement of the brain inside the skull.

Croninger moved on to the next injury, "acute intraparenchymal microscopic thymic hemorrhage, multifocal." Dr. Stier said, "I don't place a lot of diagnostic weight on the presence of microscope thymic hemorrhage, because it can be caused by so many things. But I have to report it. It is extremely important, cerebral contusion, not only is the skin of Kyson bruised in 200 places, but there is direct bruising to the brain. That is a lethal injury. It's direct impact to the head." Dr. Stier reads from Exhibit 26, "The findings are that of extreme inflicted blunt trauma (beating), and shaking, or impact cranial deceleration injury. Some lesions are patterned, which indicate the use of a physical weapon."

Croninger asked Dr. Stier to "walk through" the autopsy process, and many photos were taken during the autopsy. They started with 2AA or 2AAA, which is the sealed red body bag tag. Shown next was a photo of Kyson, genitalia covered, with much of the medical equipment still in place, a line on the left leg to apply blood products, some sensors, endotracheal tube in the oral cavity that supports the airway, a nasogastric tube entering the nose, hospital band on the right ankle, defibrillator pads on the chest, and a hospital gown.

Kyson weighed 36 pounds and was 41.5 inches in length (height). The clothing was documented and removed, the body was cleaned, followed by an external examination, then traumas were identified, starting with the head and face, chest, back, arms, and legs.

Exhibit 2CCC was of the left side of the face and showed many bruises (contusions).

Dr. Steir told the Court, "Part of my approach to cases like this is to offer the most conservative number, meaning when I counted this lesion, I considered it at minimum one lesion. It could be two, but I'm going to minimize it. So, in my report, all the lesions are a minimal number. For example, you'll see lesions to his back and his chest. If you have an impact, to say the upper mid back and create a bruise, that's a bruise. But if the same area is struck again, and again, and again, it could be many bruises all in one spot. But I'm going call it one, because that is all I can really say that it is. It could be more. So, when I offer a number, as I have offered many in my autopsy, that is the low number."

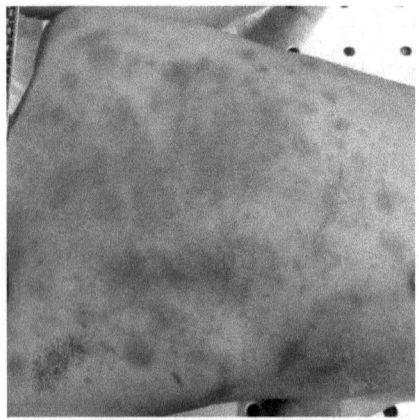

The autopsy photos shown to the jury were gruesome and horrific. Shown here is Kyson's back.

Many gruesome photos were displayed. To summarize Dr. Stier's lengthy recitation of injuries: 14 independent lesions on the left side of the face, hemorrhage to the left lower eyelid, 9 injuries to the right side of Kyson's face, lesions of the left forehead, hemorrhage, bruises on the lips, absence of an adult tooth, contusions to the chin. A total of 31 injuries to the head. Members of the jury cringed, some quietly sobbed or used facial tissues to mop their tears.

They moved on to the rest of the body. Exhibit 2HHH showed left shoulder, left arm, left forearm. The count of injuries was 17. Dr. Stier pointed out, "All the injuries are fresh. Once a bruise appears to be yellow, then it is older than a day or two. We don't see any of that here." There were 24 lesion injuries on the left arm and 23 on the right arm and 30 individual bruises on the chest area.

Dr. Stier and Croninger moved to the lower extremities. The tibia, shin, 20 injuries on the left leg, 21 on the right leg. Dr. Stier directed that Exhibit 2UUU be brought up on the courtroom screens. During the autopsy, Dr. Stier had incised, literally cut into an area of the bruise indicating massive hemorrhaging under the skin. He stated, "The deeper it goes, the more serious it is." There were audible gasps from the jury box.

Next it was on to Kyson's back, Exhibit 2JJJ. Here injuries melded together, making it difficult to count, but he came up with 25, again a minimum. There was a fractured rib. Some injuries were parallel, a repeated impact by a similar object. Exhibit 2MMM showed 11 bruises on the buttocks. The total count was about 187. Stier said, "I made an incision on the back of one of Kyson's legs. That's not routine. I did that for purposes of demonstrating the depth of some of these lesions."

Stier performed an autopsy of the internal organs, "There are two incisions made for internal examination. One in front of the body in the shape of a capital Y. Then the internal organs, heart, liver, lungs, all the stuff that is inside, are removed and examined. The second incision is across the top of scalp, looking for the integrity of the skull. The skull is sawed, and the brain is removed and examined. There is bruising to the top of the skull. Dr. Stier told the Court that one does not have bruising on the top of the head in a fall.

Dr. Stier explained, "When people fall, they sustain bruises to the scalp in the distribution called the hat brim distribution. So, imagine me wearing a cowboy hat or a derby. I'm making a line across my forehead and above the ear. This is where bruises are sustained in a fall. Not the top of the head."

The Court exhibited 2TTT, the brain. Dr. Stier said, "The brain is very soft, like a semihard pudding. There is blood in the brain and there should not be any. This type of hemorrhage is common in a shaken baby. And it's this brain injury that is ultimately fatal. We have bruises all over the body, but this is the fatal lesion. There are at least 12 injuries to the hair-bearing scalp. That would put the total injuries to around 198. And when I reexamined Kyson on May 6, I came up with three more on the feet. His body had injuries to every part except the bottoms of his feet, the palms of his hands, and his genitalia."

Dr. Stier testified for close to two hours. Flanagan cross examined, doing his best to illicit a response from Dr. Stier that the injuries could be caused by a fall. His job as defense counsel was to create doubt. Any courtroom observer realized that he got nowhere. He asked Dr. Stier about Kyson's nose. It had been established that there was no injury to the nose, but the autopsy indicated that bloody fluid was found coming from the nose. Dr. Stier explained that happens in the normal process of dying. "It happens all the time. You can die in your sleep, in a nursing home, and you can come to the autopsy suite with a bloody nose. It's a very, very common artifact of dying."

Dr. Stier was asked about the time frame over which the injuries occurred. He said the time frame in a car accident or suicide is very short, the injuries happening at once. He contrasted that with the autopsy on a chronic drinker, who may be injured by falls, and "bouncing around" all over the place. The injuries would be all different colors. But in Kyson's case, they were all of a pinkish color, which meant they occurred over a short time frame.

Dr. Stier delivered a stinging attack, "I consider the number of lesions, the locations and the time and what is going on psychologically, this constitutes, medically, torture." Stier emphasized the word "torture," actually shouting this word twice, startling the people in the courtroom. There were nods of agreement from the jury. This was a word they would remember and consider in their deliberations.

Judge Goodman dismisses Dr. Stier and wishes him safe travels back Madison.

Judge Goodman addressed the jury, "Remember what we talked about. This has been a tough day and so when you go home, it's not something you want to talk with whoever you see at your house. Afterward, you can—tell the story or not. So, we'll see you tomorrow at 8:30."

The courtroom clock reads close to 5:00 p.m. It had been a long day for everyone. With all in the courtroom standing, jury members departed, some still dabbing their eyes with tissue.

Chapter 31

Day 5: Eight Witnesses Called by the State

April 1. It may be April Fools Day, but it is all business inside Monroe County Courtroom Branch 2. The trial of Marcus Anderson was beginning Day 5 and attendees were not thinking April Fools' jokes or pranks. As promised by Judge Goodman the day prior, there would be a lighter agenda with jury dismissal slated for 1:30 p.m. Eight witnesses would be called to the stand.

District Attorney Kevin Croninger addressed the Court by stating that some issues concerning Marcus Anderson are off-limits: his record of drug-dealing, his previous criminal history, and his prison time. Croninger said, "Obviously I can't fully control what someone says when they're on the stand, but I don't want there to be any idea that the State's trying to go around the Court's order of yesterday, your Honor."

Witness #28 Clayton Tester

With that, the jury was brought in at 8:37 a.m. and Clayton Tester was sworn in. He was retired from the Monroe County Drug Investigative Task Force and as a detective for the Monroe County Sheriff's Office.

Investigator Tester reviewed the footage from security cameras installed at 1009 Jodi Circle. Shown on Courtroom screens is a short video of Larry

Quarles visiting Marcus for 25 minutes starting at 10:04 a.m. and again at 11:13 a.m. for 45 minutes.

Mr. Tester testified that with camera footage and evidence found at his residence, that Marcus Anderson and Kyson Rice traveled to Sparta, stopped at Walgreens, went to McDonald's, then to Cenex, and back to Walgreens.

One piece of evidence was a receipt from Walgreens with a time stamp of 3:14 p.m. Exhibit 7N was camera footage from Walgreens in Sparta, with Anderson wearing No. 7 football jersey and using a cane. Time stamp on the video was 3:06 p.m.

A receipt, Exhibit 40, from McDonald's, time stamp of 3:36 pm. was recovered at the 1009 Jodi Circle residence. One Big Mac, one medium coke, one four-piece Happy Meal, one barbecue sauce, one apple slices, one apple juice, and one Avengers 4 toy.

Croninger played a video clip, Exhibit 70, from the McDonald's security cameras, with a time of 2:53 p.m. The video from Walgreens indicated Anderson walking with a cane. It's quite a contrast with the video from McDonalds that displayed Anderson dancing and moving around easily, backwards, and side to side.

A video segment from Cenex was played. Anderson purchased gas and lottery tickets. Then it was back to Walgreens, Exhibit 36, with a time stamp of 4:07 p.m. on the Walgreens receipt for two prescriptions. Security camera footage, Exhibit 7T, with a time stamp of 4:38 p.m. from the Anderson residence showed the black Ford Fusion car.

Investigator Tester was asked questions by DA Croninger concerning the contents of Marcus' Ford Fusion, including Kyson's car seat.

DA Croninger moved on to a search warrant obtained to investigate the crime scene. Exhibit 2M, a photo of a red plastic straw found in the kitchen that had a white powdery substance on it was shown.

Q. How does one use a straw to consume drugs?

A. They use it to snort.

Tester explained, "The whole area is photographed before anything is touched or moved. Then additional photographs are taken of the evidence we are going to take. Everyone is wearing rubber gloves. An item is put into a bag and documented where it was found and what the item was. The bag is sealed."

Croninger asked about Exhibit 2N, a photo of a closet shelf in the master bedroom displaying the butt end of a gun. Exhibit 2O was a photo that showed items laying on top of the rifle, and photo 2P, the weapon itself. Investigator Tester explained that the gun can be traced through the Alcohol, Tobacco, and Firearms (ATF) agency. The gun was in their database. The gun was originally purchased by Mike Ayala (Witness 19) from Moe's Hardware in Black River Falls.

Croninger played a 20-second audio segment of a phone call, Exhibit 7W, from Marcus Anderson, locked up in the Monroe County jail, to Regina Hall on May 10, 2019, one week after the murder of Kyson Rice. Anderson was talking about a gun and knocking out B'dag (Brandon Crampes).

They moved on to Exhibit 2Q, the inside of the washing machine at 1009 Jodi Circle. Exhibit 2R showed the inside of the washing machine with the clothing items removed. The photo showed .22 caliber rifle rounds. Exhibit 2S showed items removed from a garbage can in the garage at 1009 Jodi Circle. Exhibit 2T was the McDonald's receipt.

Officers Tester, Walensky, and Heckman inspect the contents of the garbage can at 1009 Jodi Circle.

DA Croninger moved on to questions about Marcus Anderson's car. Tester recalled that the Ford Fusion was towed from downtown Tomah to the police impound site and that a warrant was issued to search the vehicle. Investigator Tester told the Court how they photographed the outside, VIN number, then opened the car, and photographed the insides, including the trunk.

Exhibit 2B was a photo of folded up cash between the driver's seat and the center console. Exhibit 2W was a photo of a twenty-dollar bill with spots of white powder. Tester explained, based on his experience in law enforcement, that a person would roll a bill, stick one end into their nose and then snort the substance.

Attention was turned to Exhibit 2Y, a recording of a May 7, 2019, phone call from Anderson in jail telling the person that Kyson hit his head on a "hard ass counter." Then Marcus said in the living room, then he said a counter in the bathroom. Croninger pointed that out in previous interviews, Anderson never mentioned any of three possible places that Kyson hit his head.

Investigators found Kyson's belt during a search of 1009 Jodi Circle the night of the murder.

Investigator Tester had been on the witness stand for almost an hour when it was Flanagan's turn to cross examine. In his three-minute cross, Attorney Flanagan asked Tester about the prescription medicines Marcus Anderson received at Walgreens in Sparta, Diazepam (brand name is Valium) and Oxycodone. Flanagan also asked questions about where the red straw was located in the residence and about the clothes in the washing machine.

Witness #29 Autumn Brandau

The Direct Examination of Autumn Brandau was carried out by DA Croninger. Ms. Brandau was employed by McDonald's in Sparta and was acting manager on May 3, 2019, when Marcus Anderson and Kyson went for a meal.

She testified, "The person who took his order was a 15-year-old kid and Anderson said his order was wrong, so I went to rectify the order, and make it correct. He appeared to be someone that had too much energy and didn't know what to do with it, moving around a lot, very fidgety. He was asking for something we didn't have. He wanted a deal that Burger King was running at the time. I refunded his original order and gave him his order. He said he wanted a Flurry in addition to that and I just gave him that, so that he would finish up and head out."

After Autumn Brandau's short testimony, the Court took a 25-minute break. The jury was dismissed and there was a discussion between attorneys concerning the next few witnesses who may have prior records. Unwary witnesses could be tripped up (impeached) by their own prior words, conduct, and reputation. Impeaching a witness refers to an attack on the witness's credibility. Opposing counsel could use this tactic to show the judge and jury that the witness's testimony should not be believed.

Motions **"in limine"** asked the Court to order the opposing party, its counsel, and witnesses not to talk about, or even mention, certain facts or evidence in the presence or hearing of the jury. If the motion was granted, nobody was allowed to bring up those facts without first obtaining permission from the Court, which must be requested outside the presence of the jury.

Judge Goodman, "Well, I don't want to have any appealable issues. To the best of my ability, that's one of the things I want to prevent. Perhaps the two of you can clean this up before we go into the witnesses that we're going to have before lunch, and then I think after lunch, Mr. Croninger said he has a few witnesses on call which I believe are probably not witnesses who have some type of criminal history." Croninger was tasked by Judge Goodman to "get the next three figures out so we can proceed."

After the break and before the jury returned, Mr. Croninger told the Court that the next two witnesses had been CCAPed and no criminal history was evident. There was a discussion between attorneys and Judge Goodman that went on for 45 minutes. It was about being asked about prior convictions and any criminal history for Jeremy Devine. The next three witnesses; Brandon Crampes, Ashley Wankerl, and Jeremy Devine, were people that knew and had some degree of interaction with Marcus Anderson.

Witness #30 Brandon Crampes

The third witness of the day, Brandon Crampes, was sworn in at 10:28 for a 15-minute testimony. DA Croninger does the Direct Examination. Mr. Crampes told the Court he had been friends on and off with Marcus

Anderson for about 10 years. Marcus, and others, often called Brandon Crampes by the name Bdog. The official trial manuscript reads Ddawg.

Q. What did you observe with Mr. Anderson's demeanor around Kyson Rice?

A. Sometimes everything was good, sometimes he would cuss him. The kid always seemed hurt, cuts, bruises, scratches, seemed like he had a lot of accidents.

When asked if he was interviewed by police in October 2020, Crampes replied, "Yes, I told them that Mr. Anderson called him (Kyson) stupid, pulled him around the house, yelled at him all the time and cursed at him when he was angry."

Summarizing parts of Brandon Crampes' testimony: Kyson appeared to be afraid of Marcus. Kyson started to be more standoffish and scared.

Q. At some point did you advise Jessica Rice of these observations?

A. Yes, I told her, hey, you know, I don't know what's going on. If there's anything, just, you know, be aware. Just be careful.

DA Croninger turned to the day of the murder and asked Crampes about his interaction with Mr. Anderson on May 3. Crampes said, "It was a phone call. I was at work. He called and said that there was something wrong with Kyson and I asked him why he was calling me and told him he needed to call an ambulance. And that's when I hung up on him."

Croninger showed Crampes Exhibit 2P, a photo of a semiautomatic .22. Crampes said he bought the rifle from Mike Ayala sometime in 2017 or 2018 and never fired the weapon. He left it in Mr. Anderson's car shortly before Kyson's murder. Marcus told Crampes that he had been in the Marine Corps. Asked if he had talked to Jessica Rice after the murder, Crampes said, "Yes, just a little, mainly to comfort her, me and my fiancé."

(Note: Brandon Crampes passed away of a fast-acting cancer on September 3, 2023, age 37.)

In his three-minute cross examination, Flanagan asked Crampes that if he put the gun in Anderson's Ford Fusion, why didn't he take it back.

"I really don't know, but I was on drugs back then, and it might have something to do with it." Crampes is dismissed with the usual, "You may go about your business."

Witness #31 Ashley Wankel

Ashley Wankel is Brandon Crampes' fiancé. She knew Marcus Anderson through Brandon Crampes. She was in high school with Jessica Rice but did not know her well but got to know her after the murder. When asked by DA Croninger her observations of Marcus Anderson, she replied, "That depends on the day. He didn't really have too many good days."

Asked about Kyson, "Marcus and Kyson would come over to our house. He would usually hang out with me downstairs while the guys went upstairs. He was a fun kid, loved to listen to music and he would start jumping around, singing, and playing."

When asked to describe Mr. Anderson's demeanor around Kyson, she replied, "Strict." When Kyson knew he was in the room, he paid attention to him, he didn't have no patience with him whatsoever. Kyson was more of a hassle."

Croninger queried Ashley Wankel about the day of the murder. Marcus called her several times, once around noon. Her testimony plus cross-examination was about seven minutes.

Witness #32 Jeremy Devine

The fifth witness on Day 5 was Jeremy Devine who worked security at Ho-Chunk. His wife is Christy Devine who was Witness #8 and testified two days earlier. They lived in New Lisbon. When asked if he had ever been convicted of a crime, he replied, "Yes, nine times." Jeremy Devine said he met Marcus Anderson through Brandon Crampes. He knew Kyson, because Kyson would be with Marcus. Devine thought originally that Kyson was Marcus' son.

Devine said he talked to Marcus a few times during the day of May 3 as Marcus was going to buy Devine's PlayStation 4. Devine told the Court that Marcus called him in the late afternoon of May 3 and Marcus told Devine that Kyson had fallen on "that thingy."

Devine testified, "I was supposed to meet him. I was at the Festival Foods and he didn't show up, so I went over to the casino to the Smoke Shop because I was going to leave, and I called him back and I said 'hey, I'm going to leave, this is taking all day, and he said that the kid had fallen off something and hit his head and he was dying.' I said call 911. And he hung up and I kept calling him back. Finally, he answered and said stop calling me, I'm on the phone with them." There was no cross examination by Attorney Flanagan. Jeremy Devine was on the witness stand for seven minutes.

Witness #33 Toni Halvorson

The last witness before the lunch break is Toni Halvorson. Assistant DA Sarah Skiles handles the direct examination. Ms. Halvorson was a 17-year medical lab technician at Mayo Health in Sparta.

Exhibit 2DD4 was a photo of a blood draw kit, seals and paperwork inside. Exhibit 2EE5 was a photo of everything that was in the kit: labels, tubes, seals, swab, bag for mailing purposes, paper that both the technician and law enforcement fill out.

Ms. Halvorson told the Court that she took a blood sample from Marcus Anderson at 11:23 p.m. on May 3. She explained that she used a butterfly type needle that has a tube from the needle to the collection vessel, so there was about a foot of play. "If people were moving about or a bit distressed, I had less of a chance of being poked."

Nurses at Sparta Mayo took a blood sample from Marcus at 11:23 p.m. on the night of the murder.

Exhibit 44A was a nine-minute video of the blood draw and Ms. Halvorson putting the collection tubes into the plastic biohazard bag, sealing it, and placing it in the foam container. The foam container was handed over to law enforcement and sent to the State Lab.

Assistant DA Sarah Skiles finished her 20-minute direct examination. There is no cross examination by Flanagan. The Court broke for lunch at 11:30 a.m.

Witness #34 Adam Robarge

The Court was back in session at 12:35 p.m.with direct examination of Adam Robarge by Assistant DA Skiles. At the time of the trial, Robarge was Deputy EMS Chief for Tomah Area Ambulance Service. On May 3, 2019, he was the shift supervisor. Robarge detailed his background, including 2,000 hours of paramedic training. Robarge had certification as Critical Care Transport Paramedic, the highest level in the EMS field, which required an extra semester of training.

Skiles turned to Exhibit 41, and the 18-page report authored by Adam Robarge, written on the night of May 3 when the ambulance service was called to 1009 Jodi Circle. Specifics were: ambulance dispatched at 5:56 p.m., arrived at 6:00 p.m., left Jodi Circle at 6:19 p.m. and transported to Tomah Memorial Hospital at 321 Butts Ave. It's about a half-mile distance, arriving at 6:22 p.m.

Three EMTs arrived at the Jodi Circle residence in the ambulance and Adam Robarge arrived in the Quick Response Vehicle, to which the supervisor is assigned. Robarge said, "When we arrived, Kyson was laying on the floor just to the left of the front door and in front of the couch. Law enforcement was providing CPR."

Summarizing several minutes of Robarge testimony: Kyson was unresponsive, not breathing, and did not have a pulse. We removed the law enforcement's AED and placed our cardiac monitor on Kyson. With no breathing and no pulse, a person is clinically dead, but that does not mean they can't be resuscitated. With CPR, electrical shock, and administering medication such as epinephrine, it is possible, in some cases, to restart the heart. After a second dose of epinephrine, we had a cardiac rhythm showing his heart was beating. We needed to secure airway passage. We started ventilating using the same bag valve mask used by law enforcement. We intubated Kyson, which involves placing a tube directly into his trachea, so we could ventilate directly into the lungs. When we arrived, Kyson was fully dressed, wearing a shirt, pants, underwear, and socks. His socks were wet, but his upper body was dry. There was vomit on his face and on his clothing. Vomit can obstruct his airway and something we have to address. When the brain is sloshed around inside the head, it can cause vomiting. We put a cervical collar to help keep his head and neck in line and in position. We noticed numerous family and friends arriving at the residence and it was becoming more chaotic, and I made the decision that we needed to move to the ambulance where it was a more secure place for us to provide treatment.

Assistant DA Skiles asked Mr. Robarge what Marcus Anderson was doing during their time at the 1009 Jodi Circle residence. He said, "When we arrived, he was walking around, pacing back and forth, claimed to have been trying to call the patient's mother, making phone calls, and at some point, yelling and speaking loudly. Once we started taking over patient care, he started to interact with law enforcement."

Adam Robarge, holding a bag valve mask, led the heroic effort to save the life of Kyson Rice.

Ms. Skiles asked the attending DA office staff to bring up Exhibit 7F, a 45-second video clip which shows the stretcher with Kyson. Sgt. Furlano is in the video. Skiles asks Robarge about the socks Kyson is wearing. Robarge confirms that the socks were wet.

Robarge told the Court that while loading and transporting Kyson to Tomah Memorial Hospital they were getting a brief pulse, but he was not breathing on his own.

Q. Is it fair to say that Kyson was going back and forth between life and death?

A. He was. Yes.

Mr. Robarge explained that the ambulance staff stayed at the hospital for 40 minutes.

Attorney Flanagan cross examined. He asked Robarge questions concerning the bag valve mask, how the AED functions, their own cardiac monitor, and placement of an IV to administer epinephrin.

Robarge was asked about the vomit. "Air can go down into the esophagus and into the stomach, filling the stomach up with air, and could cause vomit to then be pushed up the esophagus," said Robarge. He is also asked about the bruises the ambulance staff noticed on Kyson.

DA Croninger did the redirect. He specifically questioned Robarge about the coloring of the bruises, "We were focused on saving his life. He did have one bruise to his upper left arm that we noted, so we place our blood pressure cuff on his upper right arm."

Witness #35 Dr. Maude Kettenmann

Dr. Kettenmann was sworn in at 1:10 p.m. and the Direct Examination is led by DA Croninger. Dr. Kettenmann was one of the emergency medical physicians at Gundersen Medical, working at the main campus in La Crosse, but also at Tomah Memorial Hospital. She was a 2009 graduate of the Medical College of Wisconsin with training in general surgery and emergency medicine.

Exhibit 42, the medical report for Kyson Rice, was handed to Dr. Kettenmann.

Q. Do you recall a child, a three-year-old you've identified as Kyson Rice, being brought into the emergency room?

A. I do.

Q. Why do you remember that?

A. It was a very significant case, so it does stick out in my mind.

Q. When you say that it was a significant case that sticks out, why is that?

A. Kyson, the patient, was very ill and ended up dying that night and so those cases tend to stick with you.

Summarizing Dr. Kettenmann's testimony: He was critically ill. His heart was not beating, he was receiving CPR, he had been intubated (breathing tube in place), his skin color was grayish, which means he wasn't getting enough oxygen. Epinephrin was administered by continuous infusion and a second medication prescribed was bicarbonate to help balance the pH factor.

Dr. Kettenmann explained, "The blood becomes more acidic if it does not receive sufficient oxygen. The bicarbonate tends to make the blood neutral and that is what you want."

Q. As Kyson was in the emergency room, did his condition change?

A. There were times when we would get a faint heartbeat and then stop.

Q. Did you ultimately pronounce him dead?
A. I did.

Q. And do you know what time that was at?
A. 7:41 p.m.

Q. What is the definition or what is required for a physician to declare someone dead?
A. We look for activity of the brain, the heart, and the lungs, and if there is none, then it fits a clinical situation that fits, we declare them dead.

Q. Prior to May 3, had you met Kyson Rice?
A. Yes, the week before, he was a visitor with another patient, Marcus Anderson.

Q. While Mr. Anderson was hospitalized during that time, what was his demeanor?
A. He was fairly agitated and became more agitated when I asked him if he used drugs or any illicit substances.

Q. What was his response?
A. He accused me of being racist.

Q. Before Kyson was brought into the emergency room on May 3, had you ever seen a child covered in so many bruises?
A. No.

Attorney Flanagan had a tough job in his cross examination. He questioned Dr. Kettenmann about the time that Marcus Anderson came to Tomah Memorial Hospital through the emergency room, a week before the murder. Summarizing her testimony: "As a result of Mr. Anderson coming into the emergency room, he was hospitalized. He was holding his legs. It is standard procedure to ask about drug use in the appropriate clinical scenario. After his hospitalization, I had no further contact with him."

On redirect, Assistant DA Skiles asked if questioning a patient about drug use was appropriate. She replied, "Yes, if I think it could be the cause for their medical problems or contributing to it." Dr. Maude Kettenmann was in the witness chair for 20 minutes and there was a murmur heard in the courtroom, "She did a good job."

Judge Goodman addressed the jury, "We'll have you come back on Monday at 8:30 a.m. And remember all of my instructions and try to have a great weekend, the weather is supposed to be a little warmer. You can leave your books on the chair, there. They won't be disturbed."

Everyone stood as the jury exits the courtroom.

With the jury out of the courtroom, Judge Goodman addressed the agenda for the next week. Croninger said he had a few more witnesses, some from out of state, and some from law enforcement. He believed the State could rest its case by Tuesday and go to the jury by Wednesday or Thursday.

Judge Goodman bid Attorney Patrick Flanagan to have a good trip back to Milwaukee. "You should get there before supper." Croninger asked that the last two exhibits, No. 41 and 42, be sealed as they are medical records. Judge Goodman agreed that the records are to be sealed. The courtroom emptied at 1:30 p.m.

Chapter 32

A Reluctant Stellar Witness

Murder trials in Monroe County, Wisconsin typically would not go beyond four or five days. The length of any trial was largely dependent on the number of witnesses the prosecution and defense will call. In the State of Wisconsin vs. Marcus Wayne Anderson trial, Case No. 19CF353, District Attorney Kevin Croninger had issued nearly 100 subpoenas and called 41 witnesses.

Monday April 4, 2022, began a new week and day 6 of the trial in Circuit Court Branch 2, following a beautiful spring weekend. Lawns were greening up. Some homeowners had done their first mowing. Farmers were looking to move into the fields. People were observing Lent with Easter just two weeks away. A ferocious and devastating air assault was carried out by Russian planes on Ukraine. The suffering and dying continued. The debate resumed on the value of Daylight Savings Time.

Friends and relatives of the deceased Kyson Rice had been drifting into the courtroom and are seated. Marcus Anderson, sporting a white shirt and tie, was escorted into the Branch 2 Courtroom by a uniformed officer, accompanied by two plainclothes personnel.

Before the jury was brought in, DA Kevin Croninger indicated he had some business to bring before the Court. Croninger stated that there were photos taken of Kyson by law enforcement personnel at the hospital showing the multiple bruising of Kyson's body and he wanted assurances the defense would not object.

Judge Goodman to DA Croninger, "Did you want to put the pictures on the screen so we can address Mr. Flanagan's objections?" Eight photos were brought up. Judge Goodman allowed four photos to be shown to the jury noting, "Thursday was a tough day for everyone and several of the jurors were in tears looking at these pictures. It's very difficult material." The four not allowed were essentially repeats of the autopsy photos already shown by Dr. Stier.

Witness #36 Shelby Anderson

The jury was brought in at 8:45 a.m. and Shelby Anderson was the morning's first witness. Assistant DA Skiles handled the questioning, beginning first with her name, residence, and occupation. She was a reluctant witness, but her 20-minute testimony was powerful. She would be described later as a "rock star witness."

Q. Do you know Marcus Anderson?
A. Unfortunately.
Q. Is it fair to say that you don't want to be here today?
A. Absolutely.
Q. Is this a situation where you had a court order from the State of Wisconsin to be here for this trial?
A. I had no choice.
Q. When did you meet Mr. Anderson?
A. I believe it was 2015.
Q. Did you then marry Mr. Anderson?
A. I did. July of 2016.
Q. Where did the two of you reside when you got married?
A. My house in La Crosse.
Q. During your relationship, did Mr. Anderson have employment?
A. Nothing that you could write taxes for.

There were knowing smiles in the courtroom.

Marcus Anderson and Shelby were married and lived in this condo on Nakomis Avenue on French Island.

Ms. Skiles questioned Shelby Anderson about Marcus Anderson's drug use, and her answers described his use of meth, weed, pills, morphine, Percocet, Oxycodone, and Norco. He used drugs every day, multiple times a day.

Q. When you were married or during your relationship, did Mr. Anderson ever walk with a cane?

A. Marcus was very good at creating the outward look that he wanted you to have. So, he would use the cane when we went out and sympathy was wanted, or he was trying to get something for himself. But when we were just in, then there was no cane and no limp.

Q. Do you and Mr. Anderson have a child in common?

A. I do have a child that, uhm, unfortunately has DNA, yes, from him. He is now five years old and was born at the end of 2016.

When asked, Shelby Anderson described the relationship between Marcus and their son. He used very vulgar language like, "I'm going to cut your balls off if you don't be quiet. He expressed the will, want, and right to kill him if that was something he chose to do. Marcus was very demanding of my time, more important than my son. I really wanted to breast feed. I'm a nurse and I know that is important. The child learned to keep quiet when Mr. Anderson was around. When we separated at the end of June 2017, I saw this whole new child that was very interactive and very smiley and very loving, which had not been the child I had experienced prior to the separation."

Shelby was asked about specific instances of Marcus' bad behavior. "My son was in the Exersaucer, (toy a young kid sits in and has a platform in front with things to play with and a bottom part that sways), and I was in the kitchen cooking, the baby was fussing and I wasn't able to get over there, and Marcus was sweeping the kitchen and was upset that my son was making a noise, he put his hand on the bristle portion and began swinging it like a baseball bat, smacking the side of the tray of the Exersaucer, nearly tipping it over. At times he would kick the Exersaucer. At times, Marcus would pick up Samir by his Onesie outfit with one hand and wave him around. Marcus was angry all the time at both me and our son. Marcus has the belief that the wife and child are his property. He would say things, like, 'I can kill you if I want to and God's not going to do anything about it.'"

Ms. Skiles referred to the statements that Shelby made to Investigator Rob Walensky about Marcus' behavior and belief systems. She described the day she separated from Marcus. An argument and child noises set him off. "I was on my hands and knees, cupping my infant child on the floor beneath me, blocking him from the blows and the kicks and the things being thrown at me."

After 17 minutes of Direct Examination, Attorney Flanagan cross examined. He asked Shelby Anderson about her filing for divorce. In the petition for divorce, the ugly stuff was brought up. She was granted full custody of their son.

On redirect, Shelby was asked about interviews with investigators after Kyson was murdered. "I was interviewed by a couple of different people, both from Sparta and from the Tomah area and from La Crosse. There were several interviews across a two-year span."

Witness #37 Lt. Jarrod Furlano.

The last five witnesses are all law enforcement officers. Looking sharp in his Tomah Police Force dark blue uniform, 14-year veteran Lt. Jarrod Furlano was the first to be questioned by Assistant DA Skiles. At the time of the

Kyson Rice murder, Furlano was the second shift Sergeant. Skiles asked Lt. Furlano about the events of May 3, 2019, nearly three years prior.

Sgt. Furlano led the officer in the arrest of Marcus Anderson in downtown Tomah.

Summarizing his testimony: I was first at the scene followed closely by Sergeant Steinborn. I requested Sgt. Steinborn utilize his body camera to document bruises to Kyson. The amount of trauma to his body was abnormal, to the point of alarming. Every available inch of skin that I could see had a bruise on it. I requested Dispatch to contact Investigator Paul Sloan to come in and begin an investigation. After transporting Kyson, and speaking with Sloan, he requested we hold the residence for application of a search warrant.

I drove the ambulance so the crew could focus on Kyson. When at the hospital, I had no means of transportation, so I stayed at the hospital. Subsequently, Steinborn arrived at the hospital and said that Marcus had left the residence a couple of minutes before him. I was in the emergency room and never saw Marcus come in there and that was very odd.

So at the scene, I instructed Sgt. Steinborn to gather an initial statement for Marcus and to get his phone number. Steinborn tried several times, including asking Dispatch for a phone number, and the two phone numbers did not come close to matching.

Under cross examination, Attorney Flanagan asked Sgt. Furlano about Marcus' demeanor when Marcus was giving his statement and phone number to Sgt. Steinborn. In words: upset, agitated, excited, and pacing.

Redirect by Skiles:

Q. Typically, you've had experience of people providing a false phone number in situations?

A. False names more than false phone numbers, it's because they're usually trying to hide something.

Witness #38 Sgt. Adam Perkins

After eight minutes on the stand for Lt. Furlano, Assistant DA Skiles called Sgt. Adam Perkins. Sgt. Perkins was the day shift supervisor on May 3, 2019. He was also the K9 handler. Sgt. Perkins said, "I have a dual-purpose K9 named Viktor and he's with me every day. We do narcotics work, apprehension work, and tracking."

Adam Perkins is the Tomah Police K9 Officer along with his companion Viktor.

Sgt. Perkins described his training, "I have a Bachelor's Degree from the University of Platteville, I went to Law Enforcement Academy in Sparta, training through the Tomah Police Department, supervisor training, and the K9 handler training."

Summarizing his testimony about May 3: "At 7 p.m., I was off duty, but was called in. I was scheduled to take over as shift commander for Sgt. Steinborn, but he was busy trying to locate Marcus' 2010 Ford Fusion. I eventually found it on Superior Avenue near the intersection with East Juneau Street. It was in the first parking stall to the north on the east side of the road. The car was running, the brake lights and the right turn signal were illuminated. I pulled up behind it. I got out and approached on foot. I saw a lone driver slumped forward towards the steering wheel. I told that person to show me his hands. He did not. I observed that he was breathing. I went back to my vehicle and Sergeant Furlano arrived and we set up a high-risk contact.

Eventually, Anderson was helped out of his vehicle. I noticed his pupils were constricted. Based on numerous contacts with individuals, highly suspect they are under the influence of drugs. Near the end of the night, I assisted in executing a search warrant of the 1009 Jodi Circle residence."

Flanagan's Cross-Examination

Defense Attorney Flanagan asked Sgt. Perkins about the location of Marcus' parked car, about the car's lights, and the field sobriety tests. Anderson told Sgt. Perkins that the dog's barking made it difficult for him to hear. Sgt. Perkins said he kept his dog quiet.

Under Assistant DA Skiles redirect, Sgt. Perkins said that a field sobriety test was not feasible because of the location. Marcus complained of leg pain and asked for EMS care. Perkins was in the witness chair for eight minutes.

Witness #39 Investigator Paul Sloan

Investigator Paul Sloan pursued the homicide investigation with dogged determination.

Next on the witness stand was Investigator Paul Sloan. Assistant DA Skiles asked the questions. Investigator Sloan had been on the Tomah Police force for 20 years, and a detective since 2013. He said, "I work any criminal case, primarily sensitive crime cases, such as sexual assault, child sexual assault, physical abuse, and child exploitation cases. I have specialized training as an evidence technician, schooled through the Wisconsin Department of Justice. I've been to Death Investigation School and also trained to work fire investigation cases, and training in the collection of DNA evidence."

Sloan was asked about May 3, 2019, "I received a call from Monroe County Communications Center by Lt. Furlano and requested to go to Tomah Memorial Hospital. I went to the Emergency Room. I saw Kyson Rice being worked on by hospital staff. Then I spoke to the mother, Jessica Rice. I documented phone calls and text messages from Marcus Anderson."

Assistant DA Skiles brought up Exhibit 2FF6, the first of 23 exhibits to be produced during Sloan's nearly one hour in the witness chair. Exhibit 2FF6 was a photo of Jessica Rice's phone. The photo showed Jessica receiving a missed call from Marcus at 5:50 p.m. "That is when Marcus would have called Jessica at work saying Kyson's not breathing."

Q. Do you know what time the 911 call from Marcus Anderson was placed to the Monroe County Communication Center?

A. Around 5:55 p.m.

Exhibit 2GG7, another photo of Rice's cell phone, showed the missed call from Tank at 5:50 p.m. then it showed four outgoing phone calls to Tank and two more missed phone calls from Tank at 5:54 p.m.

Exhibit 2HH8 was a photo of Kyson's entire body, deceased, showing bruising on the right side of his body. Exhibit 2JJ10 showed injuries to the right side of Kyson's face.

Q. Were there particular injuries that you were concerned about?

A. All of the injuries. The one to the forehead, the one to his lower chin, the ones behind his eye and into his hairline.

Exhibit 2MM13 was a photo of Kyson's left side of his face. Several in the jury turn aside. One audibly gasps. There was stirring and shuffling on the side of the courtroom reserved for family members. In Exhibit 2NN14, hospital staff had positioned Kyson so that Sloan could take a picture of Kyson's back.

The last four photos brought up on the two large screens in the courtroom, plus a smaller screen at each jury position, were gruesome. The previous Thursday's testimony by Dr. Stier from UW-Madison, who performed the autopsy, was searing. Now, as the trial was winding down, the District Attorney's office wished to highlight once again, the deadly beating Kyson Rice took at the hands of Marcus Anderson.

Q. When the medical examiner arrived, did you assist in placing Kyson into a human remains pouch?

A. Yes.

Q. Are you the individual who went to the autopsy?

A. I was not. That would be Investigator Walensky.

Prosecutor Skiles produced a brown paper bag, Exhibit 49, hands it to Mr. Sloan, and asked him to hold up the contents. It was a white/blue/black striped sock that Kyson was wearing when brought to the hospital. Sloan confirmed that the sock shown is the same sock on a surveillance video that was taken about 5:05 p.m. on May 3, 2019, at his 1009 Jodi Circle house.

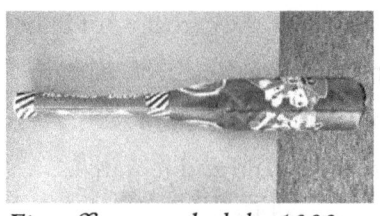

Five officers combed the 1009 Jodi Circle residents, cataloging, photographing, and collecting any possible evidence, including Kyson's toy bat.

Investigator Sloan confirmed that he reviewed the footage from 5:45 p.m. to 8:30 p.m. from all 24 cameras located at Tomah Memorial Hospital and Marcus Anderson did not show up on any of the videos.

Assistant DA Skiles moved on to testimony concerning the search warrant at the 1009 Jodi Circle residence. Sloan detailed the procedure, photos taken, and evidence collected, that was used to carry out the search warrant and how the evidence was processed and who has access to the evidence.

Q. Who carried out the search warrant?

A. Detective Tester, Officer David Heckman, myself, and later Detective Walensky and Sergeant Adam Perkins.

Assistant DA Skiles brought up several photos taken at 1009 Jodi Circle during the time of the search warrant. Exhibit 2A was a photo of the living room. Photo 2B was the kitchen area. A black and orange smoking device, or one-hitter pipe, was found in a drawer at the island counter. It was noted the garbage can had no garbage and no garbage liner in it. Photo Exhibit 2C displayed a kitchen cabinet above the microwave.

The contents of the garbage can were located in the southeast corner of the garage. Officers dumped the garbage on the floor and rifled through it. Four containers of THC wax were found among the discarded medical supplies used by the police and EMTs to revive Kyson. THC wax is a cannabis concentrate that has a wax-like consistency and contains very high levels of THC, the main intoxicating compound in cannabis. Wax is not edible, but when smoked or vaporized, can provide a potent high.

Heckman had placed medical equipment in the garbage can before leaving the residence. Sloan says, "Somebody took the garbage out in between the officers treating Kyson and then executing the search warrant."

Exhibit 2S was a photo of a red straw containing some residue that was sent to the crime lab which tested positive for heroin and fentanyl.

Exhibit 2D was the living room looking toward Kyson's room, with a red picture on the wall. A child's belt was found just inside the doorway on the floor to the left. It was collected and sent to the crime lab, which tested positive for Kyson's blood and DNA. Marcus' DNA was also found on the belt as previously testified to by crime lab technicians.

Exhibit 2I was the bathroom. Sloan gives the dimensions of the bathroom, tub, toilet, vanity counter, a damp green and white shirt on the floor, broken toilet holder on the wall, adult shoes, and an anti-slip mat in the shower.

There was a safe in the bedroom. A marijuana grinder was found in the safe and a scale with a white powdery substance. Items were sent to the crime lab and tested positive for fentanyl and heroin.

Exhibit 2L was a photo of the garage looking into the residence. Sloan said he found no evidence of any fire. Sloan went through the procedure of collecting the evidence, sending it to the Tomah Police Department, and then on to the State Crime Lab.

Skiles asked about blood found on the wall between the full bathroom and Kyson's bedroom. Exhibit 2F, 2G, and 2H showed blood droplets. Investigator Sloan explained the tedious process of collecting the blood spots using a DNA collection kit, "The first thing I do is I put on a clean pair or a new pair of latex gloves and I take a sealed package of swabs from that kit. In cases like this where it was dried, I will moisten the Q-Tip or swab with distilled water and then I'll just rub the Q-Tip on the sample to collect the sample. After I collect the sample, the swab is placed back into the original packaging and then the packaging swabs are placed in what's called a swab box. On the swab box, I put my name, date, time, and a brief location of where I collected the sample from." Three swabs were tested and two found to have Kyson's blood. The third had insufficient material to do a test.

Assistant DA Skiles asked Sloan to hold up Marcus' car keys, Exhibit 48, that were confiscated after his arrest. There were two lanyards, a black and red one with the US Marine Corps logo and another green one with the USMC logo.

Flanagan's cross examination takes three minutes. He had Sloan admitting that when Sloan interviewed Jessica Rice in the hospital that she said Kyson was a clumsy kid. He also asked questions about the floor being wet, the garbage, and the age of the blood spots.

On redirect, Sloan was asked about the time frame in which Jessica was asked if Kyson was clumsy, but in subsequent questioning, Jessica described Kyson as graceful. Why the two different answers? One can surmise that the first questioning was done before Jessica came to terms that Marcus was a violent, vengeful man, and she was, in some small way, protecting him. Sloan was excused and the Court took a 15-minute midmorning break.

Witness #40 Patrol Officer Brennon Scallon

Mr. Croninger handled the questioning, establishing that Officer Brennon Scallon was a City of Tomah Police Department patrol officer, starting in 2016.

Summarizing his testimony: "On May 3, I was supposed to come in at 10:00 p.m., but was called in early-at about 7 p.m. I was called to assist in a high-risk traffic stop downtown. My body camera was automatically activated by my squad. The body camera recorded for over 8 hours. I asked people to get back in the businesses along Superior Avenue.

I took a position parallel to Marcus' vehicle on the other side of Superior Avenue, took cover and was armed with a duty rifle. After he was taken into custody, I made my way back to the other squads parked behind his vehicle. I was told to go obtain my car and bring it behind theirs, so Marcus was going to be placed in my squad to be transported to the police department."

Over the next 45 minutes, DA Croninger questioned Officer Brennon Scallon while showing Exhibit 44A, a total of 19 video segments from Scallon's body camera. The first is a 54-second segment of being parked south of Mr. Anderson's 2010 Ford Fusion car on Superior Avenue. Croninger asked Scallon if it was a normal route for Anderson to take if he was preceding to the Tomah Memorial Hospital, to which Scallon replied, "No." After Anderson was brought out of the car, Anderson told Scallon that he didn't deal with weapons, and Anderson asked Scallon about his (Anderson's) son.

The next segment showed Anderson in the back of the squad car at the Tomah Police station. Another clip had Anderson being put in an ambulance because he complained about being in pain. A clip showed Sgt. Steinborn entering the ambulance and talking to Anderson. Anderson asked Steinborn if his son is still alive, to which Steinborn replies, "He's not doing well."

The next video segment showed Anderson in the ambulance being transported to Sparta Mayo Hospital. Anderson continually described what took place at the residence, even though Scallon advised him several times, "It's not in your best interest to talk."

In the next segment, Anderson told Scallon, "I don't do no illegal drugs." During the entire ride from Tomah to Sparta, Scallon did not ask Anderson any questions. On the contrary, Scallon told Anderson not to talk.

In the next segment, Dr. Julia Casner, the emergency room doctor on duty at the Sparta Mayo Hospital on May 3, 2019, explained to Anderson what would cause rhabdo (rhabdomyolysis). When muscles were severely injured or inflamed, muscle cells burst and release their contents and can cause muscle weakness, soreness, and kidney failure when the proteins accumulate in the kidneys. It's possible to treat it by flushing out the toxic proteins with intravenous fluids, but it takes time to recover, and muscles may be weaker after the breakdown.

Near the end of the video segment, Investigator Walensky appeared and Scallon muted his body camera so he might talk to Walensky. The next few videos showed medical personnel at Sparta Mayo Hospital giving Anderson an IV and Anderson mumbling several times, "It's my fault. My life is over." The next segment indicated Anderson settled into the hospital bed and Scallon sitting in a nearby chair. Anderson proceeded to tell Scallon he was on the way to the hospital and stopped to get cigarettes. Anderson also questioned Scallon about what happened to his vehicle.

In the next clip, Anderson said cops told him to get to the hospital, that he left, and then returned to get his driver's license. Video segments showed Anderson requesting and receiving a TV remote. He said he likes to watch CNN. Dr. Casner told Anderson she would not give him narcotics for rhabdo, and the levels for rhabdo, "were not that high."

A segment showed Scallon handing Anderson a search warrant, which made Anderson extremely agitated. Then Anderson again reiterated his version of what took place at the residence. Soon Investigator Walensky entered the room. Scallon's body camera was good for four hours, then it starts a new recording. Scallon already had over eight hours of video.

A nurse told Anderson why they took a urine sample. The nurse told Anderson that the medical staff does not believe he is suffering from anything significant. Scallon told the Court that Anderson continually wanted to give his account of what happened and at no time did Scallon ask Anderson any questions.

In his cross examination, Attorney Flanagan drilled Scallon for five minutes. Scallon was asked about the arrest procedure. Deputy Geyer assisted in the arrest. Anderson complained about leg pain, and talked about when they get to the hospital, they gave him fluids, ibuprofen, but not narcotics. He rehashed the time when Marcus was at Sparta Mayo, seeing Dr. Casner, and was told that his rhabdo levels were not that bad. Marcus was upset with Dr. Casner because he could not receive medication, such as oxycodone.

The Court broke for lunch at 11:30 a.m. because DA Croninger explained that the next witness will take an hour or more. After the jury was dismissed, Croninger brought up the issue in Count 13 that the State be held to a higher burden of proof for Mr. Anderson's use of controlled substances. DA Croninger explained, "This is related to Operating with a Restricted Controlled Substance. A first offense for this type of violation is civil in nature in the State of Wisconsin, meaning the burden of proof is lower than beyond a reasonable doubt. However, the State is allowed to agree to a higher burden of proof if they believe it is appropriate. In this case, we agreed to a higher burden of proof, so that the burden of proof would be the same on every count. We believe having the same burden of proof on every count would ensure there was no confusion in the jury room about what the proper burden was for each count."

Chapter 33

Investigator Walensky Takes the Stand

Investigator Robert Walensky

At 12:45 p.m., the jury was ushered in and the court case resumed. DA Croninger calls Investigator Robert Walensky to the stand. At the time of his testimony Walensky was the investigative coordinator with the Western Metropolitan Enforcement Group, a five-county La Crosse based, drug task force that includes Monroe County. Walensky told the Court, "I was employed with the Tomah Police Department for the previous 22 years prior to February of 2021."

Croninger detailed Walensky's extensive training and experience, especially in handling death investigations and vehicle forensics. For some time, Walensky was the only investigator on the Tomah Police Department staff. When asked about Mr. Anderson's general characteristics, Walensky notes that Anderson is a big man, 6 foot 4 inches, with a weight at 240 pounds on his driver's license.

Walensky was asked about the surveillance camera footage from the house at 1009 Jodi Circle on May 3, 2019. The Court views Exhibit 44C, Jessica Rice leaving her residence at 9:24 a.m. Nowhere in any footage did it show Jessica Rice returning to the house until late afternoon. The only person shown was Larry Quarles coming and going. There were three mounted cameras: one on the front door, one on the garage and one on the side door. One camera video showed a person mowing the lawn at about 3:00 p.m., but that person never entered the house.

Walensky said, "My role on May 3, 2019, was to follow the ambulance to Sparta Mayo Hospital with the intent of interviewing Mr. Anderson. I obtained a search warrant and had a blood draw on Mr. Anderson, read him his Miranda rights, which he agreed to, and the conversation was recorded on Officer Scallon's body camera."

For the next 3.5 hours, many video clips were shown in Court. These videos were from Officer Brennon Scallon's body camera. Anderson is cuffed to the restraints or side bars on the bed. The jury was handed a written copy of the interrogation of Mr. Anderson by Investigator Walensky that took place at Sparta Mayo Hospital. It is long and rambling. Foremost, Anderson was evasive and incoherent, often talking about things he was not asked about, and never really giving a direct answer to a question.

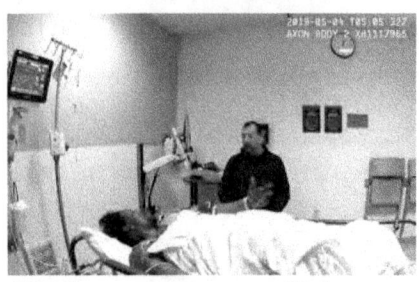

The first interrogation of Marcus took place at Sparta Mayo Hospital by Investigator Robert Walensky. The time is 12:32 a.m. on May 4.

Anderson never made it to the Tomah Memorial Hospital and made no attempt to do so. He talks about his girlfriend, Regina Hall. He acknowledged that he and Kyson went to McDonald's. He said that a Larry had come over. He tells Investigator Walensky that he, Anderson, is African American and he "doesn't want people to blame him for stuff." He claims that Tomah just wants to put him away. Anderson says he was in his underwear and had his socks on. Yet when law enforcement arrived, he was wearing a Michael Vick jersey, a do-rag, and chains.

Q. So, if what Mr. Anderson is telling you is correct, that would mean that after Kyson fell in the shower, Mr. Anderson clothed himself in a jersey, chains, and do-rag?

A. Yes.

Anderson provided Walensky several explanations for Kyson's injuries: he is light skinned, bruises easily, falls a lot, bad CPR, Kyson had a rash, Kyson had something wrong with his nervous system, or Kyson had something wrong with his blood. Someone called Jenna had a flat tire. Kyson had spots. Kyson has a brain disorder, his eyes are not closing, and Kyson has seizures.

An example of an answer to the question after the ninth explanation for Kyson's death, "You know what I'm saying? Kyson was laying in the shower, you know what I'm saying, like, you know what I mean? I'm liked 'oh, shit,' you know what I'm saying? So, he's kind of like turning his head, almost like, you know what I'm saying, he turned around and sat up, you know."

Anderson started talking about the warrant and the blood draw, and whether he was going to get into any trouble. He made allegations that Jolene (Glynn) did things to Kyson. Then he said that John Glynn could have done it. Then it was somebody called Grandpa. Then he was worried that Jessica is not there, and that Jessica had not been trying to find him.

When Walensky asked Anderson about his discipline methods, he claimed he never used an instrument on Kyson. "I took him from Madison just to get him away from his dad spanking him because I don't like to see kids get whoopin's." Yet, it has been revealed that Kyson's biological father was never involved in his life.

At another point in the interview interrogation and after he is informed that Kyson is dead, Anderson claimed, "You know what I'm saying, I'm automatically getting in trouble, you know what I'm saying, because I'm black. I'm black, man. You know what I'm saying? You know what I'm saying? The Tomah police hates my guts, man."

Anderson reverted back to CPR done incorrectly, how he would never harm a child, how he has custody of his little sisters. That he had been on the phone all day with Gina (Regina) who lives in Arizona.

Anderson claimed he "does Marcus discipline" by having the kid stand against the wall. It contradicts earlier testimony by Shelby Anderson on how Marcus Anderson disciplined children. Marcus provides a lengthy discussion about how his car window was broken, about his medical condition, and his dancing at McDonald's.

At 2:41 p.m. the Court takes a 15-minute break, having gone through two hours of testimony. Walensky tried to elicit an answer from Anderson on what he was doing on May 3, and he started talking about medical problems and going to Alma Center, then mentioning Jenna again, something about a tire.

There were a total of 16 explanations that Anderson has given of what happened to Kyson Rice. Anderson then claims he and Kyson went to the garage to start the car, before calling 911. He called Jeremy Devine, Brandon Crampes, and Ashley Wankerl before calling 911. Walensky informed Mr. Anderson that there was going to be an autopsy and he would have more information the next day. *Note: Walensky did attend the autopsy and visited Anderson the next day.*

Anderson said that any blood on himself was because Kyson's gums bleed when he brushes his teeth. Anderson talked about his performing CPR on Kyson, "I was blowing in his mouth, you know what I mean? Like, I see CPR. I did learn CPR. I was in the Marine Corps, you know what I'm saying, Like, Like, ---so like you know what I mean?"

It was 1:40 a.m. May 4, the day after the murder. The initial interrogation is over. Walensky left a few hours later to attend an autopsy in Madison. He told the Court he has attended 130 to 140 autopsies.

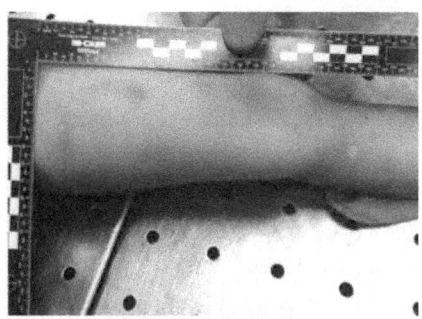
Investigator Walensky witnessed Kyson Rice's autopsy at UW Medical Center.

Q. In those 130 or 140 autopsies, have you ever seen a victim with that much bruising on them?

A. No.

Walensky told the Court that he went to see Mr. Anderson after the autopsy, in the late afternoon of May 4, accompanied by Detective Clayton Tester, and toting an audio tape recorder. DA Croninger played a 5:34-minute clip, and each jury member has received a written transcript of the audio. The two investigators are questioning Mr. Anderson about the events of the previous day, May 3.

Anderson's responses to questions were rambling, evasive, and contradictory. His accounts of what happened to Kyson vary widely and Walensky had difficulty pinning him down to the order of any events. He gave different answers to the clothing he wore that day.

The following is a snippet.

Q. He talked about getting back from McDonald's, chicken nuggets, Walgreens, getting his prescription. And then he changed the subject and talks about being charged for OWI. Is that correct?

A. Yes.

Anderson talked at length about irrelevant things, about how he, Anderson, made everyone happy. He claimed that Jessica went to work and left Kyson all alone. He claimed that when Kyson went down, he was unconscious.

In the interview, Walensky asked Anderson, "I'm wondering if this kid was beat to hell." Then Marcus said, "Wow. And there's no way. Do you know what I'm saying? I couldn't did it. I couldn't did not shit like that-all right. You know what I'm saying? First of all, you know what I'm saying?

How? Like, first of all, did you – I - I been gone for over two and a half weeks."

Marcus blamed the Tomah Police Department. He blamed Jessica Rice who he claims smacked him. At one point Anderson said, "I popped him in the mouth. It was---I was like "Ky,' you know what I'm saying? 'You don't need to say those cuss words no more.' You know what I'm saying?"

Walensky reminded Anderson several times that he should man up and he should not talk about irrelevant things. At one time, he accused Jessica Rice of being a habitual liar.

The clock on the north wall of Courtroom Branch 2 read 4:30 p.m. It had been a long exhausting day for everyone; Judge Goodman, the prosecuting attorneys, defense council, friends and visitors, and especially the jury. There were six witnesses in an eight hour session.

Judge Goodman addressed the jury, "We'll be back at this tomorrow at 8:30. Leave your notebooks on your chairs and have a great supper." It is Monday, April 4, 2022.

You know the adage, "the best laid plans..." COVID-19 reared its ugly head, as Judge Mark L. Goodman tested positive, so the trial was postponed for one week.

Chapter 34

The Trial Resumes

During the week of the trial postponement due to COVID-19 striking Judge Goodman, the world went on.

The Russian invasion of Ukraine continued. A mass grave of Ukrainian civilians was discovered near the village of Buzova. Bombs exploded in a playing field in Afghanistan, killing five. Yemen's civil war continued. The Israelis and Palestinians traded insults and gunfire. COVID-19 made headlines every day. Sacramento Police arrested a 26-year-old man who left six people dead and 12 others injured. There were rumblings in the press that Roe v. Wade was being looked at by the Supreme Court.

Gov. Tony Evers traveled to Volk Field to speak to Air Guard soldiers who are being deployed to the Middle East. Four young people vandalized Tomah Middle School and were caught. Practice began for softball, baseball, soccer, tennis, and track at Tomah and Sparta High Schools. The Amish up on Highway A, south of Tomah, were planting oats. Trees all over Monroe County were leafing out, taking on that light green hue. The songs of robins, mourning doves, cardinals, and red-wing blackbirds greeted the new season. At three weeks past the Vernal Equinox, March 22, the sun rose each day a bit more north above the eastern horizon.

On Monday morning, April 11, 2022, it was all business at the Monroe County Justice Center, District Court Branch 2. At 8:30 a.m. the jury entered the courtroom. Jessica Rice and her troupe of family members were present: Michael and Mary Ravet, Desiree Glynn, Reid Rice, Katherine Rice, Tara Eckelberg, and Rhonda Burch. So was John Glynn, who attended every hearing and every day of the trial. Detective Paul Sloan, clad in a smart light-blue suit was seated at the prosecution table. Marcus Anderson was escorted into the courtroom by two plain clothes officers.

Judge Goodman, wearing a mask says, "Have a seat everyone. We'll go on the record in 19CF353, State vs. Marcus Wayne Anderson. Mr. Anderson is present in person along with Defense Counsel Patrick Flanagan. The State of Wisconsin appears by Monroe County District Attorney Kevin Croninger and Assistant District Attorney Sarah Skiles. We are now down to 13 jurors, eight women and five men. One of your fellow jurors called in Friday reporting he wasn't feeling well and called in again today. And because of his illness, I am excusing him, and so we only have to worry about picking one alternate when we are done with the evidence in the trial. Mr. Croninger, you have more witnesses?"

Because the trial had resumed after a one-week hiatus, DA Croninger reviewed Investigator Robert Walensky's testimony from Monday, April 4. Walensky had a lengthy interview with Anderson on the night of the murder, taking place at the Sparta Mayo Hospital with Anderson handcuffed to the hospital bed.

Walensky attended the autopsy in Madison the next day, May 4. When Investigator Walensky returned from Madison, he again interrogated Marcus at the Monroe County Jail on that same day of May 4. Once again, Walensky confirmed that Marcus waived his Miranda rights.

Croninger played numerous sound bites from Exhibit 53. Anderson had provided sixteen different explanations for what happened on the late afternoon of May 3 and what led to Kyson Rice's death. It was an exercise in dodging, weaving, avoidance, misdirection, and outright obfuscation, sprinkled with frequent use of "I'm trying to process it all."

In the interview at Sparta Mayo, Anderson was asked about the gun found in the closet of the Tomah 1009 Jodi Circle house shared by Jessica

Rice, her son Kyson, and Marcus Anderson. Anderson told Walensky that he's not sure what gun he was talking about.

Walensky showed Anderson some autopsy photos showing Tyson's injuries. Walensky was met with the familiar denials. Croninger asked Investigator Walensky about the group that took Kyson's body to Madison for the autopsy. He replied, "Kyson was taken to a funeral home the night of May 3. The next day, early May 4, there was kind of a procession of cars. Funeral personnel followed me to UW Hospital. That way we can keep kind of a chain of custody, so to speak, on Kyson's body pending autopsy."

Anderson was asked about his drug use. He claimed he did not use illegal drugs. He wanted to talk about the $700 that was found in his car and taken from him. Anderson claimed he can't remember things, yet he was able to recall his trip to California, his stay in the hospital, going to Walgreens and McDonald's in Sparta.

Cross examination of Investigator Walensky

Attorney Patrick Flanagan questioned Investigator Walensky concerning the interrogation at the Sparta Mayo Hospital, the conditions, the hours, and food available. Flanagan brought out that Marcus said to Walensky, "Give me some time to process this, man. Give me some days to process." Walensky talked to Mr. Anderson two days later, on May 6.

There was a short redirect by DA Croninger starting at 10:02 a.m. Investigator Robert Walensky was Witness #41 and the last to be called by the prosecution. The jury was excused at 10:09 a.m. for the first morning break. Walensky was also excused from the witness stand. Over the next hour, the jury was called in and dismissed several times as wrangling continued between the State and Defense.

The Court was asked to decide which exhibits should be entered as evidence. Marcus had filed a request for a mistrial. Both the State and Defense agreed that the request lacks merit.

DA Croninger talked about a Tuesday Zoom call to all jurors to report back on Monday. Then there was a discussion about what exhibits had been offered and which had been admitted. Marcus Anderson had another filing with the Court, a pro se Motion for Amended Complaint. Anderson wanted Kathy Mahnke called as a witness and he felt there should be a mistrial. Kathy Mahnke was a supervisor at the Wisconsin State Crime Lab. According to Anderson, DA Croninger pressured Ms. Mahnke to get him the things that he wanted. Croninger explained that the State Crime Lab has procedures and protocols that require law enforcement officials to give explanations of why and what should be tested. Those protocols were put in place four or five years ago to try to work through the backlog of cases at the State Crime Lab.

DA Croninger presented four stipulations he wanted read to the jury.

1. April 29, 2019, Anderson had been charged with a crime and was released from custody on bond and a condition of his bond was that he "shall not commit any crime."

2. On May 3, 2019, Anderson had been charged with a crime and was released from custody on a bond with the condition that he commit no crime.

3. On May 3, 2019, Mr. Anderson was prohibited from possessing a firearm.

4. May 3, 2019, Mr. Anderson had previously been convicted of a drug offense and misdemeanor possession of marijuana.

The stipulations were read to the jury. The jury departed and Judge Goodman asked Mr. Flanagan if his client would testify. Flanagan said that Anderson told him that he wanted to talk to Flanagan about that. A recess was taken at 10:46 am. After the break, the lawyers and Judge Goodman discussed the issue of counts of bail jumping and felony bonds and how it was tied to a case in La Crosse County.

The Court (Judge Goodman): Okay, Mr. Anderson, I have to ask you these questions because this is a crucial moment in the trial. Do you understand that you have a constitutional right to testify in this matter?"

The Defendant: Yes.

The Court: Do you understand that you have a constitutional right not to testify in this matter?

The Defendant: Yes, Judge.

The Court: Do you understand that the decision whether or not to testify is for you alone to make?

Another courtroom at the Monroe County Justice Center, but the jury selection process is the same, many called but few are chosen.

The Defendant: Yes.

The Court: Have you had ample time to discuss that decision with Attorney Flanagan?

The Defendant: I had a little bit of time, but we had some time.

The Court: Have you had enough time to discuss this with your lawyer?

The Defendant: I think I could use more time but, I mean, uhm, just continue, Judge.

The Court: I need to have an answer because your answer is going to decide what we do the rest of the day.

The Defendant: I don't need no more time, Judge.

The Court: Okay. What is your answer?

The Defendant: I will testify, Judge.

The State rested its case at 11:23 a.m. on April 11, 2022, the seventh day of the trial. The jury was brought back into District Courtroom Branch 2. Judge Goodman read the four agreed upon stipulations.

At 11:24 a.m. Marcus Wayne Anderson, age 37, head clean shaven, was called to the witness stand and took the oath. Flanagan began by taking Anderson back to the beginning of 2019. Anderson revealed that he was living at Larry and Cheryl Quarles' house and also in Madison. He left April 9 to go to California and then Arizona. He was back in Tomah on April 24, where he lived at 1009 Jodi Circle. When back from California, he suffered pain in his legs, a condition of rhabdomyolysis, which breaks down tissue in the legs and causes pain. He was prescribed Oxycodone, Diazepam, Lyrica, Tizanidine, Amlodipine. Anderson says, "I was on quite a bit of meds."

Marcus testified, "When I got out of the hospital I went to Jodi Circle, then, Alma Center, then Madison on May 1, and then to 1009 Jodi Circle. I met Jessica online in 2014, then I didn't talk to her for five years." He revealed it was a romantic relationship.

Flanagan asked questions about Kyson. Marcus replied, "He was in daycare, and Jessica asked me to look after him. To which I agreed because she was working. In the beginning, I would pick him up from daycare at four or five in the afternoon and watch him until Jessica got home."

Questions turned to the happenings of May 3. In his words, "Jessica left at about 10 a.m. for work." Unexpectedly, Flanagan switched gears.

Q. You have other children of your own?
A. Yes.

Q. And one of those is a child you have with a woman who testified in this trial, a Shelby Anderson. Is that right?
A. Yes.

Q. You and Shelby were married. Is that right?
A. Yes.

Q. Did you two divorce?
A. Yes.

Q. Was it a fair, friendly divorce or were there problems in it?
A. Uhm, it was kind of ugly?

Q. She testified that you were abusive to your son that you have with her. Remember that?

A. Yes, that was her comments, but that's not true. She used that in a divorce to try to get full custody of him. My son was only like eight months at the time. He couldn't walk. He barely started to crawl.

The questioning turns back to the happenings on May 3, 2019. Anderson said, "I got back late from Alma Center and fell asleep on the couch in the living room. I woke up to her screaming and hitting Kyson. She was screaming at Kyson to watch TV, to get him under control. Amber took her to work. Larry came over."

Asked to describe his relationship with Kyson, Anderson said, "It was good. He always wanted to go with me, to be around me. He called me Tank. Out of nowhere he started calling me his dad. We would be at the park, to eat, I would buy him clothes and shoes."

When Flanagan asked about what they did that day, May 3, Marcus said, "We left the house about noon, made a stop, headed to Sparta to get my medications, along with Kyson, in my black car, went to Walgreens, McDonald's, Cenex to get gas, back to Walgreens.

Q. Where was Kyson when you were doing your business at Walgreens?

A. He was in the back seat, asleep.

Anderson said, "Then we headed back to Tomah. I stopped at an old buddy of mine for a few minutes to just talk to him. Then we went to Jodi Circle. We ate our meal in the car, that's what we usually do. When we got back, he was watching cartoons for a minute then my plan was to pick up Jessica, then I was going back to Madison."

Via Flanagan's questions, Mr. Anderson gave his version of what went on in the late afternoon of May 3 at 1009 Jodi Circle. Marcus said, "I was getting ready to take a shower and get him dressed. I started the water and told him to get ready to go take a shower, and I was on the phone. I was on FaceTime at the time, and I told him to get his stuff ready to take a shower so I could get him dressed. Probably ten minutes, he headed to the bathroom to get in the shower. I left the bathroom to go get his clothes and then I heard a thud. It was loud. I could kind of tell the way it sounded that I needed to get back in there. I rushed to the bathroom. The water was running. He was laying outside the tub on his back. I did not see any blood and did not see any marks. His face was red. I wasn't paying attention to details. I wanted to call an ambulance and get him some help. He wasn't talking. I was trying to get his attention and I was padding him like Ky, Ky, Ky. I ran and grabbed my phone and dialed 911. Then I was doing CPR on him. I felt his heartbeat, but I was also giving him CPR. I was blowing in his mouth trying to give him CPR the best I could. I was pushing on his chest. Then I turned him over. I was patting his back like this. I was panicking. I was freaking out. I tried shaking him to revive him. I seen some bruising on him but my main focus was to get him help. When I shook him, he gave a gasp like I thought he was getting air into his lungs. I kind of felt a heartbeat, but I was just waiting on the ambulance at that time. I don't recall calling anyone before I called Jess. I can't recall the order, but I think I called the ambulance first."

Pressed with more questions, Anderson provided the following narrative. "The police showed up first and a couple of minutes later, the ambulance was there. I was frantic, trying to figure out what was going on and making sure he was okay. I never had been in a situation like that before."

Defense Attorney Flanagan brought up the issue of the gun found in the house. "It dawned on me that the gun was in the house because Brandon never came back and got his gun, which he should have picked up. It was his gun. He should never have left it there. And he left it there when I was out in California and Arizona because he had my car the whole time when I was out of state."

Name: ANDERSON, MARCUS W
DOC #: 00681080
Birth Year: 1984
Age: 38
Height: 6' 2"   Weight: 324
Race: BLACK
Ethnicity: NOT HISPANIC OR LATINO
Hair Color: BALD
Eye Color: BROWN
Sex: MALE
Dexterity: AMBIDEXTROUS
PhotoDate: 07/05/2022

Booking photo of Marcus Anderson.

Asked about the marijuana found in the house, Anderson responded, "I wouldn't say it was marijuana. I guess when you're using a marijuana grinder, it flakes at the bottom. I don't know if it was any marijuana, an actual bag of marijuana. I didn't see no bag because once you use a grinder it's in there for a long time and I don't think you ever get it out."

About the time Anderson was in the hospital. Jess came to visit and brought Kyson with her.

Q. There was testimony that she claimed you hit him in the chest?
A. That's blatantly false.

Q. There's testimony that you were jerky or belligerent at the hospital. What can you say about that?
A. I wouldn't say I was belligerent. I wanted them to contact my doctor and have my doctor make some decisions on my health care and they wasn't trying to do that. They were trying to give me medications that I did not take.

Q. Previous testimony pointed out that Kyson had teeth knocked out. What happened?
A. I was told that Jessica says she was out in the garage with Kyson and he slipped on a shower rod or something and fell and hit his mouth and if I could come help her. I was on the freeway heading back to Tomah from Madison. What she explained to me that he fell on the pole in the garage and he hit his face.

Q. Is it true you kicked him in the mouth?

A. That's absurd. No, I did not.

Flanagan questioned Anderson about how he disciplined Kyson. His response, "I would like give him time out or he couldn't watch tv. It was non-contact, non-physical."

Flanagan asked Anderson what he did when they took Kyson to the hospital by ambulance. "They told me to drive to La Crosse because they were going to transport him to La Crosse. So I was getting ready. Then Amber came back and told me to get some stuff for Jessica, and that's what I went to go do."

Q. The police were outside and they say they're going to search he house, do you have any concerns or worries?

A. Yes. They didn't have a search warrant and that's her house. I can't authorize somebody to search her house.

Q. Was it occurring to you that there was stuff inside the house that the police may find?

A. Probably her grinder. I thought that the weapon may still be in the house.

Q. At some point you do leave the house. Right?

A. Yes, they told me to head to La Crosse and I was driving, and well, at first, I told the police that I did not feel comfortable driving. I'm not in good shape to drive but they proceeded to tell me to drive. So, I got in my car and I drove and I passed out. The next thing I know, the police shot out my window. I was in the hospital and a lot of medication in my system. I take a lot of Oxycodone throughout the day.

Q. So you weren't trying to drive away somewhere where no one could find you?

A. Right. I parked in an open area where police travel all the time. They didn't find me 30 miles away in a whole 'nother town. So I wasn't trying to flee.

Attorney Flanagan's questions turned back to the discipline Anderson may have meted out to Kyson.

Q. Did you ever use anything to discipline him other than just verbal instructions?

A. I popped him on the hand before but everybody does that to their kids. It's not abuse, right?

Q. Did you ever use a belt, like your belt or his belt.

A. No, I did not.

Q. There was some testimony from the crime lab indicating that there's a connection of DNA on his belt and your belt. How do you explain that?

A. I purchased his belt. I purchased his clothes. And if my DNA is in that house, if I get him undressed, of course, my DNA is going to be on there. They found multiple DNAs on that belt.

Q. OK, what about your belt?

A. He's always with me when we're in the house so I don't see why that would be a big deal. There's times when we're walking, he would hold onto my belt because some of my belt is sticking out so my hands could be free.

With a series of questions by Flanagan, Anderson responded, "I was pulled out of the car. They took me to Sparta Mayo Hospital. I tried to explain to the people that I was in pain, dealing with rhabdo. I have had four or five back surgeries. I wanted them to call Dr. Fitzgerald. He knows what treatments I need. They didn't care about my medical issues, especially when you are handcuffed to a bed. I was questioned by Walensky. I didn't have anything to eat since McDonald's. I was questioned the next day in the jail. They put all my stuff in a bag, my keys, prescriptions for Oxycodone and Diazepam, wallet, money, phone. They had a warrant to draw my blood."

Q. When we see the video, you appeared to become extremely emotional after you looked at that paper (warrant)?

A. Correct. It definitely affected me. I was in shock. I wasn't doing anything that I wanted Kyson to die.

Q. And you didn't do anything that caused him to die that you did intentionally. Right?

A. Right.

Q. Well, how would you characterize what happened to him?

A. A tragic accident.

Flanagan wrapped up his 44-minute direct examination at 12:08 p.m. It was DA Croninger's turn to cross-examine. He started off by questioning Anderson about his rhabdomyolysis condition. In a 13-minute exchange, Croninger tried to pin down Anderson's medical condition as related to his mobility; his use of a cane, walking at Walgreens, behavior at McDonald's, walking in the residence at 1009 Jodi Circle and outside on the lawn. Anderson was evasive. At one point Croninger brought up the testimony of Larry Quarles, "Marcus is good at playing the victim."

The questioning pivoted to Marcus' relationship with Jessica. The exchange was testy, yes, combative. The narrative pieced together: Marcus says he splits his time between Tomah, Madison, and Alma Center. In Madison he would stay with a friend Dwayne Jett, and sometimes take Kyson with him for a night or two. He would watch Dwayne Jett's son, Davonte. I took him May 1 and I got a speeding ticket. There's days I would stay at Brandon's house.

Q. You testified you were also in a relationship with Regina Hall. Correct?

A. You got to understand that that is a situation. So I got married and we just stayed friends. We were just there for each other.

Q. So you were in a relationship with Regina when you married Shelby?

A. It wasn't a relationship with Gina. We weren't together at that time.

Q. Are you claiming you weren't together with her at the time Kyson died?

A. I was out of town with her, yeah.

Q. Were you in a relationship with Regina Hall in April or May of 2019 or not?

A. Yes, kind of.

Q. So you have these ongoing two relationships, one with Jessica, one with Regina?

A. Yeah.

Croninger asked Mr. Anderson how he supported himself. There was an immediate objection from Defense Council Flanagan. After a spirited exchange, Judge Goodman ruled the objection sustained. Anderson did not have to answer the question.

Croninger asked where he gets the money to buy Kyson clothes and shoes. Anderson said he was a journeyman electrician. When Croninger asked when was the last time he worked as an electrician, Flanagan cries, "Objection." After Goodman sustained the objection, he tells Croninger to move on. Croninger grilled Anderson about his relationship exchanges on the day of the murder, May 3, 2019. It's an extensive series of questions and answers. Here is a partial exchange:

Q. Fair to say you were upset with Jessica Rice in the days leading up to Kyson's death?

A. No, not really.

Q. There's wasn't any distress in that relationship? Things were going just fine?

A. I mean, other than me telling her she needs to spend time with her son, and she needs to clean up.

DA Croninger displayed a series of text messages, screen shots of a cell phone with messages on them, many had been shown earlier in the trial. Starting with 2EE at 11:06 a.m. "I see you don't care about me anymore. So you want to move on, want to be somebody to make me happy and love me and not treat me like a doorstep."

Jessica and Marcus lived at 1009 Jodi Circle, just north of the Fairgrounds in Tomah. It is a quiet peaceful neighborhood.

Jessica replied by text message at 11:16 a.m., "Talk to you when I get off. I'm busy at work." Over the next 2 hours and 40 minutes, Anderson sends six text messages without getting a reply from Jessica. Each text he sends expresses irritation, frustration, and anger.

Typical items, "Oh, so you're busy now. So, from now on, don't ever call me or text me from work again so when you having a bad day don't come to me when something go wrong. Don't call me anymore. So you need to find a permanent babysitter."

Croninger chided Anderson; I thought you loved Kyson and wanted to be around him all the time.

Q. Why would you want her to get a different babysitter then?

A. Because it's not my child.

Q. You told officers he was like your son. When you split up with Shelby, you still wanted to have contact with Samir, right?

A. That's my son.

Q. So when you told officers that Kyson was your son, there was a different definition of the word son than you meant when you called Samir your son?

Anderson stammered, hemmed, and hawed.

For each text message he sent, Anderson was asked to explain. He had a difficult time, squirming in the witness chair. Perhaps he did not realize that the time period from about 11 am to 2 pm was a busy time at Taco Bell, and Jessica was unable to spend time texting or talking on the phone.

Between 2:10 p.m. and 3:09 p.m., Marcus and Jessica talked on the phone about their relationship. The content of that exchange cannot be printed here because telephone conversations, unlike text messages, are not recorded, so there is no written transcript. The text messages could be exposed in Court due to a warrant served.

DA Croninger showed Exhibit 2GG, a text message Marcus sent to Jessica while he was at the Walgreens Drug Store in Sparta, a 3:09 p.m. message. Video surveillance indicates Marcus was in Walgreens from 3:06 to 3:15 p.m. The message read, "Hey, I love you. I want this to work out. So, you need to stop making me cry and feel like shit. I'd rather having you hitting me than doing that."

For several minutes DA Croninger was attempting to have Anderson confess that he, on May 3, was upset, irritated, angry, and very unhappy. Anderson danced around the questions but did admit he was deeply hurt and not in an upbeat frame of mind.

Exhibit 2HH was a 4:01 p.m. text message from Marcus to Jessica. "I need help. I'm in pain. You know I suppose to be on bed rest." Jessica texted back, "Go lay in bed or on couch and no, didn't know that. I'll call a cab home, babe." Marcus texted back, "You supposed to be taking care of me, but you abandon me."

DA Croninger said, "You claim that you're supposed to be on bed rest, but you were fine to drive to the City of Sparta." Marcus replied that he had to get his medications. DA Croninger brought up several men that could have driven him.

DA Croninger again said, "So you felt good enough to go to Sparta, go into Walgreens, go to McDonald's, go to Cenex to pump gas, and walk into the store and buy lottery tickets, and despite your claim that you were supposed to be on bed rest, you're fine going and running all those errands?"

Another text from Jessica to Marcus at 4:09 read, "I didn't abandon you. I'll be home soon to take care of you. I have the next three days off to take care of you." At 5:58 p.m. "I'm coming home. And we can talk about that later." At 6:53 p.m. Marcus texted Jessica, "Call me ASAP." DA Croninger told the Court, "This would be the timeframe where you were messing around the house not leaving to go to the hospital."

Croninger continued, "You called Jessica at 5:50. You called Brandon, you called Jeremy, you called Ashley, you called Jessica multiple times and then finally at 5:55 you called 911." Anderson disputed some of the calls and the timeframe.

It was 12:51 p.m., it had been a long morning session, and Judge Goodman broke in, "I think this is perhaps a good time to break for lunch. The jury has been going for a while here. And I'm going to give them until 2:00 to eat something, And Dale, do you want them to do the usual, come into Branch 4."

Bailiff: How long are we having?

Judge Goodman announced to the assembled, "We're going to reconvene at 2:00, you all deserve a break."

All stood and the jury exited.

Chapter 35

The Defendant's Day in Court

With the jury out, Judge Mark Goodman addressed the Court, "My Judicial Assistant has been at work on the jury instructions. I know that she has sent both lawyers working drafts and I've made some changes to those, and I'll have her follow up and send them to you again so that we can kind of refine as we go along. Is there any business we need to take up before we all get to eat lunch?" Both attorneys said, "No."

The jury filed back in at 2:01 p.m. DA Kevin Croninger grilled Anderson about the weapon found at 1009 Jodi Circle.

Q. You knew that firearm was in your residence. Right?

A. Well, it dawned on me that it probably was there, yes.

Over a series of 40 questions about the weapon, Mr. Anderson took on the role of the artful dodger. Summarizing his responses, "I thought Brandon left it there. Kyson being unconscious, somehow popped in my mind that a gun was

The firearm found in the Rice-Anderson residence was traced by its serial number.

there. I did not touch that gun. My DNA found on the gun? If the police doing searches in the house and they picked up the firearm, they could have transferred DNA on there. I do paralegal studies. I do follow up on a lot of things about DNA. Brandon had my car when I was in California and he shared that he put the gun in the house."

Q. You asked Ms. Moseley to take it out of the house?

A. I don't recall asking her that question.

Q. You were worried about other things in the house, too, like the straw in the kitchen that has fentanyl on it. Right?

A. Why would I be worried about that? I didn't know about no straw with no fentanyl.

Croninger asked his assistant to bring up Exhibit 2M, a photo of a red straw that tested for fentanyl. Exhibit 2M was first introduced in Court by Investigator Clayton Tester, Witness #28. Anderson dodged the question, saying they gave him fentanyl in the hospital. Croninger countered with the testimony of Ms. Jungbluth who explained that fentanyl does not remain in the bloodstream for four days. Anderson claimed he does not know where the red straw came from. Croninger went to Exhibit 2V which was also introduced in Court with Clayton Tester on the witness stand. It was the photo of cash found stuffed between the seats of his Ford Fusion car at the time of his arrest. Exhibit 2W was a photo of a $20 bill.

Q. We have testimony from Detective Tester about those white spots that are sort of between the T in "the" in the picture and then sort of around that side of it. That's from your vehicle. We have testimony that the white substance was heroin and fentanyl. And so that's just another coincidence that your money had heroin and fentanyl on it and it was also in your system?

A. I'm not saying it's a coincidence or anything like that. Money transfers a lot of people hands, so.

Anderson cannot account for heroin and fentanyl on his money in the car, on a straw on the floor, on his belt, on a baggie, and on his pants. Croninger questioned Anderson on the marijuana grinder, who claimed it belonged to Jessica, and the black and orange smoking device, and the THC wax in the trash.

Q. There was testimony from several people on this case that the trash can in the house had been emptied into the garage one, and

they knew that because some of the equipment from the medical first responders was in that trash. So, you were the only one in the house. So you took the trash out before you went to the hospital, Right?

Anderson denied it, saying the police might have done it. He also disputed testimony that he prevented the police from entering the residence. After a bit of coaching, Anderson admitted he has THC in the house.

There were a series of questions from DA Croninger concerning his accusation during Flanagan's direct examination that Jessica was "hitting Kyson." Exhibit 44B was played again. Anderson danced around the questions, admitting he never said that Jessica hit Kyson when he was interviewed by Investigator Walensky on May 4, 2019.

Anderson was asked about the blood draw in the hospital after the warrant had been issued. He found out he could be charged. He said he was advised by counsel to say nothing more to the police. There were a series of objections raised by Flanagan, some are sustained and some overruled.

Judge Goodman admonished, "You can ask him about that but then it seems that he invoked his right against self-incrimination at some point and that's where we sail into forbidden territory. Move on."

It was 1:12 p.m. and the questions to Anderson from Croninger continued. Exhibit 7W was a 10-minute phone call Mr. Anderson made to his girlfriend Regina Hall, the call being from the jailhouse where he was held at the Monroe County Justice Center.

Q. You were upset with Mr. Crampes about the gun, weren't you?

A. Yeah, I was upset because he brought it into the house.

The audio recording of the conversation with Regina Hall showed that Marcus was going to knock out Crampes (B'dag) if he were charged, to which Croninger indicated is an assault. The questioning turned to the ammunition found in the washing machine.

Q. Why did you put the shells to the gun in the washing machine?

A. I didn't put no shells in the washing machine. Why would I put some bullets in the washing machine?

Q. Well, the same reason you'd take the trash out. You don't want that evidence to be readily found.

Croninger played a segment from 7W.

Q. And you said that B'dag turned on you. What does that mean?

A. When you been best friends with somebody for so long and they just turn their back on you. He didn't answer my calls. If your friend is in trouble, you're supposed to come and find out what's going on regardless.

Q. Well, we have testimony from Mr. Crampes that you called him and said that Kyson was unconscious, and he told you that you should call 911?

I had already prior called 911. I think I made that call. Why don't you pull up my phone records to show what time I called. Why are you basing it on just what Mr. Crampes says?

Q. When you were asked for the code to your phone, by Mr. Walensky, you gave him a false code?

A. I think it was the same as Jessica's phone, but I probably changed it.

DA Croninger asked Anderson about who visited the house on the morning of May 3.

Based on previous testimony and surveillance cameras, it had been established that Larry Quarles came over twice just before noon.

Croninger once more hammered Anderson on the reasons or causes of Kyson's death, asking about each of the 19 probable causes that Anderson had given. Anderson called the Glynn family and the Tomah Police racist.

DA Croninger probed the relationship between Anderson and his former wife, Shelby.

Anderson said, "She's a bitter woman. She told me I wasn't going to have my son around other women, period."

Q. You view you control children and you get to decide whether they live or die. Correct?

A. I did not say that. She made that up in the divorce to get custody.

Croninger again asked about the events leading up to the murder.

Q. By 5:50 you're calling Ms. Rice, by 5:55 you finally decide to call 911. So we know at 5:50 Kyson is non-responsive. Let's talk about how we get to that. You pull Kyson around the garage. What happens next?

A. (Several answers to questions strung together) I told him to get ready to shower, we're going to get ready so I can leave. I was in the living room ironing my clothes-my jeans. I keep like ten outfits of clothes and like 20 pairs of shoes in my car. I'm different. Kyson was watching TV. When I get done ironing, I was on Facetime with Regina Hall. And then I told Kyson to get ready so he can get in the shower and then leave. I went in the room, I got his stuff, then I turned on the water and told him to get undressed and get in the bathtub.

This bathroom was the site of the brutal killing of Kyson Rice.

I was going to get the towels, and I heard this thud. I started to take my clothes off to shower with him. Sometimes it takes me like four hours to get dressed. I was in my boxers and my socks. I get Kyson in the shower and then I leave the room. I was on Facetime with Gina. I take showers with my chains on. I had a do-rag on my head.

DA Croninger asked his staff to bring up Exhibit 21, which was introduced during the testimony of Investigator Paul Sloan. The DA asked Anderson various questions about the bathroom scene, the position of Kyson when Marcus found him, where Anderson was at the time he claimed he heard a thud, and whether Kyson was inside or outside the tub.

DA Croninger played a six-minute segment, Exhibit 44B, part of the questioning done by Walensky and recorded by Scallon the night of the murder. In this segment, Anderson told Walensky that Kyson was lying in the shower, "I don't know how he fucking—I don't know, man. All I know is when I ran back in the bathroom, you know what I'm saying, Ky was laying in the shower, you know what I'm saying, like you know what I mean. I'm like, oh, shit, you know what I'm saying. So, he's kind of like turning his head like, almost like, you know what "I'm saying, he turned around and sat up, you know."

Croninger tried to pin down Anderson, but Anderson was elusive and contradictory. Many questions followed but Anderson attempted to dodge them. Croninger revisited the phone call situation, with Exhibit 2JJ. Anderson claimed on the stand that he called 911 before he called Jessica. Phone records indicated he called her at 5:50, called her again at 5:52, a minute-long conversation. Called twice more at 5:54, Exhibit 2LL. Four phone calls to Jessica before he called 911 at 5:55.

Q. So you're so worried about Kyson, he's unconscious and not breathing and you call his mom?

A. What, I'm not supposed to call her? Why are you being aggressive?

Q. I thought you wanted to call 911 first?

A. I called 911 to get him help, yeah.

Q. I'm getting aggressive because your answers don't make any sense.

A. Okay.

Q. And Kyson deserves to have the truth told. This jury deserves to have the truth told.

A. Exactly, and that's what I'm doing, Mr. Croninger.

Mr. Flanagan: I'm objecting, argumentative.

Judge Goodman: Don't argue with the witness.

An exchange ensued about Anderson calling Jeremy Devine. Devine testified that he told Anderson to call 911 when informed on the phone that Kyson was unresponsive. Anderson said Devine called him several times during the day because he was trying to borrow some money to get rid of a PlayStation.

Q. He testified while he was at the casino and he told you to call 911 and get an ambulance.

A. No, he call me.

Questions arise as to the height of the bathtub and ease of getting in and out. And more questions about bruises on Kyson. Exhibit 2CCC was brought up again. It was previously shown in Court during the Dr. Stier testimony. Exhibit 2DDD is another autopsy photo, followed by 2EEE, another gruesome autopsy photo.

Any observer in the Courtroom could determine what is going on. DA Croninger was nearing the end of his cross-examination of Anderson. He wanted the jury to once again see the destruction wrought upon Kyson Rice at the hands of a much larger, powerful, and angry individual. It was clear to this observer that Anderson had not helped himself by taking the witness stand.

DA Croninger asked Anderson why he went to the garage and started the car, with the garage door closed. Anderson claimed he constantly leaves his car started. The car was running when Officer Steinborn arrived.

Flanagan objected, saying the questions are getting repetitive, and Judge Goodman advised Croninger to move on.

Q. When law enforcement gets there, we see video. You're now wearing a do-rag, a jersey, an undershirt, necklaces, jeans, socks, and a pair of shoes. And we have testimony earlier from you that when Kyson fell you weren't wearing shoes.

A. I said I don't recall if I was wearing shoes.

Q. You weren't wearing shoes, you weren't wearing jeans. So after Kyson fell, you decided to put more clothes on?

A. OK.

Q. We also see you in the video at 5:05 yanking Kyson around the garage in your shoes, your jeans, your jersey and your other clothing. You testified today that you didn't have shoes and you didn't believe you had jeans on?

A. I told you I don't know exactly what I had on.

Q. After Kyson is unconscious, you took time to put shoes on and your Michael Vick Jersey back on?

Anderson was having a difficult time answering the questions from Croninger. DA Croninger questioned Anderson about what Kyson was wearing when lying on the floor. Anderson pled ignorance. There were more questions about Kyson being wet and about the floor being wet.

There was a dispute in testimony on the time frame in which Marcus was wearing shoes.

Q. How did you get so wet? You told Officer Scallon that your pants were wet multiple times. How did your pants get so wet?

A. I don't know how my pants got wet.

Q. Law enforcement tries their best to perform life-saving measures on Kyson and obviously, as we've seen, that's not successful. The ambulance leaves at 6:20 or so. You then remain at the house for a significant period of time. Is that right?

A. Yes.

Q. And your claim is that law enforcement told you that you should go to La Crosse?

A. Yes.

Q. We know that's not true from the video, right, because Sergeant Steinborn even offered to give you a ride to the hospital?

Anderson stuck to his story about the police telling him that Kyson is to be airlifted to La Crosse.

Q. It's 6:40, you get in your car and drive around the circle and come back?

A. Yeah. Because I forgot my wallet.

Q. And you got in the house and 10 minutes later, you still haven't left? Because you didn't leave the house until after 7:00 p.m.? So you took over 40 minutes to leave the house after Kyson left the house?

A. Well, actually, twice I was leaving. The first time, Amber pulled up and she told me to get Jessica some clothes and then go to La Crosse.

Q. And you even brought the suitcase you packed, didn't you?

Anderson explained that his suitcase was already packed from coming back from California and he didn't unpack. Said he had 20 pairs of shoes and had four suitcases when he went to California.

Croninger asked why his car was facing north, in the opposite direction that he would want to go to get on the Interstate to go to La Crosse. Anderson did not have a good answer. He claimed he pulled over in a safe area across from the Break Room and passed out. He cannot explain the fentanyl found on the $20 bill in his car or the fentanyl found on a straw in the house.

Q. You spoke to Investigator Walensky twice and you testified here today now for several hours and you still have no explanation as to what happened?

A. No, I do not.

Q. You have no clue how this child who was only in your care ended up with a massive injury to the top of his head, injuries to both sides of his head, to more than 200 bruises, to 40 bruises on his head alone, you have no explanation for that?

A. I didn't do it.

DA Croninger: I have no further questions.

DA Croninger cross examined Mr. Anderson for 3 hours and 40 minutes.

In redirect Defense Attorney Patrick Flanagan asked Anderson questions about the time Anderson left the house. Anderson said he was ill, his body was weak, vision was poor, and when he pulled over, he passed out. The redirect lasted about one minute. Judge Goodman told the defendant he could step down. It is 3:57 p.m. and Defense Attorney Flanagan told the Court he had no other witnesses.

Judge Goodman said, "I think what I'd like to do, and we've been working on the instructions as we've gone along and I think I have -- I know Mary (Mary Miller is Judge Goodman's assistant) has sent to both of you the most recent iteration of the instructions, but perhaps we can bid the jury adieu and we can do a little bit of that work now."

Judge Goodman told the jury they can leave their notebooks on their chairs. The jury was escorted out of the courtroom by the bailiff at 3:59 p.m.

For the next 40 minutes, Judge Goodman and the two attorneys discussed the wording of the instructions he will deliver to the jury. Both Croninger and Flanagan have drafts of the instructions and now it is a matter of updating and refining.

Issues involved absence of mistake or accident, bail jumping, intent, drugs charges, character evidence, and impeachment of a witness. One of the witnesses had been convicted of a crime, so that was discussed. Court recessed at 4:45 p.m.

Chapter 36

Jury Instructions

A strong spring weather system brought rounds of thunderstorms to the area on Tuesday, April 12, 2022. Scattered storms produced pea to ping pong ball sized hail over southern Minnesota into central Wisconsin during the afternoon. A total of nine tornadoes were documented in neighboring Minnesota and northern Iowa. The highest clocked winds were 130 mph. A rainstorm hit Sparta and Tomah around 3:00 p.m.

The stormy weather outside the Courthouse was perhaps a portent of the fate of Marcus Anderson, for on that date, April 12, a jury of 12 men and women would determine if he went free or to prison for a long, long time.

Judge Goodman, District Attorney Kevin Croninger and Assistant District Attorney Sarah Skiles, and Defense Attorney Patrick Flanagan were in Branch 2 at 8:55 a.m. to finalize the instructions to the jury. It was a late start to Court proceedings as Judge Mark Goodman had an 8 a.m. and an 8:30 a.m. session concerning guardianships. For 45 minutes, the Court officials dealt with the wording of Judge Goodman's upcoming instructions to the jury.

Judge Goodman said, "I want to take up something we talked about yesterday and that is the April 7th Defendant's Motion to Amend the Complaint. It's something he filed pro se (for himself) while I was unavailable last week. And I've read it a couple of different times and I want to make a ruling on that for the record and that as a threshold consideration, the motion is improper for a couple reasons. One is that it's unsupported by a notarized affidavit. Our local rules require that. And Mr. Anderson tried to satisfy that rule by making his own self-declaration that he's making the motion under the penalty of perjury, but it is not the equivalent of a notarized affidavit.

"The thrust of the motion involves emails from a supervisor at the State Crime Laboratory, and what the District Attorney explained yesterday that those emails were sent to the District Attorney because the District Attorney has to provide an explanation and reason why this lab has to test certain items of evidence.

"That supervisor was not called as a witness by the State. Other technicians who were employed by the crime lab and who did the analysis, did testify. They were subject to cross-examination by defense counsel. And so any possible testimony from the lab supervisor would either result in needless presentation of cumulative evidence or a waste of time. It's hard for the Court to wrap its head around this type of pro se motion, but for a lot of different reasons I'm denying it." It is clear what is going on here.

Anderson believed he could be his own attorney. Perhaps he is throwing a Hail Mary pass here, one that even his own attorney won't support, so feels he must do it on his own.

At 9:41 a.m. the State rested its case and DA Croninger asked for a brief break before bringing the jury in. The State will provide a hard copy of the Judge's Instructions to the jury. Judge Goodman said there was time because he wanted to talk to the jury before he read them their instructions. The jury is brought in at 9:53 a.m. The courtroom is tense.

Jury Instructions

Judge Goodman addressed the jury, "Remember ancient history, when you first came to Court, I talked to you about a pink checklist that I have of 23 different things I need to do to run a jury trial. We are now on

Checkpoint 15. What I need to do next is read Closing Instructions to you. There are 47 pages of Closing Instructions. You don't have to memorize them. You will get a written copy of the instructions."

Judge Goodman continued, "Once I get done reading these instructions, I will then ask the lawyers to give their closing arguments. What that means is you're not taking any more notes. Mr. Croninger, or Ms. Skiles, will go first. Mr. Flanagan will go second. Because the State has the burden of proof, the State gets to make what's called a rebuttal argument. Then we will swear in the bailiffs. We'll find out whom among you gets to go home early. The clerk will tumble the list. If you are that person, you can leave your phone number with the clerk, you can find out how this turned out, we'll have the clerk call you, and let you know what was decided in the case. Then you'll go in and get the case and you'll deliberate it. And once you come back and we'll read the verdict in open Court. I may ask you to raise your hands if I've read the verdict correctly and then your service will be done. So, members of the jury, the Court will now instruct you on the principles of law which you are to follow in considering the evidence and in reaching your verdict. Consider only the evidence received during the trial."

Judge Goodman started in with Count 1. It is not feasible to copy word for word all the instructions to the jury. After all, there are 47 pages and Judge Goodman requires 41 minutes to deliver the instructions.

Count 1 was the most important, so here it is in its entirety. "Count 1 of the information in this case charges Marcus W. Anderson with first degree intentional homicide of Kyson Rice on or about Friday, May 3rd, 2019, in the City of Tomah, Monroe County, Wisconsin.

First degree intentional homicide, as defined by the Criminal Code of the State of Wisconsin, is committed by one who causes the death of another human being with intent to kill that person or another.

Before you find the Defendant guilty of first-degree intentional homicide, the State must prove by evidence which satisfies you beyond a reasonable doubt that the following two elements were present:

No. 1, the Defendant caused the death of Kyson Rice. Cause means the Defendant's act was a substantial factor in producing the death.

Element No. 2, the Defendant acted with an intent to kill Kyson Rice. Intent to kill means the Defendant has the mental purpose to take the life of another human being or was aware his conduct was practically certain to cause the death of another human being.

The Defendant contends that he did not act with intent to kill Kyson Rice but rather what happened was an accident. If the Defendant did not act with intent to kill Kyson Rice required under first degree intentional homicide, the Defendant is not guilty of that crime.

Judge Goodman issues instructions to the jury who will decide the fate of Kyson's accused killer. Kyson was an intelligent lad with much potential and a full life ahead.

Before you may find the Defendant guilty of first-degree intentional homicide, the State must prove by evidence which satisfies you beyond a reasonable doubt that the Defendant acted with intent to kill Kyson Rice.

While the law requires the Defendant acted with intent to kill, it does not require that intent exist for any particular length of time before the act is committed. The act need not be brooded over, considered, or reflected upon for a week, a day, and hour, or even a minute. There need not be any appreciable time between the formation of the intent and the act. The intend to kill may be formed at any time before the act, including the instant before that act, and must continue to exist at the time of the act.

You cannot look into a person's mind to find intent. Intent to kill must be found, if found at all, from the Defendant's acts, words, and statements, if any, and from all the facts and circumstances in this case bearing upon intent.

Intent should not be confused with motive. While proof of intent is necessary to a conviction, proof of motive is not. Motive refers to a person's reason for doing something. While motive may be shown as a circumstance to aid in establishing the guilt of a Defendant, the State is not required to prove motive on the part of the Defendant. Evidence of motive does not, by itself, establish guilt. You should give it the weight you believe it deserves under all the circumstances.

If you are satisfied beyond a reasonable doubt that the Defendant caused the death of Kyson Rice with intent to kill, you should find the Defendant guilty of first-degree intentional homicide. If you are not so satisfied, you must find the Defendant not guilty.

To this charge, the Defendant has entered a plea of not guilty, which means the State must prove every element of the offense charge beyond a reasonable doubt." End of Count 1.

Judge Goodman moved right into Count 2: Physical abuse of a child which requires two full pages of instructions. Count 3 is a charge of possession of a firearm. Counts 4 through 7 and Counts 9 through 12 concern bail jumping. The elements of bail jumping include: Defendant was charged with a crime, the Defendant was released from custody on bond, and the Defendant intentionally failed to comply with the terms of the bond. One of those conditions was that the Defendant would commit no crime. Count 8 deals with the physical abuse of a child on April 29, 2019. Count 13 charges that Anderson operated a motor vehicle with a restricted controlled substance in his blood on or about May 3, 2019. Count 14 is a charge of possession of drugs, heroin, and fentanyl. Count 15 concerns Anderson's possession of THC on May 3, 2019. Count 16 deals with repeated Misdemeanor Intimidation of a witness, Regina Hall, on about March 4, 2022. Anderson tried to prevent her from testifying. Regina Hall was granted immunity, which means she cannot be charged with a crime based on testimony given during the trial.

Judge Goodman went over the usual admonitions to the jury, "The law presumes every person charged with the commission of an offense to be innocent. The burden of proof is on the State. Reasonable doubt means a doubt based upon reason and common sense. You are not to search for doubt, you are to search for truth."

Further instructions, "The District Attorney and Defense Counsel have stipulated or agreed to the existence of certain facts which you must accept as conclusively proved.

Number 1, on April 29th, 2019, Marcus Anderson had been charged with a crime and was released from custody on four separate bonds. A condition of the bonds was that Mr. Anderson, "Shall not commit any crime."

Number 2, on May 3rd, 2019, Marcus Anderson had been charged with a crime as was released from custody on four separate bonds. A condition of those bonds was that Mr. Anderson, "Shall not commit any crime."

Number 3, on May 3rd, 2019, Marcus Anderson was prohibited from possessing a firearm.

Number 4, on May 3rd, 2019, Marcus Anderson had previously been convicted of a drug offense, specifically misdemeanor possession of marijuana."

Judge Goodman told the jury about circumstantial evidence, the difference between intent and motive. Concerning the testimony of witnesses, Judge Goodman said, "In everyday life, you determine for yourselves the reliability of things people say to you. You should do the same thing here."

Chapter 37

Day 8: Croninger's Closing Arguments

District Attorney Croninger addressed the jury with his closing argument, requiring one hour and 40 minutes. It was a masterful presentation, covering all the bases, a complete review of the six days of the trial and needing 61 pages of transcript.

DA Croninger began, "Thank you, your Honor. Good morning, Ladies and Gentlemen. I want to start by thanking you for your attention and service over the last two-plus weeks. This is an extremely difficult case as far as the evidence that you have been required to view.

I thank you for your attention, as I noted to you when I was in front of you at the beginning of this trial, this is one of the things that makes this the greatest country in the world, and in my opinion, the greatest country in the history of the world, is that we have a process like this that a person like Mr. Anderson, even though he's accused of this heinous crime, is given the respect of this type of proceeding. So, I want to thank you for your service. I would also take the time to encourage you to be conscious of what this may cause you. There's a lot of difficult things you've had to look at, so I would encourage you, if you need to talk to someone about this, do that. These are difficult things we've been showing you, a lot of difficult images. So, thank you for your service.

In opening, Ms. Skiles told you this case was about numbers, and I want to focus on a couple of those numbers, 200, 5, and 1.

Two hundred, or almost 200, is the number of injuries that Kyson Rice had on his body. That tiny little three-year-old boy's body. 200.

Five. Five minutes from the time that Mr. Anderson called Ms. Rice to the time he called 911. Now, Mr. Anderson, you saw him on the stand yesterday, couldn't explain that, tried to make some excuse about the different phones. I'll show you the CAD, show you the number that called 911. That's in evidence. We'll show you that, we'll show you the number he was calling Ms. Rice from. Five minutes. Five minutes Kyson's non-responsive and he's calling Jessica, not calling 911. I want you to think about that and what that says about what he did to Kyson and what his intent was to do to Kyson.

A veteran prosecutor, DA Kevin Croninger, grilled Marcus Anderson relentlessly.

And one. There's only one reasonable explanation of what took place here. Mr. Anderson was alone with Kyson and he tortured Kyson and he killed that beautiful little boy. He did it intentionally. There's no other reasonable explanation. There is no other reasonable hypothesis. He can sit up on the stand and spew all the crap he wants. He can spew all the crap he wants to Investigator Walensky. He can talk and talk and talk and talk. He can say whatever the hell he wants. It doesn't change the evidence. It does not change the facts. It doesn't change the fact that he was alone with that little boy, and he tortured that little boy and that he killed him. So, I ask you to consider those things."

DA Croninger used a PowerPoint presentation. Because his closing argument was 61 pages of transcript, the highlights are presented in this narrative. He had 16 counts to deal with and obviously spent the most time on Count 1, first-degree intentional homicide. It was the overriding thrust of the trial.

Croninger emphasized intent, "The law requires that Mr. Anderson acted with intent for him to be found guilty. It doesn't require that he had some long-standing plan. The process of Kyson being tortured took time. Kyson didn't get 198 bruises on his body in one slip in the shower. He didn't get it from one slap. This took time. Kyson was a happy, healthy little boy until that man came into his life."

DA Croninger showed a photo on all courtroom screens as part of a PowerPoint. He played a video of Kyson being alive at 5:02 p.m. on May 3, 2019. Then another still shot of both Mr. Anderson and Kyson, noting the size difference between the two.

Croninger intoned, "Kyson is a little boy. Marcus is a fully-grown man, a large man, He is not a small human being. And that size difference helps to explain how he caused all those bruises to Kyson, how he was able to torture Kyson because he's so much bigger than Kyson. This is the kind of person Mr. Anderson is, a big tough guy when it comes to beating on three-year-olds."

Croninger continued, "Nineteen explanations he gives to Investigator Walensky, none of which align with what's on the autopsy. His body shows that Kyson was tortured. You don't torture someone unintentionally. He killed him intentionally."

DA Croninger took the jury through Dr. Stier's report, enumerating the bruises to Kyson's body. It was a devastating gut-wrenching account, with color photos, of the brutal beating Kyson took at the hands of Mr. Anderson. A few jurors briefly looked away from their computer screen. There were audible gasps. Some reached for tissues.

Croninger moved to the testimony of law-enforcement officers, "They went all the way to Arizona to search for the truth. They spend countless hours investigating this case to make sure that they got it right."

Although he did not have to prove motive, DA Croninger hinted at the mindset of Marcus Anderson on the day of the crime. He said, "There is ample evidence that Mr. Anderson was upset on the day he killed Kyson. He was upset he had to watch Kyson. There was turmoil in his relationship with Ms. Rice."

Croninger played a jail phone call Anderson made on May 26, 2019, 23 days after the murder. He's talking to his girlfriend, Regina Hall. "He repeatedly refers to Jessica Rice as 'that bitch.' It tells you what his mindset was that day. He was mad. He was upset. We also have evidence from his ex-wife that Mr. Anderson believed that children are his property. That he controls them. He decides if they live or die. And his decision that day was that Kyson would die. So he tortured him, and he killed him."

DA Croninger took the jury back to the day of the murder with a video of Jessica Rice leaving for work at 9:24 a.m. "She had to find a ride. Mr. Anderson didn't want to give her a ride. We heard that in the jail phone call. We see videos of Mr. Quarles coming and going twice. After that point at 11:57 a.m., Mr. Anderson is alone with Kyson until First Responders arrive."

Croninger played the text messages between Mr. Anderson and Jessica, showing there was extreme turmoil in that relationship. "Marcus has business to take care of. He's got stuff to do. Mr. Quarles is coming over. I believe the exact quote was, 'It fucked up my whole little day.' He kept texting her throughout the day. He's angry. She's not responding. He's used to Ms. Rice doing what he wants. That simple little bit of control he can't have. She won't respond to his text. It makes him mad, and he continues to text her. Eventually she ends up talking to him on the phone."

DA Croninger told the jury about the medical and physical condition of Marcus Anderson. "A text message at 4:01 p.m., 'I need help. I'm in pain. You know, I supposed to be on bed rest.'" We see him at Walgreens walking with a cane, hobbling like he's somebody who really struggles, and then we see him at McDonald's just walking around just fine. So ask yourself, does he actually have a physical issue that limits his mobility or is he just playing the victim well?"

A phone call from jail seven days after the killing is played. Anderson said he was going to knock out B'dag and his momma. Mr. Anderson mistakenly believes at that point in time, that B'dag has told law enforcement about the gun. B'dag hadn't, not at that time. Mr. Anderson thought he had done a good enough job of hiding it up on the shelf underneath all the blankets and thought he'd done a good enough job of hiding all the ammunition in the washing machine."

Croninger went back to those five minutes. He told the Court, "He waited five minutes to call 911. If he didn't do this harm to Kyson intentionally, why would he wait? You only wait if you're trying to figure out a way out of this. You call Jessica because he hopes she comes home and then he can blame her. He called Brandon and hoped he comes over so then he can blame him. He called Jeremy Devine, he hoped he can come over so he can blame him. He called Ashley Wankerl and hoped she'll come over so he can blame her."

Turning to the phone call to 911 (Exhibit 6), the CAD operation report showed the number that Marcus used to call 911, (920) 517-7422. "Mr. Anderson's testimony doesn't make any sense. He didn't take Kyson to the hospital, only a few minutes away. The ambulance got there in two minutes. Croninger emphasized the 5 minutes by pausing the proceedings for 5 minutes.

He then resumed, "Kyson leaves at 6:19, Mr. Anderson hasn't even gotten out of Jodi Circle until after 7:00 and at 7:50 is not at the hospital. He packed a suitcase that he left on the floor. When Officer Heckman is trying to get back in the house, Mr. Anderson's pants are half down. There is an iron plugged in. He drove around Jodi Circle and back. Anderson claims that he just wanted to go back and get his wallet. It's 6:44. He doesn't leave the house for at least another 15 minutes. His key lanyard says he was in the United States Marine Corps. He told just about everyone he met that he was in the Marine Corps. That is patently false. He told Investigator Walensky that he'd been through Afghanistan."

The inconsistency of what Marcus was wearing on May 3, 2019, is presented by DA Croninger. "He tells Investigator Walensky that he was down to his boxers and his socks. Yesterday when I asked him about that, he couldn't give a straight answer. Well, maybe I had my undershirt on. I know I had my chains and my do-rag on. Maybe I had my jeans on. I didn't have my shoes on. Before law enforcement got there, he decided he needed to put his Michael Vick jersey on.

Croninger continued, "He emptied the cupboard above the microwave, took out the trash, asked Amber Moseley to remove his gun, and he went back to the house for his wallet. We had testimony the cupboard door was closed. It was open when law enforcement came back. There were drugs in that trash. Officers offered Marcus a ride to the hospital. He refused. He says the Tomah PD hates him, that they are racist. Testimony shows that law enforcement people treated Marcus with the utmost respect."

It is now 11:42 a.m., and Croninger used about an hour and 15 minutes on Count 1 and now moved on to Count 2, physical abuse of a child. "It's very clear that when you are a six-foot-four 270-lb man and you are beating a three-and-a-half-foot tall child, that you're going to cause significant injuries to that child."

While showing multiple PowerPoint slides, Croninger continued, "Only three areas of Kyson's body was not bruised, his hands, the soles of his feet, and his genitals."

Count 3: Felon in possession of a firearm. Mr. Croninger said, "Ms. Rice told us she told Mr. Anderson to get the gun out of the house. What does he do? He hides it in a closet. He knew full-well the gun was there. That's part of the reason he didn't go to the hospital, he was worried about this gun."

Kyson at EAA show in Oshkosh.

There were eight felony ball jumping charges. "The stipulation of a bond is that Mr. Anderson is not to commit a crime while on bond. Four bail jumping charges are for the May 3 date and then there's four for when he punched Kyson at the hospital."

Count 13 was a charge of OWRCS, Operating with a Restricted Controlled Substance, Delta 9 THC and fentanyl were detected in his bloodstream. Croninger detailed all the places authorities found illegal drugs: on a $20 bill, plastic straw, garbage, and weighing scales.

Count 16 was intimidation of a witness for his conduct toward Regina Hall. In a March 4, 2022, phone call, Anderson told Regina Hall to plead the Fifth Amendment. Phone calls from Anderson to Hall are played, showing his threatening and demanding tone when he says that she should not come to testify.

At the end of his closing argument, Croninger intoned, "At 5:04 p.m. Kyson could walk around. By the time First Responders got there at 5:58, that is what his head looked like. (picture shown) He took that beautiful little boy and instead of nurturing that little boy and helping him grow up and letting the brain develop and letting him be a man, letting him grow to be a loving, caring child, instead of letting him grow to continue to bring smiles to all those people's faces, to his mother, to his family, instead of that, Marcus Anderson was alone with Kyson and tortured him and he killed him. I ask you to think about what he did to that beautiful little boy and convict him of what the evidence shows. Thank you."

It is 12:12 p.m. and it was another long, grueling morning for the principals in this case. A 15-minute recess was taken.

Flanagan Rebuttal

At 12:25 p.m., it was time for the closing argument from Mr. Flanagan. He talked about how sad it was to lose a boy so young and so full of life. Frankly, Defense Attorney Flanagan didn't have much to work with.

Flanagan told the court, "We're here to decide whether the State met its burden of proof in this case, and that burden is beyond a reasonable doubt. When they say that Mr. Anderson intended to kill, they had to prove that beyond a reasonable doubt. They haven't done that, but that's their burden."

He casted doubt on much of the testimony and went with Anderson's version of what happened in the early evening of May 3, 2019, at 1009 Jodi Circle, of Kyson being clumsy, of hearing a thud and Kyson lying on the floor, and how he tried to resuscitate Kyson.

He attacked the testimony of Anderson's former wife, Shelby Anderson, saying that she is bitter toward Marcus about what happened in their divorce and the custody battle.

Flanagan contradicted the testimony of how Kyson lost his front teeth, and about the hospital incident of Anderson hitting Kyson in the chest. He evoked the testimony of Cheryl Quarles who said in Court that Kyson told her that Marcus hit him in the chest, but Ms. Quarles did not see any marks and didn't report it to anyone. He touched on the drug evidence, the gun issue, and the intimidation charge.

Mr. Flanagan's 15-minute closing argument ends with, "do the job that you all promised you would do when we started this and that is to be fair jurors and render a verdict that's just and true. Thank you."

There is no lunch break today. At 12:41 p.m., Mr. Croninger began his 6-minute rebuttal of Mr. Flanagan's closing argument. Croninger stated, "Mr. Flanagan has a hard job. Mr. Anderson is entitled to have an attorney represent him and somebody has to do that job for him, and Mr. Flanagan has done a very good job for Mr. Anderson. Mr. Flanagan did not talk about the autopsy. Our system and our law require evidence, and we've presented that evidence. The Defense doesn't speak of evidence in his closing. He doesn't speak of the autopsy by a pathologist who has done over 4,000 autopsies after 17 years."

Final Instructions to the Jury

Judge Goodman gave the jury final instructions by showing and reading the verdict forms, "There are 16 counts, and each sheet has either not guilty or guilty for the foreperson to sign. The foreperson must sign each sheet in ink, not pencil."

Judge Goodman read each of the 16 Counts. He says, "This is a criminal, not a civil case. The verdict must be reached unanimously. When you retire, select one of your members to preside over your deliberations. If you need to communicate with the Court while you are deliberating, send a note through the bailiff signed by the presiding juror. If you have questions, the court will talk with the attorneys before answering, so it may take a little time to give you an answer. When you have agreed to the verdict, have them signed, and dated in ink by the person you have selected to preside. After you have reached a verdict, the presiding juror will notify the bailiff, Nick, that a verdict has been reached. Everyone will return to the courtroom. The verdict will be read into the record in open court. The Court may ask each one of you if you agree with the verdict.

The clerk swore in the bailiff at 1:08 p.m. Next, the alternate juror was dismissed. There were originally 14 jurors selected out of a pool of 80. One was dismissed due to an illness. The name drawn is Cheryl Jean Lakowke.

Judge Goodman told her, "If you want to give your phone number before you leave, we will have someone call you, hopefully not too late in the evening, and tell what happened in this case."

Judge Goodman continued, "The rest of the jurors will go with Nick to our jury room. We will have the clerk bring you some menus. We're going to feed you lunch, and so it takes a little while for the food to get here, so you should start your process while you wait for the lunch. And, Nick, I'm going to give you the verdicts. All right, now everyone stands for the jury." The jury exited the courtroom at 1:09 p.m. Court is recessed at 1:12 p.m. following some remarks by Judge Goodman.

Chapter 38

The Verdict

Family members and supporters of Jessica Rice met in a small room next to the District Attorney's offices. They could eat any lunch they brought with them. The mood was one of quiet anticipation, just small talk. At 3:16 p.m. the jury notified the Court that they have a question about count 8, "Are counts 9 through 12 (Felony Bail Jumping) in regards solely to count 8 (physical abuse of a child)?" The answer from the Court to the jury, "Yes."

At 3:40 p.m., the jury returned with a verdict, having deliberated for 2 hours and 30 minutes. The defendant, Marcus Anderson and his lawyer were present in the courtroom. A gallery of 25 people sat behind the prosecutor's table.

Judge Goodman said, "The jury has returned, and I've been told by the Bailiff that we have a verdict. Could you hand that to the Bailiff, the verdict, please?" The verdict is passed from the Bailiff to the Judge who read the verdict, "Okay, **Count 1:** We the jury, find the defendant, Marcus Anderson, guilty of first-degree intentional homicide of Kyson Rice, as charged in Count 1 of the Information, signed by the jury foreperson today." There is an audible gasp of "yes" in the courtroom, and a few sighs of relief. Marcus appears emotionless. Defense Attorney Patrick Flanagan puts his hand on Marcus' shoulder.

"**Count 2:** We, the jury, find the Defendant, Marcus Anderson, Guilty of physical abuse of a child, Kyson Rice, intentionally causing great bodily harm, as charged in Count 2 of the Information. Signed by the jury foreperson dated today."

Judge Mark L. Goodman insured that jurors and witnesses felt comfortable.

Judge Goodman read the verdict of all 16 Counts.

Count 3: Guilty of felon in possession of a firearm.

Counts 4 through 7: Guilty of bail jumping, and all occurring on May 3, 2019, the day of the murder.

Count 8: Physical abuse of a child, Not Guilty.

Count 9 through 12: bail jumping, concerning events on April 29, 2019, Not Guilty.

Count 13: Operating with a restricted controlled substance, Guilty.

Count 14: Possession of a narcotic drug, Guilty.

Count 15: Possession of THC, Guilty.

Count 16: Misdemeanor intimidation of a witness, Guilty.

The scorecard is 12 Guilty and 4 Not Guilty. The big one, Count 1, is the one everyone cares about, Guilty of First Degree Intentional Homicide.

Finally, at end of the verdict for Count 16, Judge Goodman asked, "If the jury, if I have correctly read your verdicts, please raise your hand." All 12 hands went up. "Is there a request that I poll the jury? Mr. Croninger declined, as did Mr. Flanagan.

Judge Goodman addressed the jury, "All right. This will conclude our jury service in this case. I know that you are eager to return home. I ask that you gather for just a few moments in the jury room. I'd like to talk to you privately before you leave. Thank you very much."

Mr. Flanagan asked the court for a Motion of Acquittal notwithstanding the verdicts. In other words, Mr. Flanagan was asking the judge to overturn the jury's findings of guilt.

Flanagan's motion was denied. Judge Goodman said that he is not going to invade the province of the jury. Mr. Croninger asked that the PowerPoint he used on a disc be entered as Exhibit 45.

It was 3:46 p.m. on April 12, 2022. The trial was over after 8 days, 41 witnesses, 2016 pages of transcript, 396,000 words, at a cost of, well, a lot.

Remarks Heard in Hallway

It was common practice for the judge to dismiss the relatives and friends of the "winning side" first, so they may clear the courtroom. A few minutes later, the judge would allow the "losing side" to vacate the courtroom. The idea was to have a bit of separation in case there was some bad blood between courtroom spectators.

Yes, there were some comments and quips picked up by an attentive listener.

"Good riddance."

"I hope he gets the death penalty." Note: Wisconsin does not have a death penalty.

"He got what he deserved."

"It was the only verdict the jury could possibly come up with."

Interview with Jurors

Two jurors graciously agreed to be interviewed. In August 2023, I had an excellent talk with Mackenzi Pearson at her place of employment, Murray's on Main, in downtown Tomah. Mackenzi graduated from Tomah High in 2014. Some takeaways from the interview: She, like all the others, kept a journal, but had to turn it in at the end of the trial. The jury foreman was selected by vote after deliberations were completed, but she didn't remember who it was. They went around the room and discussed each count and the evidence in each count. An evening meal was brought in and they kept right on discussing while they ate. There was no doubt about Marcus Anderson's guilt. They thought the evidence on bail jumping was insufficient to convict. Judge Goodman talked to the jury after the trial, thanked them for their service. She received $190 for being on the jury, and $300 for mileage. Note: Jurors are paid, but the enumeration is very small considering the hours required.

On January 15, 2024, I talked to Jessica Clark, who worked at the BP Mini Mart on Clifton Street in Tomah. Some tidbits from that interview: It was her first time serving and she was thrilled to be chosen to be on the jury. She noted that only one person came to support Anderson and was only there for about 10 minutes the first day before leaving. Jessica Clark took many notes during the trial but did not have to go back and rely on them. Deliberations were held up on the bail jumping charge and the second child abuse charge, Kyson being hit by Anderson in the hospital room. She had kept in contact with Mackenzi Pearson, who comes in as a customer. She put a stone gift on Kyson's grave and told other jurors about it. She felt that Regina Hall was brainwashed and was socially backward or inept. Jessica Clark felt that Regina Hall's testimony was powerful, the same with Dr. Stier's. She said that Anderson made friends, girls, with those he thought he could control. She found Anderson to be an annoying person. She thought that Croninger and Skiles did a great job and she perhaps wanted Skiles to do the examination of Anderson, rather than Croninger, because Anderson resented women in general and especially strong women. She was surprised that the cane was not introduced in testimony, because the wounds appeared to have come with the beating by a cane.

Chapter 39

Victim Impact Statements

I attended the sentencing for Marcus Anderson on June 29, 2022, at the Monroe County Justice Center in Sparta. It was a bright sunny day at 8:45 a.m., temperature at 80 degrees and climbing, when I entered. The two guards just inside the door screened all who entered. The infrared thermal imaging device to read your forehead temperature had finally been removed as COVID restrictions were being lifted. Previously, a person entering the building stood on two outlines of a person's feet on the floor, looked at the device, and in two seconds, there was a readout of your body temperature. You placed your laptop carrying bag on the rollers, and put your billfold, keys, and iPhone in a plastic bowl and through the machine they went—just like at the airport.

I climbed the stairs to the second floor. A dozen people were in the hallway waiting for the doors to Circuit Court Branch 2 to open. I spotted John Glynn, great-uncle of Kyson Rice, and Steve Rundio, ace news reporter for the Lee Enterprise newspaper group, mostly out of La Crosse. Mr. Rundio covered the crime beat for western Wisconsin. His plate was always full.

The doors opened at 8:55 a.m. and the interested filed in. Most are friends and relatives of Kyson Rice and sat on the right-hand side, behind the seats of the District Attorney and his staff. I took a seat next to Rundio. Rob Walensky, retired Tomah police detective and now heading the West Central Metropolitan Enforcement Group (WMEG), is among the throng. Jessica Rice, Kyson's mother, was comforted by close friends. This would be the day of reckoning for the killer of her son. People attending were wearing a white bracelet that said, "Kyson's voice" and T-shirts that said, "Every child has a voice."

Marcus Anderson, clad in prison orange, was seated on the left side along with his attorney, Patrick Flanagan. Two marshals are seated behind Anderson. Railings separated the Court officials from the spectators.

In the back right was a small media room with a large window. Cameras had been set up to record the proceedings. Channel 19, from La Crosse, was covering the sentencing. The substitute court reporter, Susan Geiger, was from New Richmond. The court reporter occupied an open cubicle near the Judge's bench. There was a big flat-screen television on the back wall, visible to the jury, judge, court reporter, and spectators. Forty people await Judge Goodman.

It had been 78 days since the jury brought a guilty verdict in 11 of the 16 counts against Marcus Anderson. Count 1 was the big one, Guilty of First-Degree Intentional Homicide. Friends and relatives did not seem to care much about the felony bail jumping, possession of a firearm, or possession of narcotics charges. They wanted to see life imprisonment without the possibility of parole. That was the best they could hope for, since Wisconsin does not have the death penalty.

Judge Goodman called the Court to order at 9:00 a.m. Judge Goodman has an informal and relaxed style, tending to put the entire courtroom at ease. But there was palpable tension in the air. This was the day family and friends of Jessica Rice have been looking forward to.

Judge Goodman asked DA Croninger, Mr. Flanagan, and Mr. Anderson if they have read the Pre-Sentence Investigation (PSI). Marcus Anderson disputed the opinions of the writer, but not the factual content.

Judge Goodman asked Assistant DA Sarah Skiles if there are any victims that wish to address the court. She replied in the affirmative: Lieutenant Jarrod Furlano, Officer Wilbert Steinborn, John Glynn, and Jessica Rice.

Lt. Furlano was first. At the time of the killing, Jarrod Furlano was a sergeant. He had been promoted to lieutenant. His statement was a powerful testament about how this murder case had affected law enforcement personnel. Here is his statement in its entirety:

"At the time of Kyson's murder, my daughter, Sienna, was two and a half years old. The day Kyson was killed, and my shift was done, first thing I did when I saw Sienna was give her the biggest hug I'd ever given and cry. Sienna was too young to understand that her dad, who was supposed to be a tough cop and took bad people to jail, was crying in front of her.

Sienna is now five and a half years old. She's hilarious. She is smart. She lights up every room she is in. She brings joy, cares for others, and makes friends easily. She is Daddy's girl through and through. If you look up pure innocence in the dictionary, Sienna's picture would be there. I've had the opportunity to watch Sienna grow the last three years. She's grown into a great big sister, into a child who loves art, singing, and dancing. She enjoys going to school and learning everything possible. She's the light of my life, and my greatest accomplishment as a human being.

That man robbed Kyson of the opportunity to have the same impact on his family, his friends, and the community. In the few short hours I was with Kyson, he changed me as a cop, as a father, and as a person. And it makes me wonder what Kyson could have done with more time with us. Kyson had approximately 200 individual injuries to his body: bruises, knocked out teeth, and multiple skull fractures. The abuse of Kyson wasn't done in an instant. It was done over the course of several days. Over that time Kyson endured unimaginable misery culminating in his death.

In my 15 years of law enforcement, nothing has scarred me more or caused me more nightmares than this incident. There is no penalty stiff enough. No sentence long enough, and no prison hard enough that can ever provide justice to Kyson. And none of those can compare to the unfathomable acts committed by that man. Kyson's future was just as bright and had just as much potential as Sienna's, and that future is gone, never to return. Kyson's future on this earth is now dark and lonely, due to the unspeakable action of him (pointing to Anderson).

I feel selfish. I get the privilege to experience Sienna throughout her entire life, while Kyson's family will forever have to experience him through memories. After my feelings of selfishness passes, it quickly turns into feelings of sadness. Sadness that I couldn't do more to save Kyson. Sadness that I wasn't fast enough, trained enough, or skilled enough to bring him back. Then comes feelings of anger and rage. Anger that there are people in this world like him that are capable of such despicable acts against children, and rage that there aren't enough penalties available to properly avenge Kyson's murder.

I hope the Court sees fit to impose the maximum penalties allowed by law, because that is only a fraction of what he deserves. While there is no punishment that can ever bring Kyson back, every second of his life from this day forward should be dark and lonely and filled with unimaginable misery, just like what he caused Kyson."

Judge Goodman: "Who would you like to call next?"

Skiles replied, "The State calls Officer Wilber Steinborn."

Here are excerpts of Officer Steinborn's address to the court:

"He (Anderson) knew what he was doing and knew it was wrong. He failed to take responsibility for his actions on that day. By not admitting guilt, he has subjected jurors, court staff, and you, Sir, to relive these instances and his unspeakable acts. The pain, terror, and torture that he caused resulted in the death of Kyson. He needs to be removed from society. He is not correctable. He is not savable, and because of this, he deserves life without parole."

John Glynn, Kyson's great-uncle was next, providing a powerful emotional narrative. Here are excerpts:

"Marcus Anderson is a highly manipulative predator who demands all the attention. Marcus is very creative. He came up with 19 different explanations for this crime.

At approximately 6:00 p.m. on May 3, 2019, I received a phone call forever seared in my brain. I was on my lawnmower. I know the exact spot that I heard my wife, Jolene, making the sound of an agonizing cry, as if her very soul was being ripped out. And I'm continually reminded of that cry every night that she has a bad dream. Wakes me right out of sleep."

Glynn does a countdown of the blows to Kyson's body. "So face. One, two, three, four and up to 16. Then mouth 17-23, and John Glynn proceeds through mouth, head, right arm, left face, legs, chest, back, buttocks, and finally ribs."

The John Glynn hangar at the Tomah airport. A statement about the value of human life.

Glynn finishes with, "I sincerely thank you, Your Honor, for this horrendously difficult trial. And please protect society from evil. No parole ever, please, thank you."

The final speaker was Assistant DA Sarah Skiles, delivering a statement written by Jessica Rice. A photo of Kyson is on the television screens while Ms. Skiles speaks. Excerpts follow.

"My handsome, loving, caring, funny son is no more and it is extremely difficult to digest."

Choking up and holding back tears, Skiles narrative continues as she relays Jessica Rice's words about coming home on May 3, how the police told her what happened, "The thought of you treating my son like a ragdoll and continuing to cause more pain and injury leaving his lifeless body in such a way that words cannot explain. Since you took my son's life, I will never get to experience any of his firsts." She goes on to express the loss of kindergarten, first sporting events, first date, going to college and getting married, first job, becoming a grandma.

Continuing, the letter read, "That night, not only did you take my world from me, you took my ability to trust and have faith in anyone. I am no longer able to hold a healthy relationship, because of what you have done. This is a pain no parent should ever have to feel."

Skiles Sentencing Argument

Assistant DA Skiles moved into her sentencing argument, starting with several slides and videos. There were slides of Spiderman, a helicopter ride, a vinyl sticker placed on Kyson's casket, a slide of John Glynn at the airfield and with Kyson on a bike, and a video of Kyson playing.

"I'm asking the Court to send Marcus to prison for the rest of his life without the possibility of parole, to send Mr. Anderson to the maximum, consecutive sentences on all of the counts that he's been convicted of."

Skiles recounted the testimony of Dr. Stier, "Two hundred bruises. Forty-three blows to the head. How many of those did he feel? Did he ask Marcus Anderson to stop? Did he scream? Did he cry? Did he ask for his mother? Did he wonder why the person who was supposed to be his father, was doing this to him?

"On a jail call that was played at the trial, Mr. Anderson indicated to the person that he was on the phone, and he was angry that day. He was angry, because he had some business that he needed to be taken care of that day, and he was not expecting to have anyone at the house that day. That's it. That's the reason that Kyson Rice died was because Mr. Anderson needed to take care of some business.

"After Mr. Anderson beat Kyson nearly to death, and he realized that this is a very bad situation, he didn't call 911. He called at least four people that we know of before calling to get help for Kyson. He called Brandon Crampes and said that Kyson was hurt. He asked Brandon to come over. Brandon told him to call 911. He called Ashely Wankerl. She didn't answer, so we don't know what Mr. Anderson would have said to her, but Mr. Anderson called her, nonetheless. Anderson called Jeremy Devine and said that Kyson fell off the thing and hit his head. That Kyson was injured. That he was hurt and that he was dying. What time did that phone call happen? We don't know. But what if Mr. Anderson had called for an ambulance at that time? Would that have made a difference? Could Kyson have been saved at that time? And finally, Mr. Anderson called Jessica. He called her several times. He first called her at 5:50 p.m. Then again at 5:52 and 5:54. The phone call to 911 didn't happen until 5:55 p.m. These are precious minutes. Minutes, that perhaps, could have changed the outcome in this case for Kyson.

"The Court needs to know everything about a Defendant when they're sentencing someone. It is incredibly rare for there to be no positive aspects, or attributes, of a Defendant that I can talk about. But there are absolutely no positive characteristics to Marcus Anderson.

"He is a 37-year-old man and has done nothing positive with his life. Outside of the criminal convictions in this case, he has eight other criminal convictions, some of which were referenced by the Agent in the PSI (Pre-sentence Investigation). The armed robbery conviction from 2008 was mentioned. Mr. Anderson, also, has a prior conviction for the possession of marijuana from 2008. There was then

Assistant District Attorney Sarah Skiles was named the 2023 Wisconsin Assistant District Attorney of the Year.

approximately a 10-year period where Mr. Anderson did not have any criminal convictions, significantly due to the fact that he was incarcerated in the State of Arizona. His next criminal conviction was for battery, felony fleeing, felony bail jumping, disorderly conduct, and then resisting. Nearly all of his convictions have resulted in either prison sentences or lesser periods of confinement. He has been in custody as a result of this case and other cases for the last three years. He went to prison in 2008, when he was in his early 20's. He was then released in 2014 or thereabouts, and he was out of custody for approximately five years before committing crimes here. He essentially spent less than a decade of this adult life out of custody, and that doesn't even take into account the reference to the fact that Mr. Anderson had juvenile interactions with the criminal justice system in another state.

"Mr. Anderson has little or no work history. He is significantly undereducated, and if someone wrote a story about his life, it would say this, 'Marcus Anderson is an untruthful, selfish, violent predator who takes advantage of and manipulates those weaker than him. And is someone who blames the consequences of all of his actions on other people.'

"I noticed in the PSI that Anderson appeared to be bragging to the agent that he wouldn't accept employment for less than $32 an hour. That is incredibly hard to swallow when we know Jessica Rice was working, the sole provider for their household during the time period that she and Kyson were residing with Mr. Anderson.

"Another comment from the PSI about Mr. Anderson's character was that he indicated he has been watching children since he was nine years old, and no one ever got hurt. We heard Ms. Shelby Anderson testify at trial about what Mr. Anderson did to their child when their child was only three months old. Mr. Anderson has a pattern of using physical abuse and physical punishment to the children that are in his care.

"Mr. Glynn mentioned Mr. Anderson's 19 different explanations for what happened to Kyson that he asserted at trial that Kyson fell in the shower. That he was light skinned. That he bruises easily. He falls a lot. Mr. Anderson did bad CPR. Kyson has seizures. He had a rash. He had an infection. There was something wrong with his brain. He had a blood disorder. Kyson's gums bleed a lot when he brushes his teeth. Other people did it. It was Grandpa. Kyson does crazy things in his bedroom. It was the First Responders. Kyson's father did it. Jessica did it. Jolene did it. John Glynn did it. It's because Mr. Anderson is black. The police treated Mr. Anderson with the upmost respect."

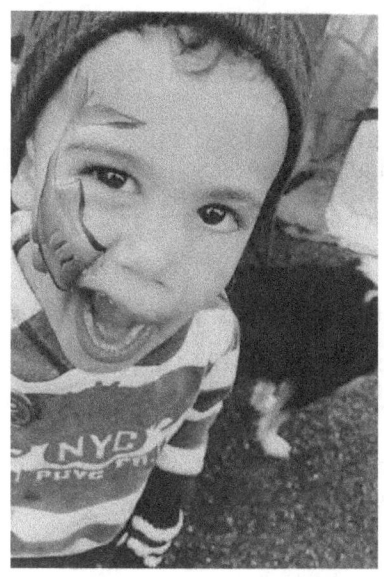

Kyson on vacation at Bayfield, WI Applefest in October 2018.

Ms. Skiles told the Court that any number of people have regrets or misgivings about their actions or lack of, centering on the concept, "'What more could I have done?' Officers Steinborn and Furlano wondering if they had been more skillful, a family member was told by Kyson that Anderson kicked his teeth out. Cheryl Quarles telling the Court about Kyson revealing to her that he wished Marcus Anderson could just tell him not to do something instead of hitting him. And John Glynn indicating at some level of, 'Why didn't I see this?'

"When the ambulance called ahead to the hospital, to let the hospital know that they had a pediatric code, one of the doctors told some of the staff members, 'It's too beautiful of a day for a three-year-old to die. Let's do our best.' The hospital staff remembers Kyson. The cops remember Kyson.

"This case has a significant impact on everyone that's involved. When we contacted Ms. Shelby Anderson, Mr. Anderson's ex-wife, about coming here from out of state to testify in this case, she had some very choice words for us that involved her yelling at me and calling me names. She didn't want to come here. She was scared. She wanted nothing to do with this case. But at the end of the day, a significant part of that boiled down to even guilt that she felt. She was the victim in the case in La Crosse County that Mr. Anderson was on bond for at the time of this offense. And a lot of her yelling at me in the beginning was 'I told you people that this was going to happen.' And when she said, 'you people,' she meant the criminal justice system. 'I told you Marcus was going to hurt someone, but you didn't believe me.'"

Ms. Skiles pulled up slide #11. It was a rendering of Kyson of what he would look like today, at age 6, put together by a professional who does age progression photos.

"Kyson's family has a life sentence, Judge. No matter what we do here today, Kyson's not coming back. Jessica Rice has told you in explicit detail about her life sentence. The firsts that she's not going to get, because of Mr. Anderson. This is essentially the last photograph that she has of Kyson's life. She's not going to have school pictures. She's not going to have sports pictures. She won't have wedding pictures, and she's not going to have grandchildren, later on, that look like Kyson. Kyson has a life sentence. There is no getting out for Kyson, or for Ms. Rice or Mr. Glynn.

"I'm asking the Court to impose a life sentence without parole, without the possibility of parole, so that they don't have to count the years down. So that, when we leave Court today, they can continue with their life. That they can remember Kyson and they can remember the good times. And that they don't ever have to worry or count how many years until it is that Mr. Anderson is going to become eligible for parole.

"Judge, I'm asking the Court to impose the maximum penalty so that they can rest. This has been an incredibly long process. And it's hard for any family to lose a loved one, but it is incredibly hard in this case because of how young Kyson was. How much life he had left, how many opportunities he should have that he won't have. Judge, please send Marcus Anderson to prison for the rest of his life without the possibility of parole. Thank You."

Mr. Flanagan Replies

Without hesitation, Judge Goodman said, "Mr. Flanagan." Patrick Flanagan addressed the Court, "Well, Your Honor, the job of a Defense attorney is, I think, most difficult at these times. Where there's been a trial, and the Defendant is insistent on his innocence and the Defense Attorney tried to persuade a jury to agree with that and they haven't. And now we have to do a sentencing hearing and the Defendant is taking the position that this is injustice. I have been wrongly convicted. And I'm still supposed to make a sentencing argument.

Yes, everyone in Courtroom 2 realized that Mr. Flanagan has an impossible task. He pointed out the Anderson is entitled to a trial, that Anderson was very respectful during the trial, that he had the right to appeal, that he felt bad and sad about what happened to Kyson.

Flanagan asked the Court for a sentence of 35 years, so Anderson would be eligible for parole at age 72, saying, "That a person can go through a process of recognizing mistakes that they've made. And if given the opportunity to get back into society to do something. To give back something."

Chapter 40

The Guilty One Speaks

Judge Goodman asked Mr. Anderson if he had anything to say before he pronounced the sentence.

Anderson responded, "Yes, there is, Judge." From a yellow-lined paper Marcus Anderson read his written narrative, "We are here today for my sentencing in this matter. I'm not happy to be here, nor do I want to. But I do truly apologize to the family of Kyson. Due to my appeal of my conviction, I can only say so much about this case.

"What I can say is that this is a very sad day, especially on May 3, 2019, when Ky died. Who in their right mind would want a child to die? I hate that this happened. Every day I think of him. And many nights I shed tears about this. Not just because I'm accused of his death, and unfortunately, he is no longer here. And it hurts to have a child die. I could only imagine the pain that Jessica, or any other parent feels or the extent of the pain because I have never lost a biological child. And don't ever want to lose a child.

"I send my prayers to the family. And to the families who lost 19 children in Uvalde, Texas, to gun violence. That was very tragic. I asked a lot every day for forgiveness. For anything I have sinned for. I have struggled with this every day to seek to more understand of what happened. And what I told this Court.

Tomah Police Officer Brennon Scallon was with Anderson from arrest to prison processing.

"I remember to the best of knowledge what happened. Trust me if I had any more information to give to the Court, the family, I would. Why would I lie? Or why would I mislead anybody. That is very dumb. To the people who really know me, I never would want to harm a child. Not only that, why wouldn't I own up to it if I did it. What do I have to lose. I hear people say things like we want justice. What is justice? By having me locked up is not justice, because it doesn't bring Kyson back. I wish every day that I could bring him back. I would give my life for him to come back. I had a chance to live a good life. He doesn't, and it pains me deeply to the core. It is very heartbreaking that he doesn't get to grow up and choose a life he wants to live.

"To Jess, I have known you for quite some time. We have some history together. It was good for the most part. You know Ky was my little man. He wanted to be with me all the time. We had some fun times. This is very tragic. That we could achieve this. I feel for you each and every day. I pray that you find some comfort. They say with time we heal. But I don't think that's true. I still haven't healed since my mom died, and both of my grandmothers are dead. I try to cope, and you have seen me hurt, cry, go through pain, and it was private. That's how I am. I can't just show my feelings in front of a bunch of strangers. But I hurt a lot. I wish I could just give you a big hug and tell you I'm sorry for your loss. And in case you didn't know, I'm still crazy about you. Peace and blessings.

"Judge, I ask that you allow me to get parole. I feel that I still have some good to do in this world. To speak to young men about choices in life and mistakes, drugs, gangs, etcetera, things to learn from. I'm not a monster or a violent person. I'm just misunderstood. No matter where I'm at, I will be a voice to young men who is heading down a dark path. I just had a conversation with my sons and my daughter about decisions that they make in their young lives. To learn from my mistakes. Don't be like me. Be better than me. I told them I would be there for them the best I could from behind these walls. To give the best advice I can. And I have failed you by not being a great support system, not financially. I always bought shoes because they're materialistic things. But to teach my boys how to be men. And I'll take full responsibility for those failures. And my daughter, daddy's little girl, who needed me and still does, I have failed. They say every man is a hero of his own story, but this is not how I want my story to end. Allahu Akbar. Allahu Akbar. (Allah is greater than all) That's all I got to say."

Chapter 41

The June 29th Sentencing

Judge Goodman said, "We're here in Case number 19CF353. The jury returned a verdict finding Mr. Anderson guilty of the following counts." Judge Goodman read Counts 1-7 and 13-16. Judge Goodman continued, "The jury returned not guilty verdicts on Counts 8-12."

"If sentenced consecutively on all these Counts, the Defendant's exposure is life in prison without parole, plus an additional 113 years after that, and maximum fines totaling approximately $195,000.

There are certain factors that comprise this Court's sentencing calculus. I look at age. Mr. Anderson is 37 years old. In a week, he will have his 38th birthday.

I look at education. According to the Pre-Sentencing Investigation (PSI_, he told his agent he attended two high schools in California and received a high school diploma in 2001. As a juvenile in California, he reported he got into some trouble and was sent to a camp where he says he earned a welding certificate.

I do consider employment. Mr. Anderson has been continuously incarcerated since 2019. He was released from Wisconsin State prisons in 2021, and immediately transferred to our county jail. And he's been held there ever since under a case bond.

Before going to prison, he reports he worked in Arizona for Sun City West Recreation. He said he gained experience working with a Master Electrician. He reports he completed an electrician apprenticeship in two years. He expressed a desire, to the Agent writing the pre-sentence, to work toward the credentials of a Master Electrician.

I do look at criminal history. Mr. Anderson is no stranger to the Court system. He has an unenviable criminal history. In 2008, he was convicted in Arizona of Armed Robbery with a Dangerous Weapon. The Arizona Court sentenced him to seven years in prison.

After serving his Arizona prison sentence, he came to Wisconsin. In 2017, he was charged in a La Crosse County case. In that case, he pled No Contest to the Class H Felony False Imprisonment as a Repeater. According to the Criminal Complaint in that case, Mr. Anderson's now ex-wife, Shelby Anderson, who was a witness in this case, told police he threw a syrup bottle at her, that he slapped her three or four times with an open hand. She said he slammed her head into a mirror and that she had to pick pieces of broken glass out of her head. She told police that he split open her lip while beating her. She quoted him as saying, 'I'm this close to killing you, bitch.' On March 25, 2019, Judge Gonzalez withheld sentence and placed Mr. Anderson on probation for four years.

In Monroe County case 2017-CF-727, which pre-dates this case, he pled No Contest to felony bail jumping and vehicle operator fleeing or eluding police. On the felony bail jumping charge, Judge Todd Ziegler sentenced him to three years and four months in prison, with 16 years (sic) to be served in initial confinement.

The Pre-sentence Investigation reports he has other Arizona convictions for possession of marijuana, drug paraphernalia, felony endangerment, and aggravated assault with a dangerous weapon. It further reports he had a 2002 conviction of possession of narcotics.

One factor the Court closely looks at is victim impact. In a word, it's severe. Kyson Rice's life was snuffed out before his fourth birthday and the Court cannot fathom a more severe impact. A young boy, described by his family as loving, kind, and generous, murdered in his own home.

Kyson lies in peace in Oak Grove Cemetery in Tomah.

His mother, Jessica, is a living victim. She told the agent she struggles with PTSD and suffers flashbacks and nightmares, and we heard more about that today from, I believe, Ms. Skiles. Jessica has sought counseling and reports that she has been placed on medication. She said at times she has missed work, because she has been physically unable to go to work. Fortunately, her employer understands and is sympathetic.

She says, and rightly so, she feels cheated out of not being able to watch her son grow up, witness his first day of school, watch him play sports, graduate from high school, and become a man. And she doesn't believe she would ever be able to have another child out of fear of what might happen to that child. She commented that it was very difficult during the trial to view the photos of her son's autopsy. And she concluded that she not only lost Kyson, she lost everything, including the ability to trust others.

The agent spoke to Kyson's great uncle, Mr. John Glynn, who personally gave a statement this morning. During her childhood, Jessica lived with Mr. Glynn for an extended period of time, and he became, later, well acquainted with Kyson. He said he and family members struggle with guilt regarding how they could have helped or done things differently. And to him, Mr. Glynn, and to Jessica, the Court says, 'It's not your fault. It's not your fault.' The victim impact is extremely severe. It is an aggravating factor in the Court's sentencing calculus.

John Glynn, great uncle of Kyson Rice, attended every hearing and every day of the trial, including sentencing.

The Court does consider the vicious and aggravated nature of the offenses. The First Degree Intentional Homicide and Child Abuse causing Great Bodily Harm were vicious and aggravated offenses. Testifying for the State was Dr. Michael Stier. He is a forensic pathologist and medical doctor. And starting in 2001, he was employed by the UW-Medical School as an Associate Professor of Forensic Pathology. He performed Kyson's autopsy. He testified he had performed between 4,000 and 5,000 autopsies over an approximate 20-year career. Additionally, he testified he'd either assisted or observed another 15,000 to 20,000 autopsies.

When Kyson Rice was pronounced dead, he was three years and eight months old. He weighed 36 pounds and was almost three and a half feet tall, according to the autopsy report. The first finding and diagnosis in that report is Battered Child, acute and extreme. Specifically, the autopsy found Kyson suffered extreme inflicted blunt trauma, beating, and shaking or impact cranial deceleration injury. Some of his lesions or visible injuries were patterned. This parallel pattern of injury indicated to Dr. Stier that a physical weapon or object was used. He ruled Kyson's demise constituted a child homicide.

His autopsy report said he counted on the body 198 bruises. He testified this was a conservative total. He testified none of the bruises were old, but they were acute or recent bruises to the boy. He said the bruises are of a similar color. They are fresh. They are new. Noting the term acute means fresh or new. The overwhelming majority of the bruises were either pink or a shade of pink, and that's because they all were fresh. He was satisfied that the overwhelming majority of the injuries were caused in a similar time frame. Dr. Stier testified he had never seen that many bruises on a child in his nearly 20 years of performing autopsies.

He said he was 'probably shocked' at the number of injuries sustained. He testified Kyson's lips were lacerated and the inside of the child's mouth was freshly torn. He said these lacerations and tears were created from pressure from outside of the mouth in contact with the inner part of the mouth, namely the teeth and jawbone. Kyson's frenulum was torn. The frenulum is a specific part of the anatomy. It's located inside the upper lip. One feels the frenulum by placing the tip of the tongue between one's upper teeth and the inside of the upper lip. A torn frenulum is a special injury. Dr. Stier testified it implies a direct blow to the mouth as opposed to an injury sustained by falling on your face. To quote his testimony. 'To lacerate the frenulum is considered a hallmark of striking of the face, particularly the mouth.'

He testified the child had sustained a right fourth rib fracture. He said this is another hallmark of a child-abuse type of injury. According to the doctor, this rib injury implies a fair amount of force, because children's ribs are softer than an adult's. They tend to bend before they break. Quoting his testimony, 'So a rib fracture in a child is special, because the ribs tend to bend. So, when you have a fracture, it implies a significant degree of force.

Dr. Stier's examination of the child's brain discovered a quantity of blood from a subdural hematoma. He said there should not have been any blood in that space next to Kyson's brain. He said there was about 100 cc of blood in the brain, and it was fresh. He compared that amount of blood to the liquid volume of one-third of a 12-oz can of soda. The doctor testified a subdural hematoma can be sustained by direct impact to the skull. He said a child's skull is softer than an adult's. He said the child's brain injury potentially was caused either by a blow to the head or possibly by shaking.

His testimony indicated the force of a blow or shaking will cause the brain to move inside the skull and tear blood vessels. That causes subdural hemorrhage. Quoting Dr. Stier, 'Because of the extent and nature of the trauma to the head in Kyson's case, I can't say whether his subdural hemorrhage is from direct impact or from shaking or from both.'

Both of Kyson's eyes were removed during the autopsy. The autopsy detected retinal hemorrhaging in both eyes. Dr. Stier testified Kyson sustained an extensive ocular injury, which he regarded as a marker of a shaken baby injury. Dr. Stier indicated the body had three lesions on the back of the leg that were parallel, indicating that they were the result of a tool, or device.

Witnessing the autopsy was a Tomah police detective. He and Dr. Stier counted 198 bruises on the child's skin. Not included in that total were the bruises to the child's brain. Starting with an examination of the child's face, there were bruises to the ear, bruises to the left side of the face, bruises to the left cheek below the eye. Dr. Stier testified there were 14 independent bruises to the left side of the child's face. He observed a hemorrhage to the child's lower left eyelid. There were nine bruises to the right side of Kyson' face. The doctor noted the tip of the child's nose was unscathed, supporting his belief that the lesions to the lips resulted from direct blows to the mouth and not from falling face first onto the floor. He testified he counted a total of 31 visible injuries to the child's head and face.

On the left arm, there were 24 independent injuries. On the child's right arm there were 23 bruises. On the chest area, there were 50 individual bruises. On the child' legs, there were 12 bruises on the front left and 13 bruises on the right front. Eight bruises were counted to the back left leg and eight more on the back of the right leg.

On the child's back, a total of 25 injuries were counted. One bruised area was so large that it could not be determined if it was a single bruise or possibly a combination of two or more bruises. On the child's buttocks, there were 11 bruises.

During the autopsy, Dr. Stier incised or cut beneath the skin to determine the extent and depth of the bruising sustained below the skin. He said the incisions showed the depth of hemorrhaging or bruising extended all the way to the surface of muscle tissue.

The doctor agreed it was fair to say the child's body was covered in lesions and bruises. The only area that was not bruised were the soles of Kyson's feet, the palms of his hands, and his genitals. Otherwise, according to the doctor, pretty much every other part of the body sustained some degree of injury.

Dr. Stier said it was his opinion that the cerebral contusion or bruising below the top of his skull was the source of Kyson's fatal injury. He explained that this type of injury implies a shaking component or an abrupt deceleration which is the same kind of shaking, where the head in motion comes to an abrupt stop. The doctor candidly admitted he really didn't know if all the bruising sustained by the child was survivable. But he said he was much more certain Kyson's brain injury unlikely was survivable.

He finished his testimony by noting the number of lesions and injuries, their location, and the time, and what was going on psychologically at the time of the child' death. As mentioned earlier, from a medical standpoint, he concluded that these injuries constituted torture.

Judge Mark L Goodman was elected to the bench in 2010.

The Court does consider as a factor of history of undesirable behavior. Testifying for the State was Shelby Anderson, the Defendant's ex-wife. She had a child with Mr. Anderson. They were divorced in 2019. During their marriage, she testified Mr. Anderson used oxycodone, Percocet, methamphetamine, weed, and any pill, in her words, that he could get his hands on. She testified he used drugs daily if not multiple times a day.

She recalled an incident where he angrily picked up their five-month-old son by the front of his onesie, waved the child around, and screamed, 'I'll cut your balls off.' She testified she could sense when Mr. Anderson was about to become angry with their child, and as a protective measure, she would do something he didn't like, so that his anger was re-directed toward her from the child.

She told the jury Mr. Anderson said to her he believed as head of the household that she and their son were his property. And she said he reminded her that he has the right to do to them what he saw fit. She said several times he reminded her that their lives were in his hands, and one time saying, 'I can kill you if I want to and God's not going to do anything about it.'

In the parties' divorce, Judge Doyle of the La Crosse County Circuit Court, found it was in the best interest of the parties' child, to have zero contact with Mr. Anderson. Shelby Anderson's testimony about Mr. Anderson's drug usage was collaborated by the State Crime Laboratory. A sample of his blood was collected in conjunction with his arrest. The Crime Lab's analysis of his blood sample detected the presence of opiates, benzodiazepines, cannabinoids, fentanyl, and morphine.

After Kyson was rushed to the Tomah Health emergency room, law enforcement secured the crime scene. Police obtained a search warrant. Police discovered in the residence, and in his vehicle, substances that tested positive for the presence of heroin, fentanyl, and THC, the active ingredient in marijuana, or weed.

Based on blood testing plus the substance discovered by the police in the home and the vehicle, there can be no doubt, at the time, Mr. Anderson was heavily involved in the drug subculture.

Other undesirable behavior included his possession of a firearm. He is a three-time convicted felon, and Wisconsin law prohibited him from possessing firearms. In connection with the evidence of the drug usage, police discovered among his belongings a Sig Sauer handgun and a couple dozen rounds of ammunition.

Another factor the Court considers in sentencing is the denial of responsibility. According to the Pre-sentence Investigation, the Defendant continues to deny he killed Kyson. 'I never harmed a child. I have mixed feelings about the situation. I'm pissed because I got blamed and sad because he died.'

When emergency responders arrived at the child's residence, they observed the child to be drenched in water. Extensive bruising covered his face, arm, legs, and body. Video evidence showed hysterical Mr. Anderson contending to first responders that he was in the process of bathing Kyson when he stepped into another room. He said he heard a thud, returned to the bathroom, and found the child lying on the floor and unresponsive. He said he attempted CPR. That he dressed Kyson prior to calling 911.

His story is a blatant, bald face lie. The fatal injuries Kyson sustained, in the opinion of Dr. Stier, was bilateral subdural hemorrhage. The pathology of this injury showed it is not the type of an injury sustained by one falling out of a shower. When someone falls and strikes his head, the point of impact does not result in a top-of-the-brain injury like the one sustained by Kyson. Moreover, nor was the extensive bruising all over his body sustained by him falling out of the shower.

The video evidence in this case also contradicted Mr. Anderson's contention that Kyson fell while taking a shower. Approximately an hour before the call to 911, there is video evidence from a residential surveillance camera. It showed a healthy Kyson walking up to the residence. About an hour or so later, other video footage showed first responders working desperately trying to revive a battered and unresponsive child. Based on the forensic pathologist's testimony and video evidence, the Court fully agrees with the jury verdict. Mr. Anderson is a child murderer. He also is a liar and a very poor one at that. Mr. Anderson's refusal to man up, to own up to his own terrible crime is an aggravating factor in the Court's sentencing calculus.

I have spent hours thinking about why this happened. What could a three-year-old, 36-pound little boy do to provide a death by torture, to use Dr. Stier's conclusion. We know from Shelby Anderson's testimony that Mr. Anderson is a violent and unstable man. And, I will say, I found her testimony to be credible.

We also know Mr. Anderson abused pills, opiates, weed, meth, and fentanyl. Shelby Anderson told us about his extensive drug usage while she was married to him. The State Crime Lab and the search warrant evidence collaborates that he continues to use various substances during his presence in the home of Jessica and Kyson.

One possible explanation this Court reached about why this homicide occurred is uncomplicated. Mr. Anderson is an inherently violent man. On the day of the murder, he was high. Poor Kyson did something minor. Something trivial in the Defendant's presence. Mr. Anderson became enraged, and he lost it. He flew into a fury and beat the life out of this little boy. The last moments of Kyson's consciousness were horrible. The Court cannot fathom the fright and agony that Kyson must have experienced as Mr. Anderson beat nearly every inch of this body. He suffered a painful and excruciating death.

The Legislature has decided the penalty for First Degree Intentional Homicide is life imprisonment. The only area of discretion for the Court in this case is to decide whether the Defendant may ever become eligible to be considered for parole from prison.

This piqued my curiosity, and I asked the Wisconsin Department of Corrections how much it would cost to imprison someone for the rest of his life. And the answer is that the cost varies. First, it depends on the institution where the Defendant is incarcerated. Notably, the cost of incarcerating women is slightly higher than the cost of incarcerating men.

Generally, the Department of Corrections says it costs around $44,000 a year to incarcerate a person in prison. Mr. Anderson is exactly one week away from his 38th birthday. His anticipated lifespan, I'm told, is 71.1 years.

And so, one way that the Courts thinks about this is he is about half-way through his anticipated life span.

If the annual cost of incarceration is frozen at $44,000 and multiplying that by the remaining 38 years of his implied or expected lifespan, it may cost taxpayers approximately $1.6 million to imprison him for the rest of his life.

Now, I've considered several aggravating factors. This was an extremely vicious homicide. Mr. Anderson showed Kyson Rice no mercy as he beat nearly every area of the small boy's body. The victim impact is the most extreme I have ever seen in my 12 years as a Circuit Judge. Kyson's death is a tragedy that neither his mother, his family, nor the Court, nor the first responders, the police officers who were here today, the people at Tomah Health, those folks will never comprehend this. Jessica and her family who knew and loved Kyson, I don't think, will ever recover from the impact of his murder. Mr. Anderson, his character, he is an unstable drug user prone to violent behavior.

And even today, in the face of overwhelming evidence of his guilt, he has no shred of repentance for this most unspeakable crime. He is a cowardly liar who refused to accept responsibility for torturing Kyson to death. While he is fully grown adult, he is by no means, in view of this Court, a man.

Mr. Anderson, the blood of Kyson Rice will never, never, come off your hands. That's what I want you to think about every day you sit in prison, feeling sorry for yourself, knowing you will never walk free again. Your crime was vicious to the extreme. Kyson Rice was one of the most vulnerable citizens in our community. You are an extreme danger to public safety, especially to our most precious and vulnerable members of the County. It will be well worth every penny the taxpayers will pay to keep you locked up until you die in prison."

Author's note. An audible sigh and murmur rippled through Courtroom Branch 2. Judge Goodman's sentencing speech had been going on for about

10 minutes. This was the first time there is a solid indication that Anderson is going to the big house and never coming back.

"With that sentencing objective in mind, I sentence you as follows: on Count 1, First Degree Intentional Homicide as a Repeater, the Defendant is sentenced to life in prison without the possibility of parole."

The remainder of the Counts and sentences seem anticlimactic after that initial sentence.

"On Count 2, Child Abuse-Intentionally Causing Great Bodily Harm as a Repeater, the Court sentences you to 46 years in prison bifurcated as 25 years of initial confinement and 19 years of extended supervision to be served consecutively to your sentence on Count 1.

On Count 3, Possession a Firearm-Convicted of a Felony as a Repeater, the Court sentences you to 10 years in prison bifurcated as 5 years of initial confinement and 5 years of extended supervision, to be served consecutively to Counts 1 and 2.

On Counts 2,5,6,and 7, Felony Bail Jumping-six years in prison, three years confinement and three years extended supervision, each Count served concurrently with each other, but consecutively to the sentence imposed on Counts 1,2, and 3."

For Counts 13, 14, and 15, Judge Goodman imposes prison sentences for possession of various drug offenses. For Count 16, Intimidation of a witness as a Repeater, an enhanced Class A misdemeanor, two years. All total, Anderson is guaranteed spending the rest of his life in prison.

The clock on the north wall read close to 11 a.m. and the sentencing hearing was winding down. There was a discussion between Judge Goodman, District Attorney Croninger, and Defense Council Flanagan concerning the use of the term consecutive as it pertains to La Crosse County case 17CF626 and Monroe County case 17CF727. Croninger asked that video discs, Exhibit 1 and Exhibit 2 to be marked and made a part of the court file.

The last photo of Kyson, taken at the family Easter Egg Hunt, two weeks before his murder.

Final Words

Judge Goodman: Anything else for today's hearing?

DA Croninger: Nothing further from the State, Your Honor.

Mr. Flanagan: Nothing from the Defense.

Judge Goodman: Okay. Then that's it. We will conclude our business today. Thank you, everybody.

DA Croninger: Thank you, Your Honor.

It's over. One of the longest trials in Monroe County history. Arguably, the most gruesome and senseless murder of a small boy. There's relief after a sentence like this, but there has to be a pervasive sadness that still extends to those who knew and loved little Kyson.

Epilogue

There are several heroes in this true-life murder saga. It's difficult to pick just one. Here are a few and not in any particular order of importance: Monroe County District Attorney Kevin Croninger, Assistant District Attorney Sarah Skiles, the Tomah Police Department, Judge Michael Goodman, John Glynn, and the jury.

District Attorney Kevin Croninger and Assistant District Attorney Sarah Skiles

Both DA Kevin Croninger and Assistant DA Sarah Skiles performed their duties above and beyond. The Marcus Anderson trial was complicated, with about 100 witnesses subpoenaed, 41 appearing, eight days of trial, the police reports, the autopsy findings. Pulling all those elements together was a monumental task. Remember, there were no witnesses, no murder weapon, such as a gun, knife, poison, strangulation weapon. They had to prove that Marcus was alone with the victim prior to the time of the murderous assault. Getting background information about Marcus was a long arduous process. It was necessary to send two police detectives to Arizona for several days. Four investigators spent hundreds of hours interviewing persons who knew or interacted with Marcus Anderson, Kyson Rice, and Jessica Rice. DA Croninger and ADA Skiles had to weave a narrative that a jury would find creditable beyond a reasonable doubt. They did that.

Tomah Police Department

Tomah has a well-trained professional police force, a far cry from the time a former principal at Tomah High School was hired, before he became principal, as deputy in the Tomah Police Department. The Police Chief gave him a uniform, badge, gun, and squad car and sent him out on patrol with the admonition to "not shoot anyone."

Lt. Jarrod Furlano reveals that the Tomah Police Department, on average, provides a total of 3,000 hours of training to its officers annually, in the areas of Leadership, Tactics, Instructor Training, K9, Medical, and School Resources. This continually professional growth is under the leadership Police Chief Scott Holum and Assistant Police Chief Eric Pedersen.

Judge Mark L. Goodman

A veteran of 15 years in the Courtroom, Judge Goodman displays the demeanor of one who knows what he's doing. He puts the jury at ease, telling them what to expect and what is going to happen next. The same disposition is exhibited when witnesses are called to the stand. Being called to the witness stand can be intimidating, even frightening. His directions and instructions are delivered in a comforting and reassuring tone.

John Glynn

John and Jolene Glynn have two grandchildren attending Queen of the Apostles Elementary School in Tomah. On December 12, 2023, at the QOTA Christmas program, John Glynn asked Msgr. David Kunz advice on how to cope with the thoughts, images, and reminders of the horrific death of Kyson Rice.

Msgr. Kunz said, "Recite the prayer to St. Michael, the Archangel."
St. Michael, the Archangel, defend us in battle.

Be our defense against the wickedness and snare of the Devil.
May God rebuke him, we humbly pray,
And do thou, O Prince of the heavenly hosts, by the power of God.
Thrust into hell, Satan, and all the evil spirits, who prowl about the world,
Seeking the ruin of souls. Amen

John Glynn attended every hearing and every day of the trial. He is intimately familiar with the key people of the case: judge, prosecuting attorneys, witnesses. He is on a first-name basis with the bailiffs.

The Jury

Mackenzi Pearson talked freely about the inner workings of the jury.

There are both joys and hardships, pluses and minuses, of serving on a jury. Some people greet a jury summons with glee, others with dread. Many simply consider it their civic duty. The prospective juror must fill out a form and bring it to the courthouse on the day prescribed by the summons. In Wisconsin, a pool of potential jurors is randomly selected from the local population of individuals eligible for jury duty. A prospective juror will not be called more than once in a period of two to four years for a one-day trial. If a longer trial, the juror may not be summoned more than once every four years.

The Marcus Anderson trial was an eight-day ordeal. I discussed the workings of this jury by interviewing Mackenzi Pearson and Jessica Clark whose recall of the trial is in a previous chapter. Both Judge Goodman and DA Croninger told the jury before the trial started that it would not be an easy task with days of gut-wrenching testimony and viewing horrific photos and videos. But how magnificently they performed.

Larry and Cheryl Quarles

Larry and Cheryl Quarles were strong advocates for Kyson.

The Quarles did all they could to prevent the murder of Kyson Rice. They took Kyson under their wing, babysitting, feeding, and nurturing. Cheryl provided Jessica Rice with warnings and things to look after. Both testified at the trial of Marcus Anderson. Both were heartbroken, attended the funeral, and to this day, ask "what if."

Stolen Valor

On November 15, 2023, another trial was held involving the Stolen Valor Act of 2013. Judge Rick Radcliffe presided over the one-day trial of Marcus Anderson. Thirteen jurors were sworn in by 10:20 a.m. The charge focused on Marcus telling a judge on December 11, 2019, that he was in the Marines, had done great things, lost a lot of men, and closed with Semper Fi. Four witnesses were called. Marcus declined to testify. The case went to the jury at 1:44 p.m. and deliberated for 20 minutes. The verdict was guilty. Marcus was given two years, added concurrently to his life prison sentence without the possibility of parole. Marcus Anderson was returned to the Supermax prison at Boscobel. He will serve out the rest of his days in a lonely prison cell, with plenty of time to ponder the enormity of his crime.

PRESS RELEASE UPON CONVICTION

Date April 12, 2022

For Immediate Release Kevin Croninger, Monroe County District Attorney

TOMAH MAN CONVICTED OF 2019 HOMICIDE OF A 3 YEAR OLD [SPARTA WI]

Today, Monroe County District Attorney, Kevin D. Croninger announced that on April 12, 2022, a Monroe County jury convicted 37 year old, Marcus W. Anderson of eleven counts including, 1st Degree Intentional Homicide; Physical Abuse of a Child - Intentionally Cause Great Bodily Harm; four Counts of Felony Bail Jumping; Felon in Possession of a Firearm; Felony Possession of Narcotic Drugs; Felony Possession of Tetrahydrocannabinols; Operating with a Restricted Controlled Substance and Intimidation of a Witness.

The convictions came after an eight day jury trial. The charges against Anderson stem from a 2019 incident in which Anderson beat, 3 year old Kyson Rice, to death in the City of Tomah. After eight days of trial the jury deliberated for just over two hours before reaching their verdicts. Monroe County District Attorney Kevin Croninger stated, "This was an extremely difficult case, as the jury had to view evidence of unthinkable acts of violence committed against Kyson, we are extremely grateful for the jurors' service and the close attention they paid to the evidence. Their verdicts help to give justice to Kyson and his family."

The prosecution of the case was handled by Monroe County District Attorney Kevin Croninger and Assistant District Attorney Sarah Skiles, along with a tremendous amount of support and assistance by the entire staff of the Monroe County District Attorney's Office.

The investigation of the case was led by Investigator Paul Sloan of the City of Tomah Police Department, West Central Metropolitan Enforcement Group Director Rob Walensky (formerly of the City of Tomah Police Department) and retired Monroe County Sheriff's Office Detective Clayton Tester. The investigation was aided by numerous members of the City of Tomah Police Department, the Tomah Ambulance Service, the Monroe County District Attorney's Office Investigator, as well as information from medical professionals in the Gundersen, Mayo and UW Health systems.

Croninger praised the work of the law enforcement offers involved, "The officers and first responders involved in this case are real life heroes. From the moment they became aware of the situation they did everything they could to save Kyson's life. When the situation transitioned to a homicide investigation the officers demonstrated the highest level of professionalism and skill in procuring the necessary evidence to obtain justice for Kyson." Following the jury's verdicts, Monroe County Circuit Court Judge Mark L. Goodman, who presided over the case, revoked Anderson's bond and remanding him to custody pending sentencing.

Acknowledgments

No one person writes a non-fiction book alone. It takes a lot of people who are generous with their time, knowledge, and talents. I give thanks to:

John Glynn said to me, "This is a story that needs to be told." Mr. Glynn attended all the hearings, every day of the trial, and the follow-up sentencing. People who granted me an interview and provided valuable feedback: **Judge Mark Goodman, District Attorney Kevin Croninger, Assistant District Attorney Sarah Skiles, Investigators Robert Walensky** and **Clayton Tester,** Tomah Police Officers **Lt. Jerrod Furlano, Sgt. Wil Steinborn, Sgt. Adam Perkins, Officer Brennon Scallon, Officer David Heckman, Adam Robarge** with the Tomah Ambulance Service, **Larry and Cheryl Quarles,** **Jessica Rice** (mother of Kyson), and Tomah Police Department Administrative Assistant **Rhonda Culpitt** who invested hours of time in providing me with police reports, still photos, and camera footage. Two jury members, **Mackenzie Pearson** and **Michelle Clark**, provided insights into the jury's structure, thinking, and deliberations. **Lynn B. Kloety,** Office Manager of the Monroe County District Attorney's Office, and **Wes Revels,** who arranged a tour of the Monroe County Justice Center. **Lt. Ryan Hallman,** Assistant Jail Administrator who conducted the tour. Editor **Valerie Biel** provided hours of work on the manuscript and cover and provided guidance and suggestions.

Biographies

KEVIN CRONINGER has been District Attorney for Monroe County, Wisconsin since January of 2014 and has been a prosecutor since February of 2010. Prior to becoming District Attorney of Monroe County, Kevin prosecuted cases in Monroe, Juneau, and Adams counties as an Assistant District Attorney. During his time as District Attorney, Kevin has handled all types of cases from speeding tickets to homicides, with a focus on serious violent crimes, such has homicide and child sexual abuse. Kevin has tried more than 45 cases to juries, with a significant number of those being child sexual abuse or homicides. Kevin received the 2017 Outstanding Victim Advocacy by a Professional award from the Wisconsin Victim/Witness Professional Association. Mr. Croninger was named the 2020 Prosecutor of the Year by the Wisconsin District Attorneys' Association.

LIEUTENANT JARROD FURLANO has been with the Tomah Police Department since 2008. He was promoted to Sergeant in 2018 and to Lieutenant in 2021. He oversees the Patrol Division, coordinates department training, the Field Training Program, the department's K9 units, and the department's vehicle fleet, while also managing the department's schedule and writing grants for equipment. Lieutenant Furlano served on the Monroe County Combined Tactical Unit for ten years, with special assignments on the team of Explosive Breacher and Team Leader. He is a Wisconsin Law Enforcement Standards Bureau certified instructor in the unified tactics areas of Firearms, Tactical Response, Defense and Arrest Tactics, and Emergency Vehicle Operations and Controls. Lieutenant Furlano holds an Associate's Degree in Criminal Justice, Bachelor's Degree in Business Management, and a Master's Degree in Management and Leadership.

JOHN GLYNN was born and raised in the Chicago, Il suburbs, attending high school and some college there prior to moving to Tomah, WI in 1985 where he met his wife Jolene. They have been blessed with two children, Sean and Desiree, and three grandchildren. He is a member of Queen of the Apostles Catholic Parish. He was a member of the Monroe County Volunteer Dive Team for 15 years. He's been employed at Cardinal GI in Tomah since it first opened in 1988 working in production and quality control and as quality manager before becoming a salesman for 25 years. He was recently promoted to the Director of Technology Marketing. One of his passions is flying. He began hang gliding when he was 14, became a certified instructor, built his first ultralight at 17, and continues flying to this day, sharing this passion with others. *"I really appreciate Tomah, and have been honored to serve on the City Council for the past four years and hopefully continue to serve the people of this community that I have grown to love."*

JUDGE MARK L. GOODMAN is a judge for the Monroe County Circuit Court in the Seventh Judicial District of Wisconsin. He was elected to the bench in 2010. Prior to his election, Goodman worked in private practice for 24 years (1986-2010). During that time, he was the vice president and shareholder of Osborne, Goodman & Tripp in Sparta. In addition to his practice, he presided as a municipal judge for the City of Sparta from 1992 to 2010. Goodman received a B.A. in journalism from the University of Wisconsin-Madison in 1978 and an M.S. in journalism from South Dakota State University in 1982. He went on to complete a J.D. (Juris Doctor) at the University of Wisconsin Law School in 1985. Goodman was admitted to practice in Wisconsin in 1986 for the United States District Court for Western Wisconsin and the United States Tax Court. From a civic standpoint, he has been involved with the Bread Basket Ecumenical Food Panty of Sparta, the Monroe County Shelter, Kiwanis, and the Knights of Columbus. Goodman also served as a coach for the Sparta High School Mock Trial Team, where his team were Regional Champs. Judge Goodman coached Little League baseball and youth basketball teams and was a Cub Scout den leader. His pro bono work included the Boys and Girls Club of Sparta, the Bread Basket Ecumenical Food Pantry, the Monroe County Shelter Care, the Sparta Rod & Gun Club, and the Monroe County Teen Pregnancy and Parenting Coalition. Goodman attended Sparta High School.

SERGEANT ADAM PERKINS is a Police Sergeant and K-9 Handler for the City of Tomah Police Department. He was hired as a Tomah Police Officer in September of 2011, was selected as a K-9 Handler in 2017, and promoted to Sergeant in 2018. He grew up in Sparta, WI, graduating from Sparta High School in 2007. He earned a Bachelor's Degree in Criminal Justice from the University of Wisconsin-Platteville in 2011, before graduating from the Western Technical College Law Enforcement Academy at Sparta in the summer of 2011. Perkins and Viktor, a 2-year-old Czech Shepard, attended a five-week training course at Jessiffany Canine Services, LLC during the months of March and April in 2017. During that training period, Perkins became a certified dual-purpose K-9 handler and holds certificates through the Jessiffany Canine Services and also through the American Police Canine Association (APCA). Perkins and Viktor were recertified in April 2019. K-9 Viktor is trained in patrol work, article detection, and narcotics detection with the ability to locate odors of marijuana, methamphetamine, heroin, and cocaine.

BRENNON SCALLON graduated from West Salem High School in 2012. He attended Western Technical College in La Crosse and the University of Wisconsin-La Crosse, obtaining sufficient credits to apply for the Police Academy at Western Technical College in Sparta, Wisconsin, graduating in 2016. He was a Patrol Officer from October 2016 until February 2024. He trained as a Drone Pilot, Field Training Officer, and OWI/SFST Instructor (Operating While Intoxicated/Standardized Field Sobriety Test). Officer Scallon received multiple lifesaving awards, unit citations, and excellence in training awards.

ASSISTANT DISTRICT ATTORNEY SARAH SKILES graduated from UW-Madison with a B.A. in Communications. Skiles graduated from Hamline Law School, St. Paul, with a Doctor of Law degree, J.D. (Juris Doctor). On November 2, 2023, she was awarded the Wisconsin Assistant District Attorney of the Year. The award is given annually by the Wisconsin District Attorneys Association, which is a group representing over 500 District Attorneys, Deputy District Attorneys, and Assistant District Attorneys across Wisconsin. The award is given to the Assistant District Attorney who provides the highest level of service in any given year. Competition for the award is strong, as there are more than 500 Assistant District Attorneys in the State of Wisconsin. The award continues a long tradition of recognition for excellence in prosecution by the Monroe County District Attorney's Office. The office has previously been recognized for prosecutorial excellence when District Attorney Kevin Croninger was named Prosecutor of the Year in 2020 and the late Monroe County District Attorney Dan Cary was named Prosecutor of the Year in 2012.

PAUL SLOAN had worked for the Tomah Police Department for 20 years at the time of the Marcus Anderson trial, nine of those years as an investigator. He was assigned to criminal cases, primarily cases involving sexual assaults, child sexual assaults, physical abuse, and child exploitation cases. Sloan is trained as an evidence technician attending the Wisconsin Department of Justice School. He also received specialized training related to fire investigations and the collection of DNA evidence.

SERGEANT WIL STEINBORN is a law enforcement officer with the City of Tomah Police Department. He was hired with the department in October of 2012 and has served as a patrol officer, field training officer, crisis negotiator, and drug recognition expert. He was promoted to Sergeant in August of 2019. He served in the U.S. Army from May 2007 to October of 2011 as an infantryman and was stationed at Fort Myer, VA where he served in the 3rd IN REG, The Old Guard. He earned an associate's degree in criminal justice from Western Technical College, completing his bachelor's degree in business administration/human resources and his master's degree in management and leadership at Western Governors University.

CLAYTON TESTER is a retired Detective for the Monroe County Sheriffs Office, retiring in 2022 with over 27 years in law enforcement. He grew up in Sparta and graduated from Sparta High School in 1984. He pursued other careers including farming, welding and construction before starting his law enforcement career in 1993. He attended the 400 hours of law enforcement certification training while working part time for the Sparta Police Department. He then worked part time for the Monroe County Sheriff's Office before taking a full time job with the Fort McCoy DOD for a few years. He was hired full time with the Juneau County Sheriff's Office before become a Sheriff's Deputy for Monroe County in 2000. He was transferred to the Detective Bureau in 2001 and was eventually assigned to the Monroe County Joint Investigative Task Force (MCJITF) which was created in 2014. MCJITF was comprised of an investigators from the Sparta Police Department, the Tomah Police Department and the Monroe County Sheriff's Office with responsibilities including narcotics and death investigations. He was one of the first TAZER instructors for the Monroe County Sheriff's Department and was also a part of the Monroe County

Tactical Team for several years. He was honored with the Meritorious Award for his work on a MCJITF homicide case.

ROBERT WALENSKY is currently the Investigative Coordinator for the West Central Metropolitan Enforcement Group (WCMEG) based out of La Crosse, WI. WCMEG is a six-county drug task force that includes La Crosse, Monroe, Jackson, Vernon, Trempealeau and Crawford Counties. The Investigative Coordinator is the administrative position for the drug task force and Robert Walensky has served in this role since 2021. In addition, he has been the Director of Forensic Services with Defense Forensic since 2021. Defense Forensic is a company that specializes in expertise in digital forensics related to computer forensic, cellular phone, and vehicle forensics. He was previously employed with the Tomah Police Department from 1999-2021 and served as an investigator with the Tomah Police Department. In that role, Walensky focused on narcotics and death investigations but also investigated many other types of major crimes. From 2014-2021 Robert Walensky was assigned to the Monroe County Joint Investigative Task Force (MCJITF). MCJITF was a task force comprised of an Investigator from the Tomah Police Department, Sparta Police Department and Monroe County Sheriff's Office that focused on major crimes occurring in Monroe County. He has received advanced training and experience in narcotics investigation, death investigations, digital forensics and many other types of training related to criminal investigations, often testifying as an expert witness in State and Federal Courts. He was the Chief of Police for the Warrens Police Department from 1996-2014 and with the Monroe County Sheriff's Office from 1996-1999. He graduated from Tomah High School in 1990 and attended Western Wisconsin Technical College in La Crosse for Police Science and Winona State University for Criminal Justice.

Why Do People Commit Murder?

While mass murders, involving five or more victims, garner the headlines, they represent less than one percent of all homicides in the United States. Dr. Peter Morrall, Professor at the University of Leeds in York, England, and head of the Mental Health, Learning Disabilities, and Behavioral Sciences program, says, "There are many reasons people commit murders because there are so many different types of murders. Motive is central to police investigations. Although a conviction is possible without a motive being discovered, finding a specific reason makes conviction more likely. Motives for murder can be condensed into four sets of 'L's: Lust, Love, Loathing, and Loot."

Dr. Morrall goes on to give an example of each. **Lust:** a lover kills a rival for his/her object of desire. The 'thrill-killer' murders people to gain a sexual payoff. **Love:** the 'mercy killing' of a baby with a major deformity or partner with incurable cancer. **Loathing:** lethal hatred directed towards one person, or a group of people, such as homosexuals or prostitutes. **Loot:** killing for financial gain, such as a robbery, inheritance, insurance payout, drugs, or contracting a hit man.

Dr. Morrall's four motives may be an overview of the reasons people kill other people. Perhaps it goes deeper than four. Murders may be a combination of two or three of the four. Another list of motives is the 'top ten' rationale and justifications or excuse for murder.

Top Ten Reasons for Murder

Revenge: Some individuals go crazy if others have not done or will not do what we think they should do. A person may believe that another fellow has done them a serious wrong. They get out of control and the ultimate revenge is killing someone. Aaron Burr and Alexander Hamilton were political enemies. The final straw for Burr was the publication of a letter in a newspaper that said Hamilton demeaned Burr's character. Burr demanded Hamilton apologize for the insults or explain them. Hamilton stayed quiet, so Burr demanded a duel.

Money and Greed: People often quip that money is the root of evil, but actually the Bible says, "the love of money is the root of all evil." (1 Timothy 6:10) In other words the problem is not about *money* but the attitude towards money and wealth. On October 11, 1984, Rick Lee Alloway robbed and shot a Minnesota shoe salesman, Roland Lampe, at a rest stop in western Monroe County. Alloway and his girlfriend drove the wounded Lampe north to Cataract, Wisconsin and finished him off with a shot to the head. They unceremoniously dumped Lamke off in the woods.

Drugs and Alcohol: After excessive intake of alcohol or drugs, people become irrational and out of control and do stupid things, like commit murder. On July 10, 1974, James Ray Mendoza killed two off duty Milwaukee police officers. Mendoza did some heavy drinking in a local tavern before the murders. In a change of venue, the trial was held in Monroe County. Mendoza was found guilty in November 1974. Mendoza claimed he was being held down by the police officers and acted in self-defense. The verdict was overturned on appeal and Mendoza was granted a second trial. He was found not guilty.

Sexual Attraction: Ah, affairs of the heart can have tragic consequences. One person may try to dominate his partner socially, mentally, and emotionally. Physical abuse is often involved. The ultimate end may be a heinous killing. A man may think, "If I can't have her, nobody can."

Pure lust may be the major motive. Jeffrey Dahmer and Ted Bundy fit this description.

Extramarital Affairs: In our society today, an extra-marital affair is one of the top reasons for creating violence and sometimes it ends in murder. Extra-marital affairs are leading causes of murder-suicides. The John Bartz killing of his girlfriend Cindy Pingel in 1981 is a prime example.

Eliminate a Witness: The October 1986 Andy Scherreiks' murder would fall into this category. Scherreiks was set to testify in Viroqua about criminal damage to a neighbor's cranberry crop by flooding it. The Court contends that two young men conspired to silence him.

Super Ego: This is your typical serial killer. An example is Joseph Paul Franklin, who killed a girl from Milwaukee, and left her body in the woods near Oakdale, a few miles east of Tomah. Franklin had life sentences from several states, and death penalty in Missouri. He died or was killed in prison.

Eliminate an Irritant: An authority figure is murdered because he trying to help a young person going in the wrong direction in life. The miscreant sees his path to freedom by removing a person he sees as an annoyance. In Monroe County, the Mogensen killing, and the Daniel and Evelyn Leis murders, are foremost cases with this motive.

Great Interest in Murder

No matter the motive for the crime, historically there's always been great interest in murder. Today this interest is fueled by the many true crime shows on television: *48 Hours, Forensic Files, I Almost Got Away with It, Cold Case Files, Forensics: You Decide, The First 48, The F.B.I. Files, A Crime to Remember, Making a Murderer, Masterminds, American Justice, Dateline NBC, Death Row Stories, Investigation Discovery (ID)*. There are some fictional murder programs: *Law and Order, NCIS, The Sopranos*, and *The Shield*.

People are drawn to these sensational stories by curiosity about the motivations of the criminals, concerns about justice and legal system, and the thrill of solving a real-life whodunnit. We want to know the criminal's motives. What drove the person? Was the person a psychopath? Was it triggered by domestic violence? Statistics show that most murderers know their victim, which makes people wonder about their own relationships.

Part of the fascination for true crime's appeal stems from a sense of justice and the feeling that the justice system broke down in some cases. This person committed a crime and should pay, is the reasoning of many. True-life crime stories are both escapism and entertainment. Many people want to see the dark recesses of someone's mind. Such is the case in *Murder in a Small Town: The Kyson Rice Case*.

Wisconsin Prison System

The Wisconsin Department of Corrections runs the state prison system. Marcus Anderson was originally sent to the Waupun Correctional Institution. The name Correctional Institution is a fancy way of saying State Prison. Waupun is the oldest prison in the system, tracing its beginnings to 1851, only three years after Wisconsin became a state. The founding fathers of Wisconsin chose Waupun due to the abundance of limestone for construction. The main building, built in 1854, is still in use. The Waupun Correctional Institution at 200 S. Madison St. is right in the middle of the city of Waupun. The Dodge Correctional Institution at 1 W. Lincoln St. is sited on the southern edge of the City of Waupun.

Waupun has some of its citizens in Dodge County and some in Fond du Lac County. It's a beautiful city of about 11,000 and the prison sits smack dab in the center, in a residential area, taking up about nine city blocks. The United Methodist Church, Public Library, and Holy Trinity Episcopal Church are sited on the north side of the prison. Pella Lutheran Church is on the east side. The Central Wisconsin Christian School is a few blocks west. Waupun Junior and Senior High Schools are a half-mile to the southeast.

The first library was established in 1858 by insurance men, William Euen and Edwin Hillyer. They ran the library out of their insurance office for 37 years without pay. That says something about the character of the people of Waupun.

In 1945, Waupun was chosen as the site of a German POW camp, constructed next to a canning factory. The 200 prisoners worked on the surrounding farms and factories. By most accounts, they were quite happy to be in Wisconsin as a prisoner, not as a soldier in the German Wehrmacht fighting a losing war. They were well fed, clothed, housed, had jobs, and were among friends. They kept track of developments in their homeland and fretted about the fate of their families and friends. Many learned the rudiments of the English language. Large numbers did not want to return to Germany when the war was over, but they had no say in the matter.

You can purchase coffee, doughnuts, and gas at the Kwik Trip, have lunch at Pizza Ranch, Butter Burgers and Frozen Custard at Culver's, and pick up a car battery at Tractor Supply. Life goes on in Waupun like it does in any small city in the United States. Contrast that life to the 2800 men inside the prison walls who have chosen a different path.

Apparently, Marcus Anderson didn't behave any better in prison than he did in society. He was transferred to the Wisconsin Secure Program Facility, better known as a Supermax prison for men. The facility is located east of Boscobel, off of Wisconsin Highway 133. Boscobel, population 3,300, is on the north edge of Grant County. Boscobel calls itself the "wild turkey hunting capital of Wisconsin", and for good reason. Boscobel is in the Driftless Area, home of some of the most beautiful scenery on planet Earth. You can find the historic Central House Hotel, the birthplace of Gideons International, the organization that places bibles in hotel rooms.

The baddest of the bad are sent to the Supermax. Even though Green Bay and Waupun are considered maximum security, the Supermax is a step above. It is home to some of the most violent men who have committed the most despicable crimes in Wisconsin. Numerous men are drug or alcohol dependent. Many are combative, family strife and broken homes and relationships. Marcus Anderson fits right in.

The Florence, Colorado Supermax (Administrative-Maximum Facility or ADX) is the most secure Supermax prison in the United States and houses some well-known scoundrels such as, Ramzi Yousef, who plotted the 1993 bombing at the World Trade Center, Ted Kaczynski, the "Unabomber", Richard Reid, the "shoe bomber", Dzhokhar Tsarnaev, the Boston Marathon bomber, and Robert Hanssen, the FBI agent who spied for the Russians from 1979 to 2001, called the worst intelligence disaster in U.S. history.

Robert Hood served as ADX warden from 2002 to 2005. "The Supermax is **life after death**. It's long term. In my opinion, it's far much worse than death. The architecture is the control. Many of the more than 400 inmates spend as much as 23 hours a day alone in 7-by-12-foot concrete cells. Meals are slid through small holes in the doors. A single window allows some natural light to come in but inmates can't see the sky. Cells have unmovable stools and the desk is made of concrete. Solid walls prevent inmates from seeing their cellmates or having direct contact with other prisoners. A recreation hour is allowed in an outdoor cage slightly larger than the prison cells. Only the sky is visible.

So sits Marcus Anderson in his cell at Boscobel, Wisconsin. He may hear the cars and trucks on Highway 133 and may catch the rumble of freight trains following the course of the Wisconsin River. He will not have a view of the beautiful tree-covered bluffs and rolling countryside of the Driftless Area. Marcus will have ample time to contemplate the enormity of his crimes.

Death Penalty in Wisconsin

John McCaffary was an immigrant from Ireland who settled in the Kenosha, Wisconsin area. McCaffary was a domestic abuser with a violent temper. On July 23, 1850, McCaffary had a noisy argument with his wife, Bridget. He held Bridget's head down in a backyard rain barrel full of water until she stopped moving. Neighbors had heard Bridget's shrieks but arrived too late.

McCaffary was duly arrested, and his trial began on May 6, 1851. Less than three weeks later the jury convicted him of first-degree murder. The judge sentenced McCaffary to death by hanging. The death warrant was signed by Governor Dewey Nelson. The death sentence was carried out on August 21, 1851. He was taken out of prison and strung up from a tree before an estimated crowd of 2,000 to 3,000 citizens. About a third were women and families brought picnic lunches.

The hanging did not go as planned. McCaffary remained alive, struggling and kicking on the end of the rope for over 20 minutes, slowly being strangled to death. McCaffary, with his elongated neck, was buried in an unmarked grave in Kenosha's Green Ridge Cemetery.

The gruesome spectacle was too much for the several thousand onlookers. Add to the fact that Wisconsin, newly admitted to the Union, was known as a "reform" state. In a few years, the anti-slavery Republican Party would be founded in Ripon, Wisconsin. The display of public enjoyment of a state sanctioned killing was too much for too many.

A Kenosha publisher, Christopher Latham Sholes, was elected to the Wisconsin State Assembly in 1852. He and his newspaper, *The Kenosha Telegraph,* took up the cause of abolishing the death penalty. He denounced the execution in his newspaper with, "the crowd has been indulged in its insane passion for the sight of a judicially murdered man. We hope this will be the last execution that shall ever disgrace the mercy-expecting citizens of the State of Wisconsin." (It's interesting to note that Sholes invented the first commercially successful typewriter with the QWERTY keyboard that became standard.)

On July 12, 1853, Wisconsin followed the example of its neighbor, Michigan, and abolished the death penalty full stop. Wisconsin Governor Leonard J. Farwell signed a law that abolished the death penalty in Wisconsin and replaced it with a penalty of life imprisonment.

There had been a few executions in Wisconsin before McCaffary's, but his was the first one after Wisconsin attained statehood in 1848. Thus, John McCaffary was the only person ever to be executed by the State of Wisconsin.

There are 31 states in the US where the death penalty is legally upheld. Also known as capital punishment, the death penalty is a legal punishment also exercised by the federal government. The U.S. is the only Western nation that currently uses capital punishment, and it is one of the 57 countries in the world that has the death penalty.

The last public hanging in the United States was on August 14, 1936 at Owensboro, Kentucky before a crowd estimated at 10,000 to 20,000. Rainey Bethea, aged 22, was convicted of the murder of a 70-year-old woman. Race made this public execution controversial.

BOOKS BY LARRY AND ANN SCHECKEL

Country School Days: True Tales of a Wisconsin One-Room School, Oak Grove Press 2021
Can People Just Burst into Flames, Oak Grove Press, 2020
I Just Keep Wondering, Tumblehome Learning, 2019
Murder in Wisconsin: The Clara Olson Case, Oak Grove Press, 2018
I Wondered About That Too, Tumblehome Learning, 2018
I Always Wondered About That, Tumblehome Learning, 2017
Seneca Seasons: A Farm Boy Remembers, CreateSpace, 2014
Ask A Science Teacher, Experiment Publishing (Workman), 2013
Ask Your Science Teacher, CreateSpace, 2011

www.ingramcontent.com/pod-product-compliance
Lightning Source LLC
Chambersburg PA
CBHW060451030426
42337CB00015B/1546